Eat, Sleep, Ride

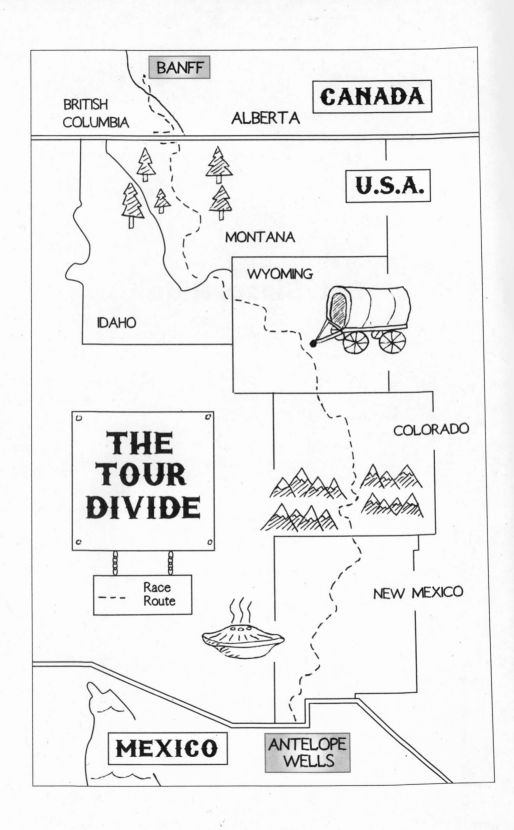

Paul Howard

EAT, SLEEP, RIDE

How I Braved Bears, Badlands and Big Breakfasts in My Quest to Cycle the Tour Divide

GREYSTONE BOOKS
D&M PUBLISHERS INC.
Vancouver/Toronto/Berkeley

To M, B, T and F

Greystone Books
An imprint of D&M Publishers Inc.
2323 Quebec Street, Suite 201
Vancouver BC Canada V5T 4S7
www.greystonebooks.com

Cataloguing data available from Library and Archives Canada
ISBN 978-1-55365-817-7 (pbk.)
ISBN 978-1-55365-818-4 (ebook)

First published in 2010 by Mainstream Publishing
Company (Edinburgh) Ltd, Edinburgh, Scotland, as
Two Wheels on My Wagon: A Bicycle Adventure in the Wild West

Front cover photographs by Kyle George/Aurora/Getty Images (top)
and Luigi Stavale/Latin Content/Getty Images (bottom)
Printed and bound in Canada by Friesens
Text printed on acid-free, 100% post-consumer paper
Distributed in the U.S. by Publishers Group West

CONTENTS

Acknowledgements 7

SUSSEX

1   Seduction 11
2   A Series of Unfortunate Events 15

CANADA

3   The Bear Necessities 27
4   A Horseshoe for Luck 40
5   Bringing Up the Rear 51
6   Where the Wild Things Are 58

MONTANA

7   Breakfast with Dolly Parton 71
8   Swan Lake 77
9   A River Runs through It 85
10   Three Kinds of Psychopath 94
11   Signs of Life 102
12   Singing in the Rain 109
13   Here's Mud in Your Eye 117
14   This Is Not Peru 126
15   Leaving Montana 134

IDAHO AND WYOMING

16   No Room at the Inn 143
17   Down the Green River 152
18   Encounter with a Cowboy 159
19   Across the Basin 168
20   Saved by a Siren 175

COLORADO

21 Moscow Calling 185
22 Eat, Sleep and Be Grumpy 193
23 I Wandered Lonely as a Cloud 201
24 Cannibal Adventure! 208
25 It's All Downhill from Here 215

NEW MEXICO

26 Independence Day 223
27 Through the Rainbow 231
28 Losing My Innocence in Walmart 237
29 Pie Town 244
30 Geronimo! 250
31 The Fall 258
32 Satisfaction 268

ACKNOWLEDGEMENTS

There are many people who helped me participate in and complete the Tour Divide, not least the people I met and rode with on the way, and of whom there are too many to name individually. You know who you are, and I hope this book goes some way to repaying the debt of gratitude I owe.

There are also several people to whom I wish to express particular thanks: to Rod Lambert – Seaford's very own Mr Cycles – for his support, enthusiasm and lessons in bike maintenance; to Eddie Start of Open Spaces in Brighton for his fund of useful advice about life in the wilds and the best kit to take.

Thanks also to Tony Harris at ATB Sales, distributors of Marin Bikes, Ian Young at Zyro, distributors of Camelbak and Altura products, and Dain Zaffke at WTB, manufacturers of Nanoraptor tyres.

I would neither have trained nor enjoyed all the riding as much as I did without the company on many rides of Ian Craig. I could still be stuck in Silver City were it not for the generosity of its cycling community in general and Barin Beard in particular.

I would like to thank all those behind the Tour Divide, especially those who made it possible for family and friends to follow the race with such enthusiasm (and to those same family and friends for their virtual support, which had very real benefits). Particular mention must also go to Matthew Lee, who found time while organising the event and preparing his own ride to guide me from novice mountain biker to Tour Divide finisher. Last but far from least, my thanks to the Adventure Cycling Association and Michael McCoy for the three years spent devising and mapping the Great Divide route, without which there would be no Tour Divide race.

Finally, thank you to Catherine, Molly, Benjamin, Thomas and Freddie. I'll only do it again if one (or more) of you wants to come with me.

SUSSEX

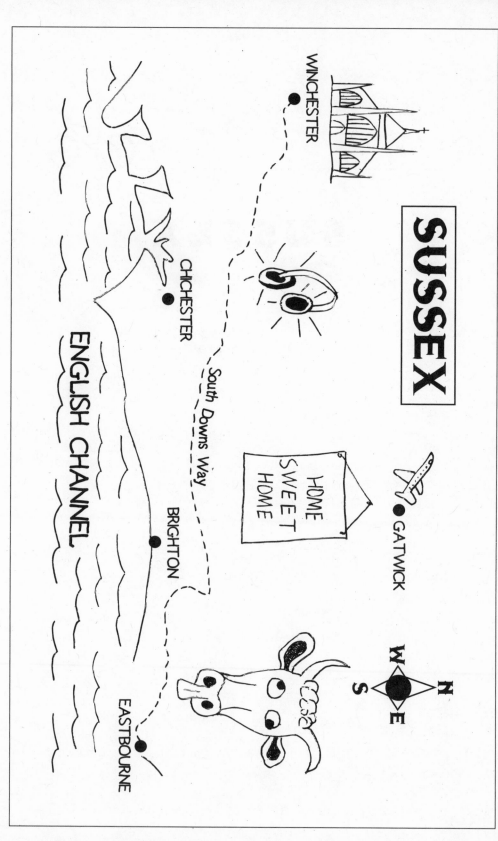

....

CHAPTER I

SEDUCTION

It seemed like a good idea at the time, though the context no doubt had a lot to do with it. Driven to despair by a prolonged stint at a grey job in a grey office in one of London's greyer suburbs, I eventually sought refuge via the virtual distraction of the Internet. After extensive and disconsolate searching through the inevitable chaff, I finally found something to fire my imagination.

That something was a news story on a cycling website about the inaugural edition of the world's longest mountain bike race. The Tour Divide was just about to start in Banff in Canada, and would take those bold or foolish enough to have signed up nearly 2,800 miles down the spine of the Rockies to the Mexico border.

Curiosity quickly became .obsession as the race itself unfurled. Although physically still very much trapped in my mundane surroundings, I was transported vicariously to the magnificent Rocky Mountains. The story of sixteen cyclists attempting to ride such a long distance off-road, to a high point of nearly 12,000 feet and with an overall altitude gain the equivalent of scaling Mount Everest seven times, was compelling. The bears, rattlesnakes, tarantulas and mosquitoes all encountered en route merely added to the drama.

It quickly became clear the story was as much one of survival as victory. Unlike the Tour de France, there were no entry criteria and no entry fee. Nor was there any prize money. There were also no defined stages to keep racers together. Riders soon became strung out over several US states. Half dropped out, not always those near the back of the field. More notable still, there was no backup or external support allowed, other than that which could be found along the route. Everybody started together in Banff, and everybody had to try and reach the same remote border post in the New Mexico desert by following the same route along the Continental Divide, but apart from that they were on their own, often quite literally.

It had everything life in an office in London didn't. I had emails and deadlines. It had solitude and timelessness. I had crowded commuter trains and a horizon broken only by shopping malls and office blocks. It had cycling and it had mountains, thousands upon thousands of them. It fulfilled all the requirements of the essential equation of Albert Einstein's ground-breaking theory of cycling relativity: $E=(mc)^2$. Enjoyment = (mountains × cycling) squared.

'I thought of it while riding my bike,' the great man had said after his eureka moment.

He also said: 'Life is like riding a bicycle. To keep your balance you must keep moving.'

Full of useful tips, that Einstein. Not wanting to contradict such a profound thinker, I decided to take his equation to heart. The Tour Divide had seduced me.

While I had been happy to be tempted when sitting in a London office at a safe distance from the badlands and the bears, a sense of guilt at having had my head turned was the overwhelming emotion when, six months later, I had bought a plane ticket and registered my intended participation. For a start, there was the small matter of not having a mountain bike. Indeed, I'd never owned a mountain bike.

The fact they had two wheels and two pedals like the road bikes I was used to was some reassurance. Yet this carried little weight in the face of my previously ambiguous experience of actually riding off-road, which amounted, as far as I could recall, to two fairly disturbing misadventures. The first came in the form of somehow becoming trapped in a bone-dry canyon in France. An hour-long lunchtime ride turned into a seven-hour survival epic as I ran out of water under a Provençal sun and ended up climbing first down and then up two twenty-foot rock walls – with a bike. The second was slightly less alarming – it was in Sussex on the South Downs – and largely involved lots of cursing at the discomfort induced by such an inefficient means of progress over bumpy ground. Nevertheless, it culminated in a silent vow never to become a mountain biker. Neither had whetted my appetite for more.

Then there were the not insubstantial reservations expressed by family and friends. Most involved questioning my sanity, which was not a particularly unusual activity. Novelty came in the form of encouragement – of a sort – from Chris Boardman.

'I really hope the adventure goes well for you. You are, of course, raving mad.'

To be considered mad by friends and family was one thing. To be considered mad by an Olympic gold medallist and Tour de France yellow jersey wearer was another level of compliment entirely.

Thus reassured, I made tentative steps towards securing a bike. A good bike, if possible. With the rider – me – possessing uncertain psychological and physical competence, an effective pedalling machine was clearly a prerequisite for success. But how would I recognise a bike good enough to cycle 2,800 miles in less than a month?

The answer came from Mr Cycles. Although strictly speaking this was the name of a shop in Seaford, rather than its proprietor, Rod, the two quickly became interchangeable. After much discussion, most of which I could only pretend to understand, I was provided with a Marin Nail Trail 29er. Marin, I was told, was the manufacturer, and Nail Trail was the name of the bike. '29er', however, had me lost.

'It means it's got bigger wheels,' Mr Cycles explained.

I must have looked even blanker than usual.

'They'll make you go faster.'

It seemed unlikely, but it was a straw I was happy to clutch at, especially when confronted with the opaque vocabulary of my few mountain biking acquaintances.

'If you want me to school you bro' we'll go out, throw down a few shapes off a booter and see if we can't stick some sick lines,' said Dom, a friend from the office in which I had discovered the Tour Divide.

He meant well, I was sure, though exactly what he meant I had no idea. By way of reassurance, Cool Dom then said something about 'berms'. This succeeded not in enlightening me but in making me think of Inspector Clouseau's attempts to single-handedly destroy the established tenets of English pronunciation.

'Not now, Kato, I 'ave fallen onto my berm . . .'

This might not be an accurate interpretation of the mountain biking vernacular, but it was certainly an accurate description of the occasionally unbalanced start to my career as an off-road rider. In fact, my first few rides involved a very convincing, if unwitting, impression of the hapless Clouseau were he to have been transferred from his 2CV to two wheels and a rocky path. Several potentially humiliating tumbles were only not humiliating because of the absence of an audience. Lying inelegantly in a clump of nettles, however, was humiliating whether the incident became a public affair or not. Still, seduction is a mysterious business. In spite of all the perfectly good reasons for not participating, not least of which were the nettles, Einstein and the Tour Divide had won me over. Whether it was a good idea or not, I had decided to give it a go.

....

CHAPTER 2

A SERIES OF
UNFORTUNATE EVENTS

Even once I had come to some sort of accord with my bike to try and avoid our causing each other mutual harm, misadventures in training were numerous.

Shortly after Easter, I decided that an attempt should be made to ride the South Downs Way in one day. Such a ride was locally perceived as the very acme of achievement, but a comparison between the South Downs and the Rockies quickly demonstrated the apparent futility of this gesture.

In purely geographical terms the difference was clear enough. The Rockies measure 3,000 miles in length; the South Downs 100 miles. The high point of the Rockies is 14,440 feet, on the imposing Mount Elbert in Colorado. In contrast, Butser Hill measures just 891 feet, a mere one sixteenth of the size. I could find no records of anyone having suffered from altitude sickness on Butser Hill.

The differences in climate are equally stark. The average minimum temperature in January in Steamboat Springs, roughly halfway along the route, is −17°C. The average high in July is +28°C. In Brighton in Sussex, the figures are +3°C and +16°C respectively. Steamboat averages 183 inches of snow per year. Brighton has no records. The extremes regularly recorded at each end of my intended ride were even more marked.

Then came wildlife. The list of dangerous creatures that inhabit the mountains of North America is enough to send shivers down even David Attenborough's spine: bears (black and brown, or grizzlies as they are more commonly known), mountain lions, wolves, moose, snakes, scorpions, tarantulas . . . In Sussex, the most dangerous animals I was likely to encounter were mad cows.

And, sorry as I was to say it, inconsiderate fellow travellers. The threat from this latter category should not be dismissed lightly. Sunny weekends, I learnt, attracted cyclists to the Downs like flies to a cow pat, often with behaviour to match. So intent were these weekend warriors on demonstrating their belief that they were Lance Armstrong's real rivals that common civility was dispensed with. Shutting gates? Not for them. Thanking others for holding gates open? A waste of breath . . . Failing to forewarn other cyclists or walkers of their impending arrival? What's it got to do with them anyway . . . I soon discovered that the only possible way to deal with such rudeness was to help already puce faces turn pucer by being ostentatiously altruistic in my own interactions with them; it helped, too, to overtake such misanthropes between gates and to repeat the dose at the next obstacle.

That most mild-mannered of figures, the rambler, was often little better. Quite why it was necessary to export road rage onto the nation's bridleways, when cars should long since have been forgotten, was a mystery. Yet the mere sight of a cyclist was enough to drive some pedestrians into a frenzy; they couldn't all be London cabbies with a personal vendetta induced by the provocative antics of cycle couriers. Other variations on the same theme included those who isolated themselves from the world around them with an iPod and headphones. Their being oblivious to others was OK; my unwittingly startling them out of their esoteric trance by passing them on a bike was not.

Even for those not cocooned in their own little world, interaction with cyclists was frequently antagonistic. It may have drawn mockery from youths gathered at bus stops, but I had fitted a bicycle bell to alert people to my presence. It generated a nice, tinkly sort of noise, designed to be a friendly compromise between no warning at all and something that might be considered too strident (such as an air-horn, or a cry of 'Get out of my bloody way, you day-dreaming path-hoggers'). Responses varied. Those a little hard of hearing, or too deeply engaged in conversation, were often oblivious to my tinkling. 'Why don't you have a bell? You should let people know you're coming . . .' they'd say, affronted at what they perceived to be my intentional impersonation of a stealth mountain biker.

Then there were those whose hearing was clearly more acute.

'You don't need to ring a bell, I knew you were there . . .' they'd declaim, affronted at what they perceived to be my impersonation of a juggernaut. I must confess to having at times dreamt longingly of a processional chariot with which to crush them, but managed to resist the temptation to turn my bicycle into one.

Nevertheless, with the start of the Tour Divide now less than two months away and the height of my off-road riding accomplishments so far having been a handful of three-hour rides, the South Downs it was going to have to be. Something – anything – had to be done, and they had the distinct virtue of being right on my doorstep.

Accordingly, one misty morning in April, Ian, a cycling friend, and I rode out of Winchester, intent on reaching Eastbourne by nightfall. Actually, intent implies a degree of earnest endeavour that was curiously lacking. We ambled through the dappled, early morning shade of the trees so characteristic of the western Downs and, while most continued to slumber, admired West Sussex at its finest. The greys and blues of the first hour slowly became infinite shades of green and gold as the mist dissipated. By Old Winchester Hill we were bathed in glorious sunshine. We were also lost, but even this couldn't wake us from our torpor. Less surprisingly, nor could the sausage rolls and pasties that I consumed, much to Ian's consternation, at the Queen Elizabeth Country Park as we crossed the A3.

Such lethargy was exacerbated by obstacles not entirely of our own making. At the pub on top of Devil's Dyke, it took over half an hour to accomplish the seemingly straightforward tasks of buying and consuming a pint of Coke and using the facilities, of which we could only find one and for which there was a considerable queue. I waited impatiently, all the while conscious that, hopping around in my cycling shoes on the tiled floor, I sounded like a demented tap dancer. Those in the queue with me, fresh from an afternoon of inactivity and alcohol consumption, clearly agreed that I was at least demented.

At last we were inspired to make a concerted effort to recoup lost time. Past Jack and Jill windmills we tried to raise our pace, but it was too little, too late. At nearly 6 p.m. at Ditchling Beacon the game was up. Stymied by impending darkness and seduced by the delightful picnic provided by Camilla, a friend of Ian's, that was designed to fuel our final push, we conceded defeat. To console ourselves, we drank tea and ate malt loaf, pouring honey into each other's ears and telling ourselves our achievements were still considerable. Nevertheless, by the time I returned to Hurstpierpoint, I had ridden scarcely 80 miles in more than 12 hours. I had also suffered noticeable sunburn on my south-facing right arm, hardly a promising portent for the deserts of New Mexico, should I ever make it that far.

The next challenge came the following day, when I had to retrace my wheel tracks to collect the car from Winchester (and hopefully turn my left arm the same salmon-pink colour as my right). I set off alone in high spirits, and made good progress for the first 40 miles or so. Then, just as I was bracing myself for another bout with the pasties from the Queen Elizabeth Country Park, disaster struck. My bottom bracket – the axle where the pedals join the bike – ceased to turn. Apart from nearly catapulting me once more into the shrubbery, this sudden seizure made it abundantly clear that any further pedal-powered progress was now beyond me. Even if I had had the correct tools and replacement parts with me it would have been beyond my skills as a mechanic to effect a repair.

Vexed as I certainly was, though, the situation was not particularly grave. By the simple expedient of pushing the bike to the top of the next hill and freewheeling down the other side I made it to the sanctuary of the café. Inspired by tea and yet more pasties, I tracked down the number of a taxi company, who promised to take me and my recalcitrant steed the remaining 25 miles to Winchester. Once safely back at the car, all that was left was for me to spend the long drive home considering what would have been my fate had I been in the great wastes of the Rockies rather than benign Sussex with a taxi company at hand.

I had already been reassured to a degree by a kind offer from my wife's cousin, Steve, a resident of Los Angeles. It turned out that he was the owner of a transport company specialising in moving crews and sets for rock groups around the whole of North America. I was unlikely to need a used Bon Jovi stage design, but logistical backup could prove invaluable in the event of a breakdown.

'As I've said, my reach is rather remarkable, so anywhere along the way that you need a hand, please call,' he wrote.

He also gave me a toll-free phone number that I could use 24 hours a day, seven days a week. That appeared to resolve my concerns about getting hold of spare parts, at least those that could be delivered to a town or metalled road. For troubles beyond that, I vowed to increase still further my emergency food supplies.

The beginnings of my second attempt were scarcely more auspicious. The previous night started gaily, with family visiting for dinner. The responsibilities of being a host should always be taken seriously, and it seemed incumbent on me to ensure a steady supply of aperitifs and then wine with the meal. An all too rare offer to retire to the local hostelry to continue the conviviality was then accepted with alacrity – too much alacrity, if truth be known. By midnight, I collapsed into bed secure in the knowledge that I could now ride un-aided to the South Pole if so required.

At 6 a.m., however, a little voice in my head could clearly be heard reprimanding me for the previous evening's excesses. At 7 a.m., as we started to ride, the voice had become somewhat more insistent, calling into question the wisdom of my chosen path, both for today and in a few weeks' time. 'Go back home, go back to bed,' the siren voice wailed. With a discomfiting wind and rain imminent, I had to rely on the resolve of Ian, once again my training companion, to ensure the day's venture didn't end before it had properly begun.

As is inevitable on the South Downs, the ride started with a stiff climb, at the top of which we were greeted by the squall that had been threatening since we left home. The cloud scudding a few feet above our heads was greyer even than the English Channel off to our left. Once more we seemed – in my mind, at least – to be doomed to ignominious failure. But while I cursed and complained in my new and highly effective waterproof jacket, Ian continued to lead at a stiff pace, clad only in a cycling jersey, seemingly oblivious to the meteorological conditions. The wind howled and the rain stung any and all exposed flesh, but as I couldn't make Ian hear my moaning above the gale I had no choice but to keep following.

At last, the weather eased. The dubious charms of the Queen Elizabeth Country Park café were once again within our reach.

Gradually thereafter I began to warm to the task. Even the unlikely traffic jams caused by more than 100 mountain bikers heading the other way as part of an organised 'South Downs Way in three days' ride could not put us off our stride.

'What's the collective noun for a group of mountain bikers?' I asked Ian.

'A bloody nuisance,' he replied, as we were once again pinned against the brambles by sheer weight of numbers.

This time we had removed the logistical hurdle of completing the ride from one end to the other by starting in the middle ('I wondered why you hadn't done that last time,' asked Catherine, my wife, when I explained our itinerary; I declined to confess that it was because we hadn't had the presence of mind to think of it). As a result, once we had made it to Winchester on our outward leg, the return was facilitated by a tail wind. Learning from our slothful progress of a few weeks previously, we pressed on and surprised ourselves by the relative speed of our return and the fact that we were not overtaken by nightfall. A semblance of progress had been made. We returned to the car exultant.

To distract from my uncertain progress as a mountain biker, I dived headlong into the logistics of preparation, reasoning – hoping – that the vast array of new toys I was collecting would provide adequate compensation for my own fallibilities.

First, it being incumbent on all cyclists to 'look the part' (even if only to disguise the reality of being a spare part), the increasingly avuncular Rod supplied me with a pair of matching black and green Mr Cycles jerseys. His concern for my sartorial welfare was touching, and he assured me that they had never been proved to attract bears.

'And if they do, at least you'll be wearing a well-designed food wrapper,' he chortled to himself.

Through Mr Cycles I was also able to procure most of my clothing needs via one of his suppliers: Altura Pro-Gel cycling shorts (with high-tech gel inserts to protect my 'ischial tuberosities', or sit bones if you prefer); similarly conceived cycling mitts to protect my ulnar nerve, which takes a considerable battering on rough tracks; top of the range waterproof jacket and overtrousers; a variety of vests, leggings and arm- and leg-warmers.

Once all that had arrived, only a few things cycling-related remained. I looked down my wish list, which had become a mass of crossings out.

'A rucksack and a pair of cycling shoes that I can also walk in,' I concluded, still conscious of my earlier mechanical failings and continuing mechanical incompetence.

'If something happens to the bike that I can't fix I might need to walk 100 miles to get help.'

This was the first time I had articulated my Plan B and, caught up in the moment, I even managed to make it sound like a perfectly reasonable proposition. Self-delusion was clearly a vital part of a traveller's armoury.

Along with tangible supplies, Mr Cycles also sought to help me overcome my phobia of bicycle maintenance.

'You might think it's all right to walk 100 miles to find help, but I suggest you try and fix your bike first,' he advised.

Over tea and a sticky bun, Rod and the equally proficient Rory performed drastic surgery on my new bike in the dungeon below the shop, all the while endeavouring to impart some of their knowledge. Their approach to curing my phobia was clearly to make me confront my worst fears. Accordingly, between them they dismembered my magnificent new machine, removing all the bits that had transformed it from an angular piece of metal into a bicycle: wheels, handlebars, saddle, pedals and cranks. Just when it seemed impossible to remove anything else, Rory produced a grinding implement that was surely better designed for use on victims of 'extraordinary rendition' rather than an innocent bicycle. Indeed, he proceeded to effect some peculiar kind of torture on the poor bike's nether regions, grinding remorselessly away at the bottom bracket housing until it seemed its structural integrity would be fatally compromised. In Seaford, no one can hear your bike scream.

'They spend so much time engineering these frames to perfection, and then they spray them with paint and leave rough edges,' said a baffled Rod through a mouthful of bun, oblivious to my mounting alarm.

'But take a bottom bracket,' he added, looking at me knowingly. 'If a bottom bracket housing has rough edges that aren't perfectly parallel to the frame it will mean the stresses aren't distributed through it evenly and it will fail, and we wouldn't want that to happen where you're going.'

I smiled weakly, and tried not to get in the way as the bike was reassembled.

Further distractions came by the way of camping and first-aid requirements. Uncertain as to whether it was possible to ask a doctor for 'something in case I fall sick while cycling in the Rockies', I nevertheless made an appointment at the local practice. I was greeted by a youthful Irishman, who listened intently as I explained my predicament. I endeavoured to make the tales of upset tummies that abound on the Tour Divide website sound as macabre as possible, and stressed the remoteness of where I was heading. Before I could make an explicit plea for antibiotics, he prescribed me with two varieties.

'This one is a general purpose, broad spectrum antibiotic, and this one is for serious, water-borne infections like Giardia. You'll know when you have that,' he said cheerily.

I had less success when requesting a generic snake venom antidote.

'There is no such thing. The best approach is to avoid being bitten.'

Nor did he have any bear vaccine.

'Sounds like a fascinating trip,' he concluded, making it sound little more than a visit to a museum. 'Be sure to come back and tell me how it goes. Next, please.'

Meanwhile, in Brighton, Eddie at Open Spaces undertook to supply me with all the necessary camping goodies. The only problem was defining what exactly was necessary. Did I need a stove? What about a water filter? Should I take a tent or a bivvy bag? Of course, Eddie couldn't answer these questions for me, but he could provide the benefit of his wisdom, even if his habit of only looking sideways at his interlocutors rendered this wisdom even more enigmatic than it already was.

'I should opt for the most comfortable approach if I were you, but then I'm not you, am I?'

I took this sagacity as an indication of great experience in the wilder parts of the world, and assumed his idiosyncratic demeanour was the result of casting wistful glances over the Downs, wishing they were the more imposing ranges on which he had previously roamed. Maybe he could come with me and act as an adviser? He declined politely. In the end I opted for two parts asceticism to one part indulgence: no stove, no water filter, but a tent rather than a bivvy bag. Food and water I hoped to be able to find from external sources; sleep would be my own responsibility.

The final piece in the jigsaw was to fashion a means by which all these belongings could be safely carried on my bike. With a rucksack, a rear pannier rack and a small saddlebag already sorted, the crux remained the handlebar bag into which I hoped to cram all my food as well as my direction notes and maps. Such vital and probably heavy fare would need a particularly resilient arrangement to cope with the rigours of off-road riding, yet off-the-peg solutions in the UK were noticeable only by their absence. The much vaunted, custom-built designs from the US that featured regularly in Tour Divide photos were unavailable due to the demand generated by a field of 42 riders. Inspiration finally arrived at 2 a.m. one anxiety-ridden, insomniac night, leading to a mad dash out to the shed in my pyjamas to check the plan would work. Confident in my design, it then fell to my neighbour, Alan, in whose own shed all sorts of metalworking wonders abounded, to turn concept into reality: a two-pronged piece of metal rod to fit through the sleeves of an existing bar bag, shaped like a shallow 'U' and held in place by passing over the handlebars but under the stem. One brief trip to the scrapyard later, plus a few grunts and groans as the steel was bent to shape, and 'Alan's patented bar bag mount' came into being. Lightweight it was not, but heavy and hopefully indestructible would do for me.

The countdown continued. With two weeks left before departure, I was joined by another Alan and Steve, two Tour Divide veterans, for a final training ride on the South Downs. The aim was to complete the entire length of the Downs twice on consecutive days, fully laden.

Just making sure I could fully load the bike was the first hurdle. In spite of considerable preparations, the moment of departure still found me baffled by the absence of a place to stow my sleeping mat. Trying hard not to betray my incompetence to such vastly more experienced companions, whose bikes and kit looked as rugged and efficient as their owners, I spotted a spare strap. Quickly tucking the mat under this strap, I announced that I was ready for the off. I also hopped immediately onto my bike, hoping to disguise the last-minute nature of my packing arrangements.

I was too late. Alan and Steve were already casting a paternalistic eye over my set-up. A few vaguely promising nods of approval suddenly halted when Steve saw my sleeping mat.

'That will fall off,' he warned. 'If it doesn't fall off today, it will definitely fall off in the Rockies.'

With no other options apparent, I shrugged my shoulders and we set out. Sure enough, within 5 miles I had to retrace my steps to collect my free-spirited mat. Eventually, space was contrived in my tent bag and the ride continued.

The pattern was set early. Alan and Steve rode cheerily uphill, chatting away and admiring the birds in the trees and the sheep in the fields. I laboured in the rear, trying to pass off my wheezing and panting as appropriate responses to their conversation. The flat sections would be spent with me trying desperately to recoup lost ground, while downhills were merely a chance to anticipate how severe the next climb would be.

The situation slowly deteriorated. New shoes and an inadvertently modified foot position caused my right knee to become first slightly sore and then noticeably painful. My inability to keep pace increased in direct relation to the discomfort induced by my knee. By halfway I was reduced to borrowing painkillers and anti-inflammatories from Alan (my own 'first aid kit' was in fact no more than a facsimile, stuffed with what I hoped would be an appropriate volume and weight of proxy materials – batteries, deodorant sprays, that sort of thing; it had seemed inconceivable that I would need a supply of real medication so close to home). At Devil's Dyke, with more than 30 miles still to ride but only a stone's throw from home, I had to admit defeat. Although endeavouring to put a brave face on it, I had no option but to leave my companions with my tail between my legs.

'See you in Canada,' said Alan. Right at that moment, nothing seemed less likely.

CANADA

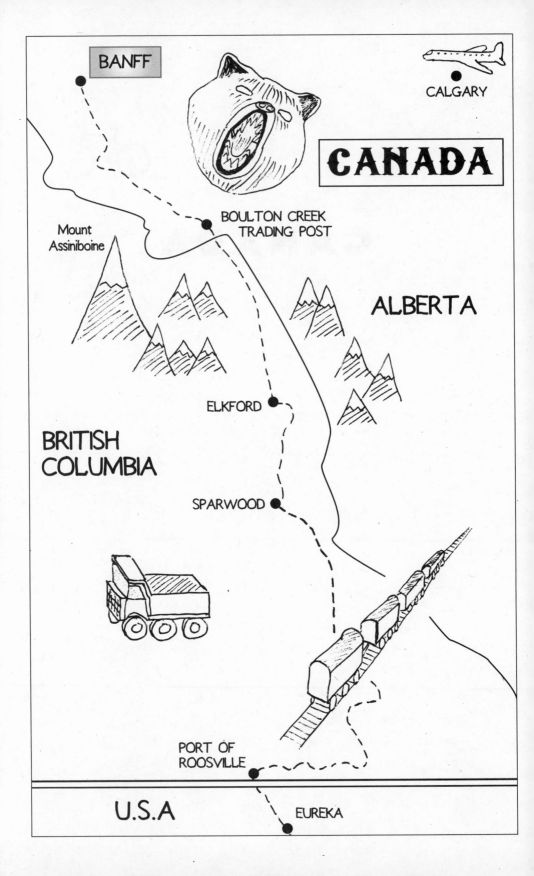

....

CHAPTER 3

THE BEAR NECESSITIES

Two weeks after the ignominious end to my training ride with Alan and Steve, my departure from the UK was suitably low key. The coach station at Gatwick can never be a fitting place for taking leave of anyone, let alone wife and children. Just finding the right place to unload a car was a minor miracle and an unwanted cause of extra anxiety. The prefabricated concrete ceiling was so low and so oppressive as to dampen even the fondest farewells.

'Don't get killed,' was Catherine's eminently sensible and comforting advice as I struggled to remove the boxed-up bicycle from the boot of the car. I assumed she was thinking of the dangers I was set to face. The possibility of an even more untimely death caused by negotiating fat concrete pillars and thin pavements with a wonky trolley and speeding coaches close at hand only became apparent shortly after she left.

In a mild state of emotional turmoil after having said goodbye to Catherine and to Thomas and Freddie, my two youngest children who had turned three only the day before, I cursed every wobble and teeter of my precariously perched load. Fellow travellers once again seduced into oblivion by their iPods and mobile phones provided moving obstacles – or sometimes targets, I confess – for my cumbersome load. As I waited, drenched in sweat, for the shuttle to Heathrow, it seemed unlikely that the Rockies could house any trickier terrain.

An hour later and my first experience of Heathrow's much vaunted Terminal Five was, if hardly the architectural revelation some may have claimed, at least much calmer. The doorways were wide enough for the bike box, and the process of checking in was smooth. Unable to fathom the machines that purported to allow me to register my arrival myself, I went to enlist the help of a rather suave chap clad in a corporate BA uniform. Fortunately, he seemed to be the check-in clerk equivalent of contemporary television newsreaders – no longer desk-bound, he was at liberty to roam the terminal's wide open spaces, dispensing wisdom and assistance to all who required it. In less than the time it had taken me to read the initial page of instructions, he had accomplished the task delegated to him and found me a sought-after seat by an emergency exit.

Nevertheless, the cost and time-saving benefits of DIY check-in, even when aided by a roving member of staff, were immediately undermined by my need to then check-in my luggage. At least there was no queue.

'Is that a bike in the box?' I was asked by the man who was studying my passport with the air of a bemused child looking for a sliver of hope in an overwhelming exam paper.

I supposed it was the large, handwritten notice saying 'BICYCLE – FRAGILE' that had given it away. Such powers of observation clearly boded well for identifying undesirable travellers.

'Is it heavy?'

'Oh, no,' I replied, lifting it up as effortlessly as I could – no mean feat with not just a bike but sufficient kit for four weeks in the Rockies also stuffed inside. I made sure not to put the box down onto the scales.

'It's amazing how little bikes weigh these days, isn't it?' said the clerk, happily oblivious to my artifice. Maybe his powers of observation weren't so great after all.

'You need to take it over to the outsize baggage department.'

As I did so, I once again passed the DIY check-in machines, where the helpful newsreader-type chap now had a queue of puzzled travellers asking for his assistance. The 'do-it-yourself' aspect of the process didn't appear to have been widely adopted.

After startling the two operators of the outsize baggage handling machine from their afternoon reverie, I placed the bike box gently onto the conveyor belt. Too gently, it seemed, as the conveyor did not engage and the two operators, doing a very passable impression of children's television favourites the Chuckle Brothers, edged it forwards and backwards to entice it to move.

'Be gentle with it,' I pleaded, nicely I hoped, before I went to buy a newspaper from the newsagents next door. Leaving the shop two minutes later, presumably just at the point the Chuckle Brothers thought I'd long since been consumed by passport control, I watched them pick up my bike box and drop it from a considerable height onto the conveyor which, gratifyingly for them at least, started to move. The Chuckle Brothers had become the Brothers Grimm. As the bike disappeared from view into the bowels of the airport, I hoped this particular fairytale would have a happy ending.

The flight itself passed uneventfully. Clint Eastwood's *Gran Torino* warned of the dangers of a side of North America that I was hoping not to encounter in the Rockies.

Once below the early evening clouds, the descent into Calgary was revealing. Circling over the city, the surrounding plains seemed to be endless. Roads and fields came and went in the vast blanket of high flatlands. The only topographical features noticeable in the midst of the myriad gentle undulations were shallow gullies carrying water courses, some natural, some man-made. The city itself, even though a classic example of North American sprawl, was dwarfed by its setting. If this was how overwhelming the flat parts of Canada were, I wondered how my arrival in the mountains would feel.

On the ground, the sense of being somewhere very big was confirmed by the wildly varying times shown on the clocks in the customs area. I knew Canada had several different time zones, but this seemed ridiculous. Maybe it was all part of a plan to disorientate newcomers and help officials flush out ne'er-do-wells. I assumed the ferocious questioning I received just as I was about to break out into Canada proper was similarly motivated.

'Is that a bike in the box?' said a uniformed woman (was this my first ever Mountie?). The sense of déjà vu from check-in was only overcome thanks to the mirror sunglasses worn by my questioner.

'Yes, it is,' I replied, trying desperately not to sound as irreverent as I felt. The large 'BICYCLE – FRAGILE' labels had survived the flight intact.

Behind her mirror shades, my interlocutor betrayed no indication of her likely reaction. Time stood still while I contemplated the hassle of unpacking the bike simply as a result of inadvertently mocking an officer of the Canadian Border Services Agency. After all, it had taken me more than three hours of incompetent fumblings in the garden to squeeze it into the box in the first place, although trying to fend off footballs aimed imprecisely at the nearby goal had contributed to the delay. At last, the silence was broken.

'Enjoy your ride,' she said, with just a trace of a smile.

The shuttle to Banff confirmed impressions of the scale of my surroundings and the incongruity of Calgary, a rapidly expanding city of a million inhabitants located in the middle of what appeared to be nothing. Downtown, a few miles to the south, was an impressive array of skyscrapers lit by the receding sun that was now peeking out under the western edge of the glowering clouds overhead. Whatever the non-downtown sections of such cities are called was a less than glittering amalgam of poorly maintained, rectilinear streets and down-at-heel malls. Occasionally, older streets at curious angles betrayed the underlying morphology and confirmed it was not entirely flat.

As the shuttle began its long trek west, the city eventually had to yield to grassland. Ranches replaced suburbs. First horses, then cows and even deer appeared out of the window. Johnny Cash sang on the radio. Every few miles an impertinent tree broke the monotony of the terrain. The excitement this generated was tempered, however, by the fact that such brazen cheek only served to magnify the emptiness everywhere else.

Everywhere else except straight ahead, that was, where the Rockies were rising ever more abruptly out of the surrounding plains. The sun glinting on snow-clad summits did its best to soften their jagged profile, but the general picture was of dark rocks and even darker trees. Closer inspection was not to dispel this assessment. The sun had set by the time I reached Banff, but it was still light. The sense of being in the heart of the mountains was palpable.

My cumbersome arrival at the Young Women's Christian Association hostel drew a good degree of attention, though not from the staff at reception. Instead, I was greeted in what I would soon learn was a West Texan twang.

'Hey, how ya doing? Do y'all mind if I ask if you're a racer?'

Even though the Tour Divide was very much a race, it hadn't dawned on me until that moment that my participation conveyed onto me such a vaunted status. Fortunately, I had the presence of mind to say yes.

'Gee, that's great. I got here yesterday and I sure been looking forward to meeting some other racers.'

My new companion was Cadet, a schoolteacher from Midland-Odessa.

'It's famous for two things. First, for being the setting for a football movie called *Friday Night Lights*. Y'ever heard of it? It's a great movie.'

I said no, football in the US being played with the wrong-shaped ball. I also assured Cadet that the village I lived in was not famous for anything, as far as I was aware.

'It's also famous for being where George W. Bush is from,' he added, with slightly less enthusiasm.

This was something about which I felt I could offer fewer assurances.

After a receptionist eventually appeared, I was concerned to find myself allocated to Room 101. Cadet put me at ease.

'Anything has to be better than where I was last night,' he said, before detailing the raucous party thrown by his Quebecois roommates. Like all good parties it involved wine, women and song, and didn't stop until nearly breakfast time.

'Ideal preparation for a near 3,000-mile bike race,' Cadet added, but he still preferred to join me in my Orwellian dorm where we could be left in peace to consider our own personal demons rather than those imposed by others.

The next morning, Cadet showed me around Banff. The setting was every bit as impressive as my brief shuttle journey the previous night had led me to believe. Timber-clad mountainsides rose sharply in every direction. Rocky ground took over as the trees began to thin out, the uninterrupted slopes culminating in serrated ridges and peaks, the highest of which – just under 10,000 feet – were dusted with fresh snowfall. Although far from overwhelming in terms of height, the mountains exuded a rugged invincibility. Perhaps it was the absence of the pastures and grazing lands that characterise the Alps. Everything was very angular, and the dry, clear air, even though the sun possessed considerable warmth, created a feeling of brittleness like that generated by extreme cold.

The town itself didn't take long to explore. Over the bridge across the Bow River at the south of town, the wide, straight main street contained mainly curio stores and outdoor shops. It seemed churlish to compare a town little more than a century old with Alpine settlements that have developed over the past millennium, but the temptation was difficult to resist. Certainly, the inevitable grid layout of the centre lacked the 'olde worlde' charm of the winding alleyways of Guillestre, say, or Aosta.

Instead, the buildings were a mix of modern functional, modern faux-frontier style and a few genuine, timber-framed buildings from the town's early days. The effect was attractive. Off the main street, the modern functional architecture took over and the roads remained just as wide. Pick-up trucks the size of small houses lay abandoned in vague proximity to the kerb. A satisfyingly wide variety of tea and coffee shops, along with more outdoor shops, provided evidence of just how much the town – population less than 7,000 – acts as a tourist honeypot for the surrounding Banff National Park, which attracts more than 4,000,000 visitors each year. Early June, however, seemed to be something of a quiet time and the streets and cafés were uncrowded. The pace of life was gratifyingly slow.

In contemplative mood I decided to confront my fears and seek advice about bears. It would be fair to say the prospect of meeting a bear had already been occupying my mind since signing up for the Tour Divide. My only previous encounter with a bear had, in fact, been a hallucination brought on by fatigue. I was uncertain whether it was better to encounter a bear or be so tired as to think that you had. It seemed as though this trip would provide the opportunity to make a direct comparison.

In the last nine years, I had learned, there had been 28 recorded fatal bear attacks in North America, though many more had ended in serious injury. I tried to rationalise this as just three bear deaths per year in a population of more than 300,000,000 and an area more than twice that of Europe. Yet such logic had seemed considerably more persuasive on the South Downs than in my current surroundings. After all, fatal bear attacks had been recorded in every state of the Tour Divide route. More alarming still, in 2005 a jogger had been killed by a bear while running near a golf course in Canmore, only a few miles from Banff. Exposure to garish fashions and reactionary opinions are the only threats encountered on golf courses in the UK.

At The Ski Stop, which, in spite of its name, was also a bike shop, I made sure to fit my bike with the latest in high-tech, audio bear-warning devices.

'You mean a bell,' Catherine said later, a touch dismissively.

The fact I also intended to carry a whistle seemed to cut little ice.

'The best thing is certainly to make as much noise as possible,' one of several Ski Stop assistants told me. 'Try singing, that sort of thing, because bears will normally run away from noise.' My questionable baritone, certainly very effective at driving away humans, suddenly seemed to have become a virtue.

'But what do I do if I do meet a bear?' I asked, trying hard not to sound too concerned. The attempt was clearly a failure. Sensing a little sport, other members of staff gathered round to swap anecdotes of bear encounters. As the extreme nature of the encounters described increased, it crossed my mind that I had become an unwitting participant in a modern, more humane form of bear baiting.

Nevertheless, some potentially useful advice was forthcoming. If an attack actually took place, it would pay to know your bear. Brown bears – grizzlies – were more likely to lose interest if you played dead. Indeed, fighting back could be seen as an act of provocation. Black bears, on the other hand, were less gentlemanly and would happily kick – and maul and bite – a man when he was down. But brown bears could appear black, and black bears sometimes brown. If you were sure it was a black bear, the only option was to fight back. Even if you were sure it was a grizzly, if the attack hadn't waned after a minute you should also fight back. I tried to imagine counting to 60 while being mauled by a 500-pound ball of teeth and claws. My face must have betrayed my inner anxiety.

'You'd better take some pepper spray and bear bangers,' the assistant concluded after his co-tormentors had dispersed. I drew some succour from the fact that they all still had all of their fingers and limbs and there were no large scars across faces.

To soothe my nerves, I visited the library to check my messages. The first one I opened was from Bob, a Canadian friend whose bear advice I had also sought. By way of reassurance, he sent a link to a local newspaper, detailing how a 15-year-old boy had been dragged from his tent by a black bear, saved only by another camper firing two shots from his rifle to scare the bear away.

'Paul, the article that I forwarded to you is an example of an isolated incident,' Bob wrote. 'Generally, when you are travelling through the Canadian Rockies, you *must* stay at a designated camp-ground. It would not be advisable to stop at the side of the road and pitch your tent. First, it is illegal. Second, it can be dangerous. There are not just bears, but also coyotes, wolves and cougars. Cougars will definitely attack a single person.'

Nobody had mentioned cougars. A quick Internet search revealed four fatal North American cougar attacks since 2000. While I was at it, I also checked for fatal snake bites – also four – and lightning strikes – 33 in the first half of 2009 alone. Maybe bears wouldn't be my biggest problem after all. I decided to ignore the link to fatal bee stings.

'In any event, bicycling in Canada is 100 per cent safe with regards to wildlife,' my friend continued. 'No grizzly bear is going to come charging out of the bush and chase you down on your bike. The bigger danger is the possibility of being hit by a car as there are lots of idiot drivers. Hope you really enjoy your adventure.'

My other messages were less alarming.

'Here is some advice from your children,' wrote Catherine. 'Molly says "be second the best and don't die". Benjamin says "be first the worst and second the best and don't fall off". Thomas says "Thunderbirds" and Freddie says "please come down". I don't know where you have to come down from but he was adamant.'

Suitably inspired, I decided it was time to put my bike together. Only one part of it was protruding from its box, which I felt was a good sign. Slowly, and by casting furtive glances to copy what Cadet was doing, I managed to put everything back in the right place, a slightly buckled wheel being the only obvious damage incurred during the journey.

The next day we went on a brief ride to make sure the bikes were fully functioning, joined by another British rider, John, from Newcastle by way of Milton Keynes. Not only had he assembled his bike quicker than I could eat my breakfast, he betrayed the self-confidence integral to success by having booked his return flight from Phoenix in Arizona over a week earlier than mine.

The seemingly gentle climb up to the Hot Springs that had provided Banff's original raison d'être in the 1880s caught us all by surprise. Either the altitude – Banff is the highest town in Canada, but still only 4,500 feet above sea level – or more likely the dryness of the air meant we rasped our way up the hill.

Then we undertook our first foray into the boundless woods surrounding the town, venturing the first few miles along the Tour Divide route. Bears might not have been the biggest actual threat to our safety, but they certainly exercised the greatest hold over our imaginations. Even though we were on a marked trail used by thousands of cyclists each year, the sense of having strayed into the wild was immediate. Elk nibbled on the grass below the imposing Banff Springs Hotel. Not for the first time I wondered quite why I'd wished so fervently for an adventure on this scale. Beware of what you wish for, it might come true.

Back at the hostel, I was simultaneously wishing for more and less carrying capacity. The way John had ridden up the hills on the track out of town made it clear what an advantage it would be to have less weight. Whenever I asked him if he had what I was just about to pack he invariably said 'no'. Even a tent had been forsaken, in preference for a bivvy bag.

On the other hand, the growing realisation at just how inhospitable the terrain would be made me wish I could carry more. More food was certainly on the agenda if I could find room, even if stories of a bear's incredible sense of smell called into question the wisdom of carrying peanuts loose in the pockets of my cycling jersey as was my wont.

The vexation of trying to resolve these packing dilemmas was unintentionally exacerbated by the presence of the first Tour Divide groupie. 'Crazy Larry' was something of a Banff character with a well-known passion for mountain biking. 'Crazy Larry' was not just an affectionate nickname.

'I've had my name changed by deed poll because I work with disadvantaged young people and they think I'm crazy,' he said proudly to a dormitory now filling with increasingly frazzled cyclists.

Larry – or maybe that should be Crazy – wore his hair in a mullet, and rattled his way around the room sporting a variety of bear protection devices. The most impressive weapon in his armoury was a machine to fire four bear bangers in one go.

'It's just not worth taking any chances with those bears,' he said knowingly.

Crazy's favourite occupation appeared to be discussing bike set-ups and bemoaning the fact he couldn't join us on our ride.

'Man, it's just gonna be awesome.'

He had hit the nail on the head, but my capacity for small talk is limited at the best of times, and I soon needed to find a quieter spot to continue wrestling with my logistical conundrums.

In between worrying about what I should and shouldn't take, I began to weigh up rivals for the prestigious *Lanterne Rouge* competition. *Lanterne Rouge* is the term used to describe the last-placed finisher in the Tour de France. As well as generating often much-needed sympathy from onlookers, thanks to the wearing of a red race number, it conveyed to the recipient a useful notoriety, facilitating invitations to the lucrative round of post-Tour criterium races that once constituted the major part of a professional cyclist's income. I wasn't sure whether completing the Tour Divide would open up similar remunerative opportunities, or even if the Tour Divide considered the *Lanterne Rouge* a legitimate race within a race, but it was clearly the only competition in which I was likely to play any meaningful part.

I also had to make sure I did my homework in case the competition developed along the lines of the equivalent award for finishing last in the Giro d'Italia. As befits the often controversial and partisan nature of racing in Italy, the battle for the infamous *Maglia Nera* was the source of great skulduggery. Shady deals were struck, long-cuts were taken, punctures fabricated – all for the sake of claiming a footnote in sporting history. Perhaps unsurprisingly, the official competition only lasted from 1946 to 1951.

First among my rivals, by his own admission, came Cadet. I had already explained my perverse desire to give up the *Lanterne Rouge* crown at the last moment – if possible – in order to be able to tell my children that Daddy hadn't come last for once. Winning the *Lanterne Rouge* or not coming last would be a tricky choice.

'I can be that guy,' he smiled generously.

Then there was Rick from Tallahassee, Florida. I didn't dare suggest as much to him but, at 63, I felt as though there were reasonable grounds for thinking he might be nearly as slow as I anticipated being. Martin, from Austria, was younger but had such a capacious and immaculate set of bright red panniers that speed didn't seem to be his priority. There were others, too, with less easily quantified *Lanterne Rouge* credentials. Would the tandem go twice as fast or twice as slowly as us singletons? Would the mechanical simplicity of those riding without gears outweigh their obvious benefits?

Some riders would clearly not be involved. Along with the superstars of the event, like last year's winner and race organiser Matthew Lee, and John Nobile, record holder for the race from the US border to Mexico, Alan and Steve had already established just how strong they were on the South Downs. John had done likewise in our short spin around Banff.

The two Italians who arrived one evening in Room 101 also looked seriously speedy. Small Italian Bruno, bald-headed and lean, looked how Marco Pantani might have looked had he lived longer and eaten more pizza. The circumference of his thighs must have been at least twice that of my own. Big Italian Dario was well over six foot and had thighs twice as big again. Maybe the extra weight would count against him.

To make myself feel better and improve my aerodynamic efficiency I went for a haircut. A very attractive lady, originally from Toronto, first washed my hair, then gave me a delightful head massage. This level of luxury felt rather like a cranial version of the Last Supper.

Showing a degree of attention to detail and pride in her work that had escaped all those who had previously been let loose on my scalp, she concluded by asking if I would like my eyebrows trimmed. I'd always been quite proud of my bushy brows, inherited from my maternal grandfather, but now they felt rather incongruous. Besides, having never been asked such a question before, it seemed possible I would never be asked it again and a unique opportunity would have been spurned. I said yes.

All that remained was to attend the eve-of-race barbecue on the banks of the Bow River. As befits a pack of hungry cyclists, burgers were consumed with relish, both literal and metaphorical. In spite of the bravado, however, they were accompanied by relatively little alcohol. Most people were too intent on trying to understand how to make sure their GPS SPOT tracker units worked to want to cloud their brains with beer.

'To send an OK message you press the OK button,' said Matthew. 'To switch the tracker on press the on button and then hold the OK button for five seconds. OK?'

I hoped so.

We also tried to digest the last bit of route information provided to facilitate our riding through a new section, the beautiful but wild and rarely visited Upper Flathead valley. With the Upper Flathead being comfortingly known as the Serengeti of North America due to the density of its big game, which to me meant bears, it seemed quite important to know where we were going. The route cards contained much less detail than those for the rest of the route. Nevertheless, when combined with the photocopied map of what was deemed to be the tricky bit – a 1-mile 'connector' between forest service roads – they seemed adequate. Besides, now was no time for doubt.

After the barbecue had run its course, cyclists scurried hither and thither in varying degrees of panic. Alan captured the prevailing mood.

'What are you doing? Should I be doing it?'

When I confessed to wrapping my new route notes in clingfilm he seemed less concerned to emulate me. I, too, wasn't sure if it set quite the right, heroic tone. Finally, the frantic activity began to diminish, even if sleep remained a distant prospect. The noises and disturbances caused by four young children were as nothing compared to the frantic attempts at relaxation of a dormitory of cyclists about to embark on such a ludicrous endeavour.

....

CHAPTER 4

A HORSESHOE FOR LUCK

DAY I

Race morning dawned clear and fresh. To remove ourselves from the hothouse and enjoy the early morning sunshine, Cadet and I decided to consume breakfast away from the hostel. Elk grazed by the Bow River as we walked into town.

The Jump Start Café was not Banff's coolest café location – it boasted little in the way of world music and organic cookies – but it had the considerable advantage of being right next door to the post office. Along with most of the other racers, we both needed to send superfluous clothing and kit home before departure, and the last thing we wanted was to be at the back of the queue.

More importantly still, the Jump Start had the calming demeanour of a place frequented by pick-up-driving locals rather than frenzied cyclists. Accordingly, Cadet and I ordered our oatmeal, pastries and coffee while Hank and Chuck and friends (it could have been Jim and John, but Hank and Chuck seemed more appropriate) ate their own vast repasts and bantered with the staff.

With pre-race nerves growing in spite of the tranquillity of our surroundings, Cadet responded to a call of nature. His departure through the door behind the serving counter prompted an unlikely flurry of activity.

'Have you still not put up that horseshoe?' asked Hank (or it might have been Chuck), motioning to the empty space above the door.

'Gee, I need a man to do that for me,' said the lady behind the counter, clearly accustomed to recognising an opportunity when it presented itself.

The response was like sticking a pin into a bear.

'Well, why didn't ya say so . . .'

If there wasn't an actual scrum to get out of the door and be the first to return from the fleet of pick-ups parked nearby with hammer and nails it was only because the cumulative effect of years of large – one might say 'man-sized' – breakfasts meant the reaction times of some of the café's regulars had begun to slow. Nevertheless, here was Banff Man in his element. Not only was there food, company and conversation that focused solely on the sports section of the local paper; now there was also a chance to show off the tools kept in the trunk of the pick-up truck.

In fact, here was a justification for a whole way of life that to more sensitive eyes might have seemed a rather ostentatious display of machismo and rampant consumption of the earth's finite resources. Following the natural presumption that it would be unmanly not to be able to help a damsel in distress, and aware that just such a crisis as the absence of a lucky horseshoe could happen at any moment, in the most unlikely surroundings, it followed as sure as night followed day that a man must have a big truck full of tools. How else could he be reasonably expected to supply a hammer and a tin of nails at short notice (and all the other accoutrements that are required to perpetuate a certain concept of manliness)? Accordingly, in less than the time required for Cadet to return, the requisite tools had been provided and a long-overdue portent of good luck had been installed.

Unaware of the level of activity that his departure had unleashed, Cadet was slightly bemused to discover we had now become minor celebrities. He had, of course, just become the first person to walk under the newly installed horseshoe, an achievement for which he was roundly congratulated. When I topped it by becoming the first person to walk under the horseshoe in both directions – success in our forthcoming endeavour was now assured – curiosity finally got the better of our fellow Jump Starters.

'You boys are cyclists, ain'tcha?'

Clad in Lycra and clipperty clopperty cycling shoes, we were in no position to disagree.

'Where ya headed?'

'Mexico.'

For the second time that morning, pandemonium ensued. Also, and possibly for the first time ever, Hank and Chuck and friends were compelled to express admiration for cyclists.

'That's one helluva trip.'

This brief conversation then inspired a demonstration of the North American penchant for spontaneous hospitality that can leave jaundiced Europeans choking on their cynicism (and their breakfast). We were offered a present to help us on our way. The present came in the form of an insulated coffee mug that our hosts thought might provide a useful means to keep our liquid refreshment cool in the New Mexico deserts. I was about to explain that it was probably a very good idea but one that wouldn't work in practice when Cadet, aware of the sincerity of the gesture, wisely accepted his gift.

'It's very kind of you, ma'am, it'll do just great.'

I agreed and, after a refill of coffee, during which time the conversation around us returned to the burgeoning success of a Calgary footballer (American, that is, not Association), we left for the post office feeling more confident than we had any right to.

An hour later, the hostel was a hive of activity and poorly disguised anxiety. Cyclists with far too little or far too much luggage milled around, killing time. Very few seemed to have settled on what I had considered the happy medium. People took pictures and made last-minute modifications to packing arrangements. John tried to fit a specially commissioned map case that had been promised two months ago but had only arrived at 5 a.m. that morning. The Tour de France it was not.

I spoke briefly to Per, who, although actually Swedish, had put down London as his home town and had become British by proxy. The fact that he had only signed up for the race a few weeks before the event had been encouraging, tempering fears about the task ahead. Clearly someone, at least, felt the years of preparation of which some riders were now boasting was over the top.

Nervous wives and at least one husband, as well as other friends and relatives, gave well-intentioned but invariably superfluous last-minute advice ('Don't feed the bears, honey'). Then merciful distraction was provided as the tandem arrived. Powered by the Petervary husband and wife team, the tandem itself was blue at the front and pink at the back. Any thoughts I had entertained that they could be among my rivals in the *Lanterne Rouge* competition were immediately dispelled. Apart from the fact that Jay Petervary was a former record holder for the border to border part of the route (and had once been described in a magazine article as having the internal energy of a small supernova), it was now clear that his wife – Tracy, or T-Race as she was better known – would hardly hinder his speed. Unlikely as it seemed, the 'Love Shack' was in it to win it.

Winning the race was definitely not on my agenda, even if I did inadvertently contrive to give this impression.

'First, to finish,' was my answer when asked by Aaron Teasedale, the one journalist in attendance, about my goals. Unfortunately, the comma seemed to become misplaced and Aaron interpreted my response as an assertion of likely victory. The way he then reacted to this interpretation made it abundantly clear that 'likely' would be that last adjective he would use to describe a victory by me. I felt oddly disappointed, but hastened to correct the misapprehension.

'No, I meant that my first goal was simply to finish. Anything else . . .'

'Yes, I realised that,' said Aaron, a little quicker than was strictly necessary.

'Why are you participating?' he persisted.

Slightly thrown by my earlier inarticulacy, the best I could manage in response was 'Why not?'

What I had intended to convey, in a George Mallory 'because it's there' kind of way, was that, once you had become aware of such an event – once you had become aware that such an undertaking was even possible – the pertinent question was not 'why?' but 'why not?' How could you not want to respond positively to such a hitherto inconceivable opportunity? It seemed to me as tenable to shun something like the Tour Divide as to not investigate a previously undiscovered room in your own house. What's more, as all the answers to the question 'why not?' were inherently unsatisfactory, the only conclusion that could be reached was that there was no reason not to do the race.

I'll concede, however, that it wasn't immediately apparent that this was how Aaron had perceived my seemingly truculent response.

At 9.50 a.m., all 42 cyclists left the grounds of the hostel for the brief journey to the official start at the Banff Springs Hotel. The hotel was commissioned in 1886 by Cornelius Van Horne, the railway baron, to attract tourists to his recently completed Canadian Pacific Railway. The hotel's distinctive, castle-inspired design was created by influential US architect Bruce Price. The end result was certainly massive and imposing, in a way no doubt intended to mirror the grandeur of the surrounding scenery. Yet it also seemed perversely fussy and intricate, which the nearby mountains, with their endless seas of green trees and pure, clean lines, most definitely were not. Nevertheless, such was its stature and the beauty of its surroundings that television directors and team sponsors the world over could easily be imagined waxing lyrical at the prospect of staging a global sporting event against such a backdrop. The Tour Divide was not yet that event.

The hotel's rear car park was a different matter completely. Tucked discreetly behind the service entrances and recycling bins at the back of the hotel, the car park was no more than a flat area of gravel distinguished only by providing access to the start of the Continental Divide Trail. A dozen spectators and some bunting was the scant evidence of our imminent departure.

As riders once again milled around, uncertain exactly what was going to happen next, a racer bolted from the massed ranks and yelled behind him as he disappeared into the forest.

'Let's go.'

Without further ado, the race had begun. There was just time to consider the fact that the rider – Matthew Lee – had effectively already stolen a 30-second advantage over those of us at the back of the field before we could start. I decided it would be churlish to complain.

I also resisted the temptation to make a fool of myself in the name of trying to lead the race, even if only for a mile or two. Instead, Cadet and I stuck to our recently developed game plan of ignoring the siren temptations to go too fast, too soon. Actually, suggesting we had the ability to succumb to these temptations would have been inaccurate, but at least the notion that we were going slowly through choice rather than through necessity made us feel better.

As we made our way south along the valley of the Spray River, the density of the trees increased as the riders surrounding us thinned out. The trail remained wide and accommodating, however, and progress was smooth. It was hard to believe that we were on our way to Mexico.

The impression that we were merely out for a spin in the woods was reinforced when, after an hour or so, we left the trail and rode onto a wide, gravel road bleached white by the sun. The glare and the heat gave a foretaste of challenges to come, and the endless ridges were spectacular: peaks of over 10,000 feet were visible on each side. But several day-trippers had parked up nearby, making it feel more like the Lake District than the Rockies.

This conundrum had not escaped the authors of the Canadian section of the route map. 'This section of Great Divide Canada showcases some of the most magnificent scenery in the entire Rocky Mountain Chain. Paradoxically, the route feels somewhat more settled, or civilized, than many sections to the south in the United States. One reason for this is that Great Divide Canada passes through a string of national and provincial parks which, not surprisingly, attract a great deal of visitors.'

To our considerable surprise there were not just visitors but also some spectators, taking photos and shouting encouragement. To our even more considerable surprise, only a short distance later we encountered one of the icons of the Rockies: a trio of male big horn sheep licking salt at the side of the road. It was immediately clear that the name 'big horn sheep' was something of a misnomer. These sheep did not just have big horns. They were big, full stop, and exceptionally muscular. Big horn, big sheep would have been more accurate, if something of a mouthful. In spite of their size they looked benign, though possessed of a self-confidence, bordering on arrogance, that shone defiantly from their unblinking eyes.

After several miles on the road, the route crossed over a dam and became rougher. Massive mountains reflected in the still reservoir, though the scene suffered from the reservoir having a dirty bath-ring around its edge, the blight of all reservoirs when not full. I hoped to catch a glimpse of the famed Mount Assiniboine, the highest peak in this section of the Rockies and, judging by the photos I had seen, as shapely a mountain as could be imagined. James Outram, the first man to reach its summit, certainly thought so. 'Its massive pyramid forms a conspicuous landmark from almost every considerable eminence for scores of miles around, towering fully 1,500 feet above its neighbours, and by its isolation no less than by its splendid outline commanding attention and admiration.'

The first white person to record having seen the mountain, the Catholic priest and explorer Pierre-Jean De Smet in 1845, was even more effusive. 'The monuments of Cheops and Chephren dwindle into nought before this gigantic architectural cliff of nature.'

A conspicuous landmark it may have been, but it remained hidden by the lower peaks on my right. Instead, I had to make do with the not insignificant consolation of Mount Shark and, later, Mount Sir Douglas, named after Douglas Haig, to admire.

Next came some rougher riding still, following a trail through dense woods. Cadet had dropped back, and I made a brief effort to catch some riders further along the shoreline in order to avoid tackling it on my own. To my relief, my new companions were more than happy to whoop and holler their way through such desirable grizzly country. Connoisseurs of the peace and tranquillity of our surroundings we were not.

The incongruity of the route again became apparent when the trail through the woods reappeared in another parking lot at the end of another dusty road. Aaron the journalist was there, along with Joe Polk, the creator of the MTBcast website that made the telephone messages recorded by riders while on the route available for friends and family to listen to. I sat and tried unsuccessfully to eat some lunch, waiting for Cadet. Joe asked if he could record an interview to post on his website, then Aaron suggested taking some pictures.

'Shall we session it?'

I'd just started the world's toughest bicycle race yet I now found myself in the middle of a radio interview and magazine photo shoot. The extent to which the whole endeavour had skewed normality was confirmed by the fact that this unlikely situation seemed quite unremarkable.

* * *

Cadet arrived, having already eaten, and we continued our journey along the dusty road. It was far from difficult riding but we both flagged. Earlier, we had been carried on a wave of relief at having finally started. Now, the anxieties of preparation seemed to be taking their toll.

Half a sun-baked hour passed. A large dog, or so it appeared, ambled nonchalantly along the centre of the broad road ahead of us.

'Coyote,' said Cadet.

'Are they dangerous?' I asked, not feeling much inclined to put in a sprint if evasive action were necessary. The animal in front of us was two foot tall at the shoulder, maybe a touch more. It was rangy in physique, rather than muscular, but it possessed a disdain for other road users, including a car that had just passed by, suggestive of an absolute lack of fear.

'Nah, they're no problem,' Cadet assured me.

We had scarcely returned to our previous companionable silence when Cadet spoke again in a slightly more urgent voice.

'Look! Bear!'

'Pardon?'

'Bear!'

'Where?'

'There, down the slope off to the right.'

'Oh, yeah!' I said, excitement temporarily getting the better of fear.

The road had been climbing for some while but had recently settled into a flat section carved across the hillside. On our left, the uphill slope, the trees abutted the roadside, but on our right, the tree line was occasionally broken by aprons of grassland. Sure enough, a hundred or so yards ahead of us, at the bottom of one such apron, was a small bear. At least, it looked small from such a distance.

'What should we do?' I asked, Cadet having now become the arbiter of all things animal related.

'Keep riding quietly, I guess.'

Along the roadside, between the road and the grass, was a motorway-style crash barrier that helped to partially obscure us from view. We rode cautiously, peering over the barrier to maintain a close eye on our furry friend. As we approached, it became clear it was not a small bear but a giant black bear. Well, medium-sized maybe. Stood quietly on all fours two thirds of the way up the grassy apron, 30 yards below the road, it was about 3 foot high at the shoulder and 4 foot long. Initially it seemed oblivious to our presence, but then it turned to look at us. Nothing happened.

As we neared the bear, we skirted briefly out of sight before returning to the barrier side. When we were in a position to see it again, it was still looking. Still nothing happened.

Another hundred yards along the road and the bear was out of sight. When, a few minutes later, it still hadn't come bounding along the road after us, we breathed again.

'Wow, that was cool,' said Cadet.

'Excellent,' I agreed. 'I definitely wanted to see a bear, at a nice, safe distance, and now that's happened I can quite happily ask the fates to make sure I don't see another one for the rest of the trip.'

By 5 p.m. the bear excitement had passed and weariness had returned. We decided it would soon be time to stop. It didn't seem very adventurous to stop so early but, as we rode along the by-now metalled road and were passed frequently by lumbering camper vans, the cloud that had been threatening for a while started mustering with a vengeance. What's more, the campsite at Boulton Creek Trading Post was the last official accommodation until Elkford, a further 50 miles away and almost as far as we had already come. We were unlikely to make it that far that night, and the prospect of camping rough in bear country at this early stage of the journey held little appeal.

The official campsite may have been self-service but how to book in was far from self-explanatory. Fortunately, a neighbourly couple explained the process, and proffered some more bear advice. Given that he looked like a bear and she looked like she had just swallowed one whole, I felt inclined to believe them when they said we must use the bear bins for food and all of our perfumed belongings as well. It seemed ungrateful to point out that we did not have many toiletries with us.

The Trading Post itself offered little by way of diversion, other than the girl behind the shop counter who had enormous holes in her earlobes, held in shape by equally enormous circular earrings. While I stocked up on chocolate bars for the next day, the lady at the head of the queue asked how long it had taken her to create her holes.

'About two years, but I had to stop for a while at certain sizes,' she explained proudly.

Cadet tucked into dinner but I could only look on enviously. My tummy made it quite clear to me that it had no desire to consume any food, even if my brain disagreed. Whether this contradiction was brought on through nerves, or exertion, or possibly the burgers consumed at the pre-race barbecue the night before, was uncertain. I made do with two bottles of Pepsi.

Slowly we were joined by other riders: Martin from Austria (he of the immaculate bright red luggage) and Floridian Rick ('You can call me the old man of the race') were followed in by Jeff from Arizona and Bruce from Iowa, neither of whom I had met before. It was quite a convivial gathering. Maybe Tour Divide racing would just be one long party?

Meanwhile, another Arizonan, Deanna, maintained a lonely vigil outside in the gathering gloom, clearly still uncertain as to whether our current mileage was sufficient to justify calling it a day. At 20, Deanna was the youngest participant in the Tour Divide and was an avowed vegan; having scarcely eaten anything other than burgers in my six days in North America thus far, I was already concerned how she would find enough food. What's more, as if cycling 2,800 miles down the Rockies without recourse to the most popular and widely available foodstuffs were not enough of a challenge, she was riding on a bike with no gears and a fixed wheel, which meant she couldn't even stop pedalling when going downhill. I was looking forward to freewheeling a good proportion of the course when gravity was on my side. She also appeared to be wearing espadrilles.

'If I come in and get warm I'll definitely want to stop,' she explained as I went to move my bike out of the rain.

I felt considerably less than heroic.

Eventually the café and shop closed and we all retired to our tents. Except for Cadet, Jeff and Deanna, that is, who retired to their bivvy bags. I silently thanked them for providing a first line of bear defence. In a rather half-hearted attempt to salve my conscience, I explained where the bear bins were.

Rick looked askance.

'Aw, gee, you're not gonna make me take it *all* down, are ya?'

'Toothpaste as well,' I insisted.

'What kind of a country is this?' asked Martin.

Snug in my tent, I listened to the rain drip through the trees above before falling into a fitful sleep.

I had ridden 60 miles. More than 2,700 still remained.

CHAPTER 5

....

BRINGING UP THE REAR

DAY 2

As dawn broke and the noises of activity among my companions increased, I slumbered lazily in my sleeping bag. It was below freezing, and my lethargy suggested my decision to stick with a combination of lightweight sleeping bag and an extra layer of clothes had been vindicated.

I eventually surfaced at 5.35 a.m. to find almost everybody else with half-struck tents and breakfast prepared. I struggled in the cold, damp shade of our shale pitch to pack everything away while keeping it clean and dry and my hands warm and functioning. In spite of the time I had spent organising my luggage in Banff, I was at a loss when it came to finding my overboots and gloves, even my hat. I packed and re-packed several times before being satisfied I was wearing all that was necessary to stave off the chill that had now enveloped me, and that everything else was safely stowed.

Breakfast was a perfunctory affair, partly because it was such a gloomy spot, partly because almost everyone else had already left and I was keen to join them. Only Cadet remained, seemingly sanguine about the distance ahead. Our mutual aim was the town of Sparwood, 80 miles away. Yesterday had taught us that we rode well together, but better when left to set our own pace, so I took my leave.

After a mile of tarmac, the trail disappeared out of the back of a car park into the trees. The going was instantly tougher than at any point the previous day. The 'trail' was little more than two lines of tyre tracks in the mud created by yesterday evening's downpour, interrupted by puddles and broken branches.

With twigs cracking beneath me as if in a Fenimore Cooper novel, I began the laborious, 1,000-foot climb to Elk Pass. The effort distracted me from concerns about early-morning wildlife. It also began to warm me, though my extremities remained mere blocks of ice.

As I approached the bottom of a steep, rough uphill section labelled 'a virtual wall' on the official maps, I saw the gear-less Deanna wheeling her bike only a short distance ahead of me. Rather ungallantly, I immediately selected the easiest of my 27 gears and set off in pursuit. At this early stage of the route, through stubbornness rather than the minute increase in speed it afforded, I was still intent on riding as much as possible. By now cursing the extra layers that had been essential only a few minutes before, I weaved my way up the track. I passed Deanna a few yards before the top.

'Awesome,' she enthused.

Unfortunately, I was too out of breath to acknowledge her encouragement.

The rest of the climb to the pass was similarly rough but not as steep. The route followed a gash in the timber cover created by a powerline. On such a pristine morning and against a backdrop of such perfect mountains this would have been a heinous crime were it not for the fact that it allowed passing cyclists to enjoy the spectacular views.

At the top of Elk Pass I stopped to admire my achievement and my surroundings. Deanna arrived and we celebrated our first crossing of the Continental Divide (from the eastern, Atlantic/Arctic watershed to the western, Pacific watershed) as well as our arrival in British Columbia. I asked where Rick, Bruce, Jeff and Martin were. They had, after all, departed our camp before me but after Deanna.

'You didn't pass them?' she asked by way of reply. They clearly hadn't passed her. On such a beautiful morning, the prospect of them enjoying an unintended excursion into the surrounding hills had us more amused than concerned.

With no one else in view, we embarked on the equally rough descent into the Upper Elk valley. It immediately became clear that Deanna's inability to free wheel would slow her going downhill just as much as the lack of gears had done the same on the ascent. Even my questionable descending skills saw me disappear ahead of her into the trees, a mix of alpine fir, Engelmann spruce and lodgepole pine. I fished my anti-bear whistle from inside my jacket and began to toot as loudly as possible. It felt peculiarly disrespectful of the surrounding tranquillity, but the vegetation on either side of the trail was impenetrable and memories of yesterday's bear encounter remained fresh.

The opportunities to take in the fabulous views over the Elk Lakes Provincial Park and neighbouring mountains increased as the gradient eased. Although only one of several hundred provincial parks in British Columbia alone, the scenery was breathtaking – perhaps literally, as I crested a blind rise having neglected my whistle-blowing duties. I noisily unclipped my pedals to take a picture across a clearing, only to be interrupted by an ominous rustling on the other side of a thicket. The invisible crashing and grunting reached its climax when a startled and clearly irate moose lolloped out of the shrubbery. Even though my camera was immediately to hand I was too transfixed by the appearance of such a large beast to take a photograph. I slowly digested the fact that it wasn't a bear. Nor was it a bull moose with antlers, and there didn't appear to be a calf present. For all its snorting, the moose also seemed to be weighing the threat posed by its new-found companion. Fortunately, it clearly concluded there was none. The scrub and saplings that would have been shoulder high on me just tickled its tummy as it slowly disappeared from view.

Before me to the south lay a magnificent valley. It would be 40 miles before I arrived in Elkford, itself a town of only 2,500 souls. Yet the happy, holidaying Calgarians of the previous night's campsite were a mere 6 miles behind, separated only by vast acres of wood and bog. The round trip by car to the trail head at which I had now arrived was more than 200 miles; it could have been a world away. Deanna was a few miles behind. Ahead, the nearest rider would have had a start of at least several hours. Once the moose alarm had passed, the sense of isolation and solitude was thrilling.

The track broadened as I rode between meadows and clearings replete with juniper and an plethora of unidentifiable wild flowers. Streams babbled busily on their way to invisible lakes. Butterflies and other insects roused themselves in the sun's growing warmth, while snowshoe hares, still with snow – or white hair, at least – on their shoes, bounded to and fro, indicating the regular absence of humans.

After 15 miles the trail, which by now had become a fully fledged dirt and gravel road, crossed to the west side of the valley. As the elevation slowly reduced, the density of the forest increased and the hand of man became more evident. Clearings in the timber were now straightlined segments felled by machine rather than natural meadows, full of the bleached bones of tree roots and forgotten branches. The intensity of the sun's glare on the pale road increased, as did the effort required to surmount each rolling undulation. In the middle of a straight section rendered seemingly interminable by the heat haze into which it disappeared, I stopped to marvel at the scale of things, vaguely hoping that somebody might join me to prove that it wasn't all a figment of my imagination. To my surprise, within a couple of minutes somebody did join me, but it was not a cyclist. Instead, it was another grizzly-bear sized man armed with tales of the real grizzly bear he'd seen patrolling these very woods the day before. I noticed that he had a powerful rifle slung across the front of his quad bike.

Shortly after, as I continued to desiccate slowly, I passed the 100-mile mark for the journey so far. It was 11 a.m., meaning that even though yesterday's ride had been brief, it had still only taken 25 hours to reach this landmark. With a total riding time of 28 days the height of my aspirations, I was reassured about the speed of my progress. A minor increase in speed and I would be at the requisite 100 miles per day. This beacon of encouragement propelled me into Elkford.

The transition from wilderness to civilisation was almost immediate. In the case of Elkford, however, the term 'civilisation' had to be used with a degree of caution. A broad, metalled road flanked by parched concrete culverts led past a few outlying houses to a crossroads, to the right of which was a small concrete mall with various assorted buildings. The central attraction was the parking lot and the vehicles in it, all of which were consumed by an air of weariness. Everything felt 20 years behind Banff, which was no mean feat given the town was only founded in 1971 as a home to those working in the nearby coal mines. The prospect of a reinvigorating lunch waned with every pedal stroke.

Appearances can be deceptive, however. The nondescript café-cum-restaurant that consisted of a narrow, windowless corridor between two external doors in one of the outbuildings turned out to provide excellent food and company. Still uncertain how to interpret the mixed signals emanating from my stomach, I ignored the long list of classic North American cuisine and opted instead for a Greek salad with garlic bread. My appreciation may have been heightened by the morning's exertions, but I was immediately transported back in time to an earlier cycling excursion in the Peloponnese where just such a salad had had similar recuperative powers.

I was brought back to the reality of British Columbia by an unlikely offer.

'Would you like to see how the rest of the racers are doing, eh?'

My initial reaction clearly betrayed my bewilderment.

'I've been following the race, eh, and I've got a BlackBerry, eh, so we can see where everyone is, eh?' explained my inquisitor, who was evidently intent on providing single-handed proof of why cousin Steve had referred to Canada as 'eh land'. As dialect foibles go, it was slightly less annoying than Antipodean rising terminals, but it was still early days.

With a mouth full of tomato and feta I must have given some silent sign of affirmation for I was then provided with an 'eh'-filled commentary on the race to date. Matthew Lee, as expected, was at the front of the field, having nearly made it to the border some 130 miles further on. Most of the other riders were between him and Sparwood, where I hoped to spend the night. More reassuringly, Cadet and the others could be seen making rapid progress to Elkford. So rapid, in fact, that Arizonan Jeff walked through the door as my Internet guide and race groupie Ken concluded his exposition. Cadet arrived shortly after and we confirmed our shared plan to stop in Sparwood. After unsuccessfully attempting to resist the lure of an unhealthily rich cheesecake, I embarked on the next leg of the journey with a stiff road climb towards one of the enormous mines that had led to Elkford's foundation. I immediately regretted the cheesecake.

After the climb, the first part of the remaining 25 miles to Sparwood ran down a narrow and rapidly dropping tributary of the main Elk River, the two separated by a small massif. The valley's sides were steep and rough, a roughness exaggerated by the scars of mining and logging activity, but the cycling was easy, thanks to the favourable gradient.

By the time I returned to the main valley the wilderness had all but dissipated, the valley having flattened out and become dotted with farmsteads and smallholdings. The sun, too, had become obscured by mid-afternoon clouds as it had the day before, and which seemed to be the predominant weather pattern for the time of year. A notice in the Elk Lakes Provincial Park had warned of the dangers posed by lightning storms, with snow or hail, that were common in early summer.

The outskirts of Sparwood, criss-crossed by railroads and strewn with workshops, revealed just how much the town, like Elkford, owed to its proximity to major coal mines. It was bigger and busier, however. It also had a certain sense of civic pride, made evident by the prominence afforded on the way into town to one of its most famous inhabitants. The mustard-coloured 'Titan', or to be more accurate a Terex Titan 38-19, was, at the time of its construction in 1974, the world's biggest dump truck, capable of hauling 317 tons of coal or earth in one load. The display signs nearby proudly boasted of its 236 ton net weight, 66 foot length and 23 foot height (56 foot when the tipper body was raised – higher than a Brachiosaurus). Modern designs and more efficient hauling techniques had rendered the Titan redundant, however, even if it still found a useful role in its enforced retirement as a draw for tourists. I wondered if Sparwood and Elkford would be able to say the same when the coal supplies had been exhausted.

I drew inquisitive glances from local residents as I hosed down my bike at a car wash and then booked into the town's second-best motel (out of a choice of two). It had been recommended by 'BlackBerry Ken' due to its relative cheapness and the fact that it had a Chinese restaurant next door. I took a bath, simultaneously washing my already filthy cycling kit, and hung out my still damp tent to dry. Cadet and Jeff arrived and we went for dinner. Rick declined to join us, insisting he had to find a pizza restaurant, even if it meant cycling a mile uphill into town, and Martin had already decided he needed the laundry facilities provided at the town's other motel at triple the cost. He obviously intended to keep his kit as pristine as his panniers.

Just as we were about to go into the restaurant we saw Deanna cycling past in the wrong direction. Of course, it turned out only to be the wrong direction if you were not stopping for the night as we were.

'I need to keep going so I can get a bit of a head start for tomorrow,' she explained.

Rather sheepishly, I asked where she intended to stop.

'Oh, I'll just bed down at the side of the road. It'll be fine.'

Our guilt at our apparent indulgence and lack of adventurousness knew no bounds. Deanna was right about the difficulties of what lay ahead. The new route through the Upper Flathead valley consisted of 105 miles of rough going, with a complete absence of services or any other form of civilisation. I told myself that a good night's sleep and a big meal would be more beneficial than a head start, but it seemed like hollow consolation.

Peculiarly, the sense of guilt lasted only as long as it took to inhale the appetising aromas from inside the restaurant. As we tucked in to chicken chow mein, sweet and sour chicken and stir-fried vegetables, my stomach having temporarily decided that a full repast was the only antidote to its ongoing tribulations and my mental unease, we were joined once again by BlackBerry Ken.

'After you left, eh, I just got to thinking about having a Chinese meal, eh, and then I couldn't stop, eh, so I decided to see if you guys had made it here, eh, and wish you good luck for the rest of the ride.'

....

CHAPTER 6

WHERE THE WILD THINGS ARE

DAY 3

The phoney war had ended. Partly through choice, but mainly through necessity, the first two days had been something of a gentle introduction to the rigours of the Rockies. The previous day's Upper Elk valley may have seemed remote, but it was only the uppermost 40 miles that had been left undisturbed by main roads and the Trans-Canadian railway. Even then, mining and logging activity had penetrated another 25 miles up the valley from Elkford.

The Upper Flathead valley, by contrast, is unique in southern Canada in its isolation. It is the only low-altitude valley to have resisted permanent human settlement or opening up to through-transport. In spite of this, it has been under relentless pressure from mining companies.

Aside from its isolation, which on its own was a major preoccupation for cyclists faced with 100 miles of solitude, the valley also represents a unique wildlife habitat, particularly dangerous wildlife. According to Flathead Wild, the group campaigning to have the area classified as a national park, the Upper Flathead supports a greater diversity and abundance of carnivores than any other area in North America. That means not just brown and black bears (there are estimated to be 100 grizzlies alone), but also mountain lions, wolves, wolverines and lynx (there have been no recorded human fatalities caused by these last two creatures, but they both possess lots of sharp teeth and I was keen not to establish a precedent).

Then there was the fact that the Upper Flathead was new to the Tour Divide this year, having previously been excluded from the official route for being too inaccessible. The area was served by a handful of rideable forest service roads, but there had always been a missing link for through-cyclists. The possibility of such a route had provoked much debate on the Tour Divide website until, two weeks before the start, the following had been posted:

> The preliminary news is in from Flathead reroute scouts, Bill and Kathy Love of Whitefish, MT. The beta can be reduced to one critical word: Singletrack! They spent the greater part of three days sussing out the passes and looking for a connector between Wigwam Forest Service Road and Rabbit-Phillips Forest Service Road. They returned with exalting news: confirmed trail between the two FSRs. It was getting pretty tenuous at two weeks out from TD's grand depart, so the beta comes as grand relief. 2009 Tour Dividians will, indeed, be rewarded with first tracks along this remote backcountry passage.

I didn't know what beta meant, but clearly the real adventure was about to begin.

At 5 a.m. the alarm sounded. By 5.05 a.m., Cadet had put the coffee machine on as I measured out the cereal bought from the poop-a-scoop section of the supermarket. I congratulated Cadet on what was a cheering, domesticated scene.

'That don't offend my sensibilities none,' he replied, which I took as a sign of approbation.

Packing after a night under canvas had been something of a trial. The luxury of a roof over our heads meant we were ready to leave in little more than half an hour, except that Cadet had to resign himself to another delayed start after realising he had left his sunglasses in the motel's reception. Given his decision the previous night to off-load a large proportion of his more essential belongings (bivvy bag, sleeping bag, camping mat) in pursuit of a leaner, meaner set-up this seemed a curious decision.

'They're prescription sunglasses. I'd like to see the bear that's about to eat me,' he explained, not unreasonably.

Once again it was below freezing as I rode back to the route. The first hour, as the sky slowly brightened into day, was along a traffic-free main road, then a perfectly smooth spur leading to a vast coal mine. I passed Bruce, who had arrived late into Elkford, and then Rick, both of whom were clearly better at early mornings than me. There was no sign of Deanna, but nor was there evidence of any bears having feasted at the roadside.

On the approach to Corbin, the pressures facing the Upper Flathead were all too plain to see. The enormous coal mine had provided the metalled road for which I had been hypocritically grateful. It had also lopped off the top of one of the nearby mountains, and created a dense network of access tracks through the neighbouring forest. Then there was Corbin itself, a camp for peripatetic miners of the sort I would have insisted had died out at about the time of the Pony Express had it not been arrayed in front of me. The decomposing remains of mine machinery were hardly picture postcard material.

My cheerless reverie was disturbed as I rounded the next bend to find the way blocked by a train, parked rather inconsiderately across the road. Actually, to describe the obstacle ahead of me as simply a train would be misleading. I now realised that I had been cycling past the train's coal trucks, partially obscured by some desultory trees at the roadside, for the past couple of minutes. Further ahead I could count another 25 wagons before they disappeared from view around a bend. I had come to the Rockies prepared for all manner of obstacles, but this was something new.

I began to consider my options. They seemed strictly limited. The map revealed no alternative route, leaving the equally unappealing prospects of waiting for the train to clear the road or finding a way through it. I couldn't help but think of Molly, Benjamin, Thomas and Freddie's likely delight at such an obstacle. Freddie, in particular, was a considerable fan of the 'troublesome trucks' that frequently wrought mischief and mayhem in the Thomas the Tank Engine stories.

Had I been a mere pedestrian, crawling under the trucks would have been an option, but there was insufficient headroom for a bike. I shuddered at what would happen if it or I became stuck. Negotiating the gap between two wagons seemed the best bet. I approached cautiously. The area below my shoulders was made impassable by the mass of couplings, hoses and chains that connected the two wagons together. Above that, however, the back of each wagon had a narrow metal walkway that provided a potential route to the other side. The difficult part would be lifting the bike that high in the first place and ensuring it remained there while I climbed up to join it. Cyclists may be blessed with strong legs and enviable lung capacity, but upper body strength is often most noticeable by its absence.

I was just about to test the extent to which my arms had become as useless as those of Tyrannosaurus Rex (relative to the rest of its impressive physical attributes – I didn't imagine a T-Rex would have had too much trouble picking up my bike) when Rick arrived, accompanied almost immediately by a crescendo of clanking. The flippant suggestion that it might have been his bike making such a terrible noise was instantly dismissed from my lips when the train – on which I was still leaning – started to move. The din was tremendous. It sounded like an iron leviathan being woken from the sleep of ages. Great, metallic booming noises shot up and down the valley as it began its slow, lurching progress. I was glad I wasn't balanced on a wagon walkway.

After five minutes of grinding and groaning, our vexation had become considerable. An early start was being squandered, and we still had the best part of 90 miles ahead of us if we were to avoid an impromptu night in the wild, all because of a train on the road. Then, the monster before us ground to a halt. In less time than it took to say 'now's your chance', 63-year-old Rick had rolled back the years and leapt onto the couplings.

'Pass me a bike,' he instructed.

I tried, and failed, to pass him his own bike. It was a good deal heavier than mine. At my second attempt I was more successful. It wedged nicely onto one of the walkways. Rick kept it steady while I clambered between the pair of them, jumped down the other side and lifted it off. One down, one to go.

Even motionless, the train shuddered and juddered alarmingly. I reached my bike and fortuitously managed to wedge it, unmoving, in the same spot, jumped up and over and then retrieved it. Rick clambered down and we endeavoured to regain our composure. Instead, we descended into a fit of giggles of which my boys would have been proud. In the freshness of the early morning we exhaled plumes of spent breath that could have been smoke from a steam engine.

'That was fun,' said Rick. 'Mind you make sure to tell your dad that I didn't make you do it.'

We set off again and began climbing through the woods towards the Upper Flathead valley. The sun was starting to win its battle against the chill of the night. It promised to be a hot day.

After cresting the pass a long, rough descent beckoned. Judging by the state of the creek at the side of the trail there had obviously been recent, heavy rain. In fact, on several occasions the stream became so frustrated by the confines of its natural course that it decided to annexe the rocky path too. At times, the water through which it was necessary to pass made riding impossible. Either it was too deep and fast-flowing, or it had shifted the shingle and created patches loose enough to snare passing bicycle wheels. Or both. The cold on feet and straining calf muscles was like a knife.

Once in the bottom of the main valley, it was immediately clear why it was deemed such a special area. The rough track apart, there was no sign of human intervention. Instead, having succeeded in resisting the overwhelming tree cover of forests grown for timber, it retained a shifting mosaic of floodplains and scrub woodland, in which no doubt lurked all the area's dangerous animals. Yet for all its isolation, the succession of open areas and the variety of shrub and tree species created a much more welcoming, less intimidating aspect than yesterday's man-made austerity.

Effort and aesthetics combined to create an equilibrium that on its own provided an explanation, if any were needed, for the motivations for such physical endeavour. I rode down the valley in a trance.

The temperature continued to rise. After a couple of hours I stopped in some shade for an early lunch of Pepperoni, pitta bread and raisins. Rick rode past. Shortly after what passed for the main meal of the day I caught him again as we finally turned away from the Flathead and began the climb of Cabin Pass. Appropriately enough, we soon passed a log cabin. The door was ajar and, in spite of the heat of the day, smoke was emanating from the little chimney. Outside stood two backwoodsmen who looked for all the world as if they might have been living there since the days of Davy Crockett. Except for the large pick-up truck parked next to the cabin. We exchanged greetings and realised how comfortable a night spent there would have been.

Sensing the effort that was to come, Rick decided to stop for a breather. Just as he did so, Cadet arrived, now reunited with his sunglasses. He had clearly been cycling well and was full of Texan good humour, providing a timely fillip in the midday sun. We had now descended to only a little over 4,000 feet, lower than the start in Banff, and the temperature reflected this.

'I just knew I had to git rid of some stuff, and since I did I been a-cruisin',' he enthused from under the brim of his sun hat, scarcely seeming to have broken sweat.

I explained that weather like this in Yorkshire occurred only once every ten years at most.

'This ain't hot,' he smiled. 'This is just a little appetiser for real desert heat.'

His promise that I would enjoy New Mexico's dry heat rang a little hollow.

The road up Cabin Pass began under dense tree cover and in considerable humidity. Chewy sweets from my back pocket and sweat from my brow offered a reprisal of last night's sweet'n'sour. Gradually, the tree cover reduced and the spectacular, snow-rimmed crest of Inverted Ridge mountain came into sight on the left. The purity of the air intensified the sun's rays. Near the top I realised I could see a mirage – a cyclist riding and then walking ahead of me. In fact, it wasn't a mirage, it was Deanna. She had clearly survived her night alone in the wild.

As I panted my way up to her it became apparent that, while I had discarded all but the clothing strictly necessary to maintain my decency (even in the wilds one must have standards), Deanna was wearing considerably more: waterproof overtrousers and a windproof smock, with several more layers hidden underneath.

'Aren't you hot?' I spluttered.

'I'm just fine,' she smiled serenely. 'It's only 92 degrees on my bicycle computer.'

I felt strangely reassured – at least I wasn't making it up. The gradient eased and we exchanged photo-taking opportunities.

'Do you mind if I ask why you're riding that bike?'

'Everyone asks, it's not a problem. I just like it. It's awesome. It's so simple, and I can get a really good rhythm on the flat on it. It stops me from going too fast, which is great for endurance rides.'

'But what about the hills?

'I just get to 4 mph and then stop. I can push the bike almost as quickly as that anyway.'

And about as quickly as you can ride with all your fancy gears, she might have added after our experience the previous morning on Elk Pass.

'But you can't even freewheel downhill,' I persisted.

'No, and I broke off my front brake before the start in Banff so I only have the back brake. I get to do some awesome skids.'

In spite of this chastening exchange, I was beginning to feel confident that the day would end successfully. The only remaining concern was the heat. We had begun to descend the other side of the pass, a descent in which I came to resemble even further a lobster in a pot as the cooking water surrounding it came slowly to the boil. When it became clear that the turn up the Wigwam valley would lead to another upstream slog, without the beneficial cooling effects of a significant gain in altitude, I decided to take action.

After the success thus far of having asked the fates to let me see one bear – at a safe distance – and no more, I ventured to make another Faustian pact. This time, I decided to ask for some cooling rain. The fluffy clouds ahead looked promising, if I could make it there before heat exhaustion set in. I should have known better.

I was on my own again. The smothering humidity continued to build, and my yearning for refreshment from the heavens grew. Yet it was quite clear that I had become like a moth drawn to a flame. No sooner had I made my compact with the devil than the clouds ahead had transformed seamlessly from visions of cuddliness into bastions of battleship grey. Worse, they had now adopted the terrifyingly familiar shape of an anvil, on which it was obvious Thor was about to beat out his particular form of devastation. The only question was when. Far away, on the other side of the valley, I saw a teepee; then I realised that in this valley, of all places, it must have been a genuine wigwam.

An hour later and the full folly of my deal was brought home to me. Even though I had been expecting it, the first thunderclap caught me by surprise. The lightning must have been lost in the clouds above, which was a sort of reassurance. I wobbled precariously in the aftermath of the blow. It would have looked comical had there been anyone to see me. At the same moment, the rain began to hammer down as heavy and as stinging as hail. Exposed muscles were instantly tetanised. It was already too late to cover up.

As a distraction, after the next lightning flash I counted the seconds like an excited schoolboy. In fact, I counted them like an over-excited schoolboy. After reaching a count of five, I consoled myself with the announcement, to nobody in particular, that things were OK – the storm was 5 miles away. Then it dawned on me that five seconds should actually represent one mile. One mile seemed a little close for comfort.

The storm intensified. Lightning and thunder began to follow in such quick succession that associating the two became impossible. My debate about its proximity had been resolved unfavourably. I was uncertain what to do. Conventional wisdom at home said don't stand under trees, of which there were plenty, even if the temptation was great. Yet being out in the open, riding across the gashes made by areas of clearcut, seemed counter-intuitive. The reality was that I was deluding myself into thinking I had a choice.

Eventually, the rain eased and the thunderous soundtrack grew more distant. I stopped to warm up – oh, irony – and realised I was at the beginning of the 'connector' section between forest roads. The only information it had been possible to glean about this much-vaunted connector before the race came in the form of an entry on the Tour Divide website by Bill and Kathy Love, who had pioneered the route:

'The connector was very nice – pretty easy-to-follow blazed trail along the river bottom with a quick grunt at the end. We saw a moose calf nursing from its mom along the river.'

'Nice' did not seem a particularly apposite description. A solitary piece of blue tape and a tree branch laid across the main track marked the point at which it was now necessary to disappear into the undergrowth, an undergrowth made freshly sodden and even more foreboding than usual by the recent downpour. The track was indeed visible, and occasionally rideable – between the recently created areas of bog – but 'nice' implied a pleasantness which, in my slightly frazzled state of mind, I could not discern.

Pushing through the puddles and shivering through my bear whistle, I noticed only slowly how the 'trail' was being squeezed between the river and its imposing embankment. This, it turned out, was the 'quick grunt' at the end. It looked neither quick, nor a mere grunt. Instead, after the passage of nearly 40 pairs of feet and bikes as well as the recent downpour, ahead lay a loose, shale rake that climbed steeply up a precipitous slope. The occasional twisted tree trunk and associated glistening roots added an extra frisson to the task ahead.

With little enthusiasm for retracing my steps, and unsure that I could even if I wanted to, I started to climb; slither and slip might have been a better description if it were possible to do so uphill. Initially I pushed the bike, although it soon became necessary to take advantage of the leverage afforded by hanging on to surrounding trees and haul it after me. Climbing over the bike on such a precipice was a delicate manoeuvre. I drew some succour from the fact it was unlikely that a fall would result in a direct plunge into the river below. Becoming impaled on a tree branch on the journey down was a much more likely fate.

After ten minutes of such 'grunting' I emerged into what for all the world appeared to be a large car park. This was the terminus of the day's final forest service road. I sat down to regain my composure, then remembered that the others were still to come. It was 6 p.m. and I was keen for the day to come to an end, but my long-suppressed conscience finally decided now was the time to make its annual appearance. I remembered the enormous weight of Rick's bike and belongings; I remembered that Deanna had still been wearing espadrilles, which I couldn't imagine offered the best traction on the ground I had just covered. Fuelled by a disproportionate sense of noble endeavour, I armed myself with a stick with which to beat off an army of grizzlies, laid down the bike and retraced my steps.

Within half an hour this unlikely good Samaritan act had run its course and my more natural desire for self-preservation had kicked in. I invented a plethora of perfectly good reasons for not waiting any longer: they were all together and would, collectively, be able to cope with what I had now decided was a simple muddy bank; even better, they had all had the eminently sensible idea of abandoning the whole endeavour and found another route to civilisation; more bleakly, they had already been eaten by bears and there was no point in my adding to their number. In reality I was cold and hungry and wanted to go home; even somebody else's home would have done. I returned to the car park and gloomily contemplated the track ahead.

The trail began to climb. At first this was tolerable as it generated some heat and the mileage already accumulated on my computer made it clear the end was in sight. Assuming whatever ascent I now faced would be mirrored by a descent, I could expect little more than a couple of miles of uphill. I would be in the US in less than an hour.

An hour and half later, after fighting my way over two vast piles of avalanche debris – stones, mud, snow and trees – I was still climbing into the wilderness. I laboriously pursued a large male elk up the track ahead of me. In other circumstances this dogged invasion of his personal space might have seemed reckless, but I was in such miserable spirits it could have been a bear or a pack of wolves and I wouldn't have desisted. After the mileage at which I had expected to reach the border had passed, I resorted to profanities.

Just as I had exhausted my not inconsiderable repertoire of Anglo-Saxon curses and diversified into French, two cyclists came round the bend in front of me. I was stunned into silence. They smiled knowingly.

'We've just ridden out to see the "connector",' one said.

'It's awful,' I replied.

'We know, everybody has been talking about it on the race website.'

My two cheery friends then told me the good news that I was virtually at the top of the climb, and that the ensuing 10-mile descent was, in the vernacular that had come to dominate the race, 'awesome'.

'There's lots of bear scat,' added one.

Perhaps they noticed my disquiet, or perhaps they had simply remembered my earlier torrent of expletives.

'Anyhow, you don't need to worry about bears, you'll be hauling ass down there.'

I wasn't entirely sure what he meant, but I knew that it implied speed. He was right. I left the top of Galton Pass at 8.22 p.m. Only 23 minutes later, at a quarter to nine precisely, I arrived at the Port of Roosville border post some 10.5 miles away, an average of 27.5 mph (including two miles of flat road covered at a meagre 16 mph). In spite of the gathering gloom and the switchback nature of the trail, the maximum speed recorded on my bicycle computer was 37.5 mph.

At the border post I was almost hysterical with delight after my thrilling descent and safe return to civilisation (calling Roosville civilised was a clear indication of my reduced mental state rather than an accurate description of the place itself). As a rule, however, US border guards don't seem to warm to semi-delirious, exceptionally smelly cyclists. This was no exception.

Nevertheless, by 9 p.m. I had become a legitimate visitor to the USA; at 9.45 p.m., just as dusk turned to night, and more than 16 hours after I had left Sparwood, I arrived on the fringes of Eureka. Scarcely had a town been more appropriately named.

MONTANA

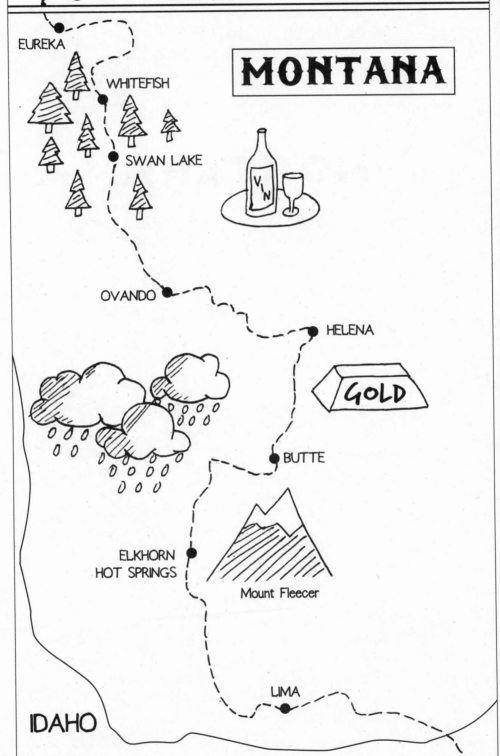

....

CHAPTER 7

BREAKFAST WITH DOLLY PARTON

DAY 4

After the previous day's exertions I had set the alarm as late as I dared. I was eventually woken from my slumbers at the luxuriously late hour of 7.30 a.m. Whitefish, the next town of any note, was a further 90 miles away. Ambitions now firmly tempered by reality, I would be more than happy if I made it that far.

Fired by a vague recollection that the café opposite the motel had been recommended for breakfast, I opened the door and was immediately shocked by the brightness. I had grown unaccustomed to rising after dawn, and last night's rain clouds had long-since dispersed, leaving a sheen of water on the car park to reflect and amplify the rays of the morning sun.

I was also shocked to see Rick, dressed and ready for action, fiddling with his bike outside his room.

'I wondered when you'd be stirring,' he smiled.

I asked what time he'd arrived.

'Gone midnight.'

I almost apologised for having had it so easy.

'Do you fancy breakfast?' he asked.

'Not really, but I'd better eat something.'

Although yesterday's ride had inspired dreams of culinary excess, overwhelming fatigue and limited choice in the end meant dinner had consisted of no more than a tin of ravioli heated up in the microwave in the motel room. Hunger still seemed a distant companion.

Rick disappeared to get some money. I poked my head in the door of his room and saw not just Rick but Cadet and Deanna too, surrounded by an explosion of wet kit and sleeping bags. Cadet looked almost as tired as I felt and was nursing a sore knee from negotiating the connector. Even Deanna had the decency to have apparently lost a little of her customary *joie de vivre*.

At the Four Corners café, Rick and I tried unsuccessfully to blend in. Figure-hugging Lycra did little to disguise the fact that we were half the size of most of the regulars. My inability to order the simplest breakfast items didn't help. The menu proposed an overwhelming variety of options but few that I understood or found palatable. Most eye-catching were the two Dolly Parton-themed breakfasts on offer. The 'Full Dolly' consisted of sausages, bacon, biscuits, hash browns and gravy, all topped with two fried eggs – sunny side up, of course. It was a visual gag. More intriguingly still there was also a 'Half Dolly' – as above but with only one egg, and dedicated to a late regular who obviously had a favourite mammary.

'Do you think they'll just be able to give me some pancakes?' I asked Rick, all references to pancakes on the menu being accompanied by a dozen variations on the theme of a cooked breakfast.

'Sure, just go ahead and ask for anything you want.'

I decided against suggesting the apparently exhaustive nature of the menu was therefore a pointless exercise. The waitress arrived and, looking disdainfully at my figure, advised against three pancakes.

'Two will do you,' she said. 'Mind, we did have a cyclist the other day who ordered six, but he didn't finish them all. He took some of them with him.'

Rick did his best to continue the trend of excess by ordering a bewildering array of ingredients otherwise known as a lumberjack breakfast. As I struggled to come to terms with even two pancakes, my attention was caught by an unguarded conversation on a neighbouring table.

'Well, hell, if we go to war with China, we're dead,' said one of the diners, seemingly apropos of nothing. Certainly, the newspapers in the café made no mention of there having suddenly been a catastrophic deterioration in Sino–US relations. One of the great advantages of cycling into the wilderness for a few days was isolation from the worries of the rest of the world.

'They've got lots of things,' went on the self-appointed military analyst to his friends. 'And they've got technology too.'

The border might have been only 10 miles away, but we were clearly now in the paranoid land of Uncle Sam. Unfortunately an influx of noisy new customers put an end to this uniquely insightful assessment of China's military prowess.

Rick stoically cleared his plate while I gave up on carbohydrates and filled up with caffeine. I couldn't even face the prospect of taking a spare pancake for later. Back at the motel, I had not had the energy to unpack the previous night so was soon ready to leave. Cadet and Deanna's plans for departure had advanced little, and Rick was now encumbered by his breakfast. I decided I couldn't delay any longer.

It quickly became apparent that last night I had merely arrived on the edge of Eureka. After the unappealing surroundings of our motel and associated roadside gas stations, it was a pleasant surprise to discover an attractive small town of frontier-style buildings and useful shops. The riding the other side of town down the old road along the Tobacco valley was equally agreeable. I had come to the Rockies for adventure, but for this morning was content to appreciate the savagery of wilderness tempered by agricultural endeavour. Farmsteads and isolated houses, some of impressive stature, punctuated the copses and meadows. The metalled road helped as well.

This softness didn't last long, however. After 20 miles I was back on dirt roads winding through oceans of forest – western larch and lodgepole pine – and facing another 10 miles of stiff climbing. Ahead lay a mountain range that was vast by British standards but here was just one small island in a huge archipelago. High, grey clouds and little wind created perfect cycling conditions but made for a distinctly chilly and lonely breather on top of the pass.

'Crest Whitefish Divide and begin descent through spectacularly wild country. Watch out for Grizzly Bears!' cautioned the route description.

I decided it was lunchtime. Maybe not being hungry myself would deter any potential predators. In fact, I still had no real hunger, and had begun to marvel at my apparent ability to cycle long distances on less food than I would consume on a sedentary day at home. I wasn't sure it was sustainable all the way to Mexico, but it was certainly cheap.

I munched on a bag of crisps and was dismayed to find my accompanying 'Grape Juice Drink' had neither grape juice nor caffeine, which I had come to see as my primary fuel. The only company was a chipmunk, which surveyed the scene from a safe distance, and dozens of invisible birds that serenaded me from the woods and scree. One, in particular, sounded teasingly like a bear-whistle-toting cyclist but, in spite of the fresh tyre tracks I had followed all morning, no one appeared.

The descent passed bear-free and returned the route to the Flathead valley on the US side of the border. It was broader and more open than its Canadian counterpart, and lacked much of its majesty. It was also infested with mosquitoes.

The return to the mountains and the day's second climb were a welcome distraction. In fact, all of a sudden I was confronted with a surprising sensation. I was enjoying the ascent. Devotees of Holland and advocates of cycling in flatlands may demur, but one of the great joys of riding a bicycle is the rhythmic harmony of mountain climbing. Finding that rhythm provides an overwhelming, atavistic sense of well-being and vitality. I started to sing.

'I've got rhythm, I've got mountains, I've got my bike, who could ask for anything more?'

The Gershwins had it right, way back in the 1930s.

Even the discovery of more avalanche debris followed by remnant snow patches could not dampen my spirits, though they proved very adept at scratching my limbs and freezing my feet. The fact that I had five hours of daylight and only 30 miles of almost constant descent remaining no doubt helped my mood remain cheery. As did the scenery. Red Meadow Lakes was everything I had hoped the Rockies would be, or at least the northern portion of them. The lakes themselves reflected the surrounding snow-covered peaks in their quicksilver waters. They were also at sufficient altitude for the intense timber cover to have begun to ease, providing clearings and meadows from which to enjoy the views. It would have proved an idyllic campground and base for exploration off the beaten track (or even the not particularly well-beaten track on which I had just been riding).

Which was exactly what the next person I saw was using it for. Actually, he was sunning himself and half asleep when my inadvertently surreptitious arrival caused him to start. He soon realised I was not a bear; his 'guard dogs' had clearly already reached the same conclusion. Nor was I the first cyclist he had seen that day, and he was already well aware of the race.

'There were two groups of two who came through a couple of hours ago,' he said as I sat down and warmed my feet for half an hour.

Of course, he couldn't tell me who they were, but my curiosity had been well and truly whetted. Since dinner in Sparwood I'd had no information concerning the whereabouts of racers ahead of me, although it was my companionable rather than competitive streak that entertained thoughts of catching them. It seemed unlikely they would stop in Whitefish if they were so far ahead as they would have time to continue the 10 miles to Columbia Falls or beyond, but, with Cadet and the others likely to already be some distance behind, there was now a chance I could find some new fellow travellers.

There was still some snow to negotiate on the far side of the pass. In the shade of the precipitous mountains I was once again cold and my feet numb, even though it was little after 5 p.m. This clearly wasn't a deterrent for the natives, however: four teenagers, two boys and two girls, clad scantily in T-shirts and trainers, came round a corner ahead of me. Closer inspection revealed the girls were carrying fishing rods and the boys rifles, slung over their shoulders at rakish angles. They waved jovially and continued their high-spirited progress to . . . to what? I listened intently but heard no shots before the snow eventually cleared and the speed of my descent increased. I followed more fresh tyre tracks past another delightful lake embedded like a jewel in the velvet of the all-encompassing forest.

The rest of the ride to Whitefish was as uneventful as yesterday evening's had been exciting. Entertainment came this time in the form of thousands of flowering grasses – 3-foot-tall stems crowned with hundreds of tiny cream flowers, the whole forming the shape of a bulb or partially inflated balloon. Then the route emerged from the darkening green at Whitefish Lake and skirted expensive houses and second homes with private jetties. Another enormous freight train shunted slowly along the far shore.

Whitefish was another pleasant surprise, more refined in its charms than the rudimentary, prosaic appeal of the towns encountered since

Banff. Unlike Elkford or Sparwood, or even Eureka, it clearly benefited from having a second source of activity and income in addition to its primary industry of logging. Skiing is big in Whitefish. In fact, the Whitefish Mountain Resort is one of the top three ski destinations in the whole of Montana.

Out of the skiing season, however, and after 8 p.m. in the evening, the town's 5,000 or so residents were evidently content to let the handful of strolling visitors have the run of the place. Strangely, accommodation seemed the one service in short supply. Eventually, the scruffiest motel I'd yet encountered presented itself. Even in my slightly reduced state I nearly balked at the prospect. I was glad I didn't. I ended the evening eating dinner – a chocolate bar and a can of Coke – while soothing my aching muscles in a rooftop jacuzzi.

CHAPTER 8

....

SWAN LAKE

DAY 5

I woke before the alarm sounded. It was 6.40 a.m. Laziness tempted me to go back to sleep but guilt at already losing valuable cycling time eventually won the battle for my conscience. I donned yesterday's clammy cycling kit, in spite of which unpleasantness my Whitefish experience continued to exceed expectations by providing an enjoyable breakfast, the first since Banff. I had a veritable feast: two bagels; four pieces of raisin toast; apple juice; three cups of coffee.

At the same time, I treated myself to the conveniences afforded by modern technology and logged on to the Tour Divide website on the hotel computer. The SPOT GPS tracker loaned to all Tour Divide riders allowed visitors to the website to follow their progress through position updates beamed to an omniscient satellite at ten-minute intervals. The system was clearly working to the satisfaction of those back home, even if it did feel as though Big Brother had finally caught up with me.

'Hello from us all,' Catherine had written. 'We are avidly watching your progress and flipping between excitement when we can see you moving and slight worry when you don't go anywhere for a while (especially at nine in the morning!).'

Yesterday's lie-in had evidently not gone unnoticed.

It also provided a means to convey other vital messages.

'What is a bear mace by the way?' asked a friend to whom I had endeavoured unsuccessfully to explain my bear precautions. 'Is it some kind of ceremonial item with which you hope to convince the bears that you are their mayor?'

My brother-in-law Dominic clearly thought the whole undertaking was not sufficiently demanding. 'It's reassuring to know I have the right website as I also found a site set up by a group of alternative crazy-men who follow a similar route but have to wear hair-shirts and be beaten to sleep every night with a totem pole.'

There was even some encouragement.

'Enjoy the suffering – pain is only weakness leaving the body.'

I must have been weaker than I thought.

Next, I checked on the position of other riders. Rick and Deanna had stopped a considerable distance short of town. Cadet was still in Eureka. Then, an initial flurry of excitement at finding two racers apparently still in Whitefish subsided when I realised that my own tracker placed me 5 miles back the way I'd come, somewhere on the shores of Whitefish Lake. Maybe the satellite wasn't as accurate as it was cracked up to be. Nevertheless, I departed in buoyant spirits. I had become a fox with a couple of rabbits up the road. I veritably sprinted through the neatly tended lawns of the edge of town. It was just a question of time before I had someone to talk to again, and to help me fend off bears.

In the meantime, I revelled briefly in the normality of my surroundings. A man mowed his lawn. Parents drove their children to school. I passed a golf course. It was soon enough to have me dreaming once more of the wilderness ways still to come.

Then I caught sight of something ahead, disappearing around a distant bend. There was no room for doubt. It had been a laden cyclist; it must have been a Tour Divide rider (as desert travellers through the centuries have made clear with their pursuit of mirages, desire can be a potent force). I estimated the distance between us was probably half a mile so there was no chance of a quick catch, but I upped my tempo a notch. The roads were straight, intersecting with each other at right angles. Yet every time I anticipated a clean line of vision ahead it was obscured by a truck, or a tree, or a dip in the road.

To pass the time, I struck up imaginary conversations with my soon-to-be new riding partner, though I couldn't quite decide if it was Rudiger from Germany or Jacob from Manitowoc in Wisconsin who was ahead. The website had had them both in Whitefish that morning. Or maybe it *was* both of them. That could be some party. Back in Banff, Jacob had displayed a laudable pride in the beer-brewing abilities of his homeland; add in some German bratwurst and Yorkshire pudding and we could have a ball.

This fictitious discourse had clearly been distracting me from chasing my quarry. By Columbia Falls, 10 miles after leaving Whitefish, I had resigned myself to a vain pursuit of the spectral cyclist ahead of me. Maybe it had all been a hallucination brought on by an almost unrecognisable sensation – hunger. After several days of contradictory messages, my stomach seemed to have finally accepted that a unilateral rebellion against the stresses and strains being placed on my body would end up being counterproductive for both of us. It wanted more breakfast and, although it meant foregoing the prospect of company, even if only illusory, I was happy to comply.

Refuelled, I continued south on another grid of interlocking roads, some metalled, some gravel, all as straight as a die. The scenery became steadily more agricultural, even if the broad, flat valley was still hemmed in on the east by lofty peaks in their coats of green. To the west lay Flathead Lake, the largest freshwater lake this side of the Mississippi. Each road provided access to a small handful of farms, interspersed with the occasional stalled housing development – a sign of straitened times. A signpost designating the residence of the Snell family caught my eye, but there the similarity with the BBC's fictitious caricature of rural English life, portrayed daily in the radio soap opera *The Archers*, ended.

The fields in between were predominantly given over to grazing – lots of horses, some cattle – or simply grass to produce winter feed. The short growing season precluded anything more exotic. Exoticism came instead from what appeared to be rudimentary trebuchets dotted here and there. I wondered if this indicated an unexpected popularity for mediaeval re-enactment societies, perhaps compensating for the relative youth of the region in the eyes of its non-native inhabitants.

In the end there was a more prosaic but equally charming explanation. These strange objects were in fact known as beaverslides and were a traditional Montana means of stacking hay for winter storage. They consisted of a large, rectangular timber frame, supported halfway up its length as if part of a seesaw. The lower two thirds of each frame was filled with slats, while the upper third was open. At the bottom of this frame was a slatted timber lip, onto which the hay was massed before being hauled up the slide and deposited through the open upper third into a pile below. The resulting stack was fenced off from inquisitive cattle and elk until winter, when it was used as forage.

Further on, the proportion of cows grew while that of horses reduced. Given the lack of variety it was a surprise to discover that gardening was something of a busman's holiday. Far from creating a bulwark against the vastness surrounding them, most front gardens, some the size of football pitches, were simple continuations of the prairie. Some even had cows grazing on them among the pick-ups and 4×4s. The only variation was provided by those who grew Christmas trees, the distance of a few miles to nature's own abundant supply clearly being too great. It was the gardening equivalent of Stockholm syndrome – people showing an unlikely affinity to the landscape in which they appeared hostage.

After three more hours I stopped for something to eat in Ferndale, which I mistakenly thought had a full range of services. Instead, it consisted of little more than half a dozen houses and a crossroads. A mile out of my way I found a gas station and began picking my way morosely round the store, looking for anything that might sate my now voracious appetite. Gradually, I became aware of the aroma of cooked food, even though its source remained so obscure that I had to ask for help in finding it. Such was my ignorance of gas station etiquette that I also needed help serving myself.

'Just use one of the boxes to take what you want,' I was instructed kindly as I stared blankly at an array of chicken wings and samosas.

The problem was that I was incapable of choice.

'But how can I get one of those?' I asked, pointing at the sign for ready meals.

'Oh, they're in the boxes at the bottom. Roast chicken, roast potatoes and green beans. You can also help yourself to an apple dumpling with cream, and a large drink.'

'And that's $5?'

'Yep, we had to put the price up a bit not long ago.'

I sat on the bench on the veranda in very heaven.

The sunshine that had massaged my muscles at the gas station soon turned from friend to foe. The valley floor was only 3,000 feet above sea level and the surrounding mountains had created a giant oven in which I was slowly baking, or rather steaming, thanks to the humidity of the impenetrable forest on either side of the track. I climbed steadily for an hour, for which effort I was rewarded only with a rough and frustrating descent. The promised vistas ('Clearcuts will offer views of the majestic Swan Mountains' advised the route description) rarely materialised, while the heat and humidity became ever more oppressive. Instead, vertiginous, crowding trees turned the trail into a sinuous prison which continued, according to the map, for another 100 miles. The trees that hemmed in the narrow road were the bars on my window, a window that gave onto a view of trees, trees and more trees. Rarely can agoraphobia and claustrophobia have been so closely intertwined.

After another hour I could take no more. It was not yet 4 p.m., but drastic action was needed to preserve my sanity and diffuse the panic that was beginning to set in. Closer inspection of the map revealed that I could find food and accommodation in a nearby lakeside resort. The price to be paid for escaping from my mute green captors was retracing my steps 2 miles and venturing another 4 miles off route, a round journey of 12 miles or an hour's riding. It was an easy decision.

The resort of Swan Lake proved the perfect antidote. Far from the garish compilation of condominiums I had feared, it consisted of little more than a smattering of houses and a few essential services spread alongside the empty main road: the Swan Lake Bar and Grill;

a community hall; a volunteer fire department; a chapel; the Swan Lake Trading Post; and the Laughing Horse Lodge.

I stopped at the trading post to replenish my supplies, feeling demob happy. If it were possible to have eaten postcards and trinkets I could have filled up for the entire journey. I asked about accommodation.

'The Lodge is cosy,' said the proprietor. 'If she's got no room, we've got space to camp. I've got everything you need – hot showers and cold beer.'

It sounded appealing, but I craved a bed as well. I picked up the local newspaper. The front page picture was of a young grizzly seen roaming earlier in the week.

'Don't worry about him, he's all right,' I was told, unprompted. 'It's the black bears that are the problem here. There's one who's been getting into the bins recently. He'd better be careful or he's gonna get some buck shot in his ass.'

Peculiarly reassured, I went to the lodge. There was no one home – not even a laughing horse – but a handwritten notice invited new guests to choose a cabin and book in once the owner had returned. The cabins – timber-framed, rustic, delightful – were at the back and formed a courtyard around an idyllic cottage garden full of aquilegia, surfinia, poppies, roses and lupins. I lounged guiltlessly in a chair in the shade and watched with fascination the swallows darting hither and thither. A sign at the front of the lodge explained there were four varieties: the tree swallow; the violet green swallow; the cliff swallow; and the gregarious barn swallow. Between them they produced 60 chicks during their six-month stay from April to September.

'They're a bit messy, but we love their electric chatter and voracious appetite for mosquitoes,' the sign concluded.

I contemplated the relief I felt at no longer having to pretend I was fearless, even if it was the trees that had got to me rather than the bears. A pair of hummingbirds arrived, seduced by voluminous hanging baskets. From the house next door, a middle-aged couple mounted their Harley Davidson and sped off, helmet free, to enjoy the open road.

After checking in I rode slowly back to the bar and grill. Happiness, I decided, was feeling hungry and having the means to satisfy that hunger. I ordered my first burger and chips since Banff from the 'ever-so-purty' waitress. In cut-off denim shorts, she was a dead ringer for Daisy from the *Dukes of Hazzard*. I felt slightly incongruous in full waterproof overclothes – the only items I possessed that were 'clean' – but she smiled sweetly anyway. Swan Lake clearly had it all.

I sat outside on the decking and watched the bar owner entertain his grandchildren and their friends with rides in his Model T Ford. Inside, a group of 20 or so locals had gathered for a wine tasting, something of a novelty in these parts. Snippets of conversation reached me through the saloon door. It was an education.

'The next wine I'm gonna move on to is a dry rosé, a kind of transition between white and red,' said the sommelier. He pronounced rosé with such emphasis on the second syllable it came out like 'row-zay'.

This was clearly a surprise to at least one of his audience.

'Yes, ma'am, some people like their row-zays. If you go to Europe, the most popular wine is a dry row-zay, drunk as an early evening aperitif. The warmer it gets, the hotter it gets, the more people drink it.'

I found myself nodding in agreement. He was warming to his task, explaining that the row-zay in question was made from Syrah grapes (pronounced 'sea-ra').

'It's been pressed twice to make it nice and dry and it's got a little bit of spice. It's good with anything, water melon, white meats . . .'

A double-bacon-cheese-burger-with-extra-fries-and-onion-rings was delivered to my table. As an accompaniment I chose not a 'row-zay' but a sweet Coca-Cola. Inside, things had moved on.

'Now, gang, we're gonna move to the red side of the tasting. Some bottles of red can fetch up to $2,500.'

He had scarcely finished this party piece before he was drowned out by a chorus of 'holy cows'. It could have been my imagination, but the audience seemed to shuffle a bit closer in anticipation of sampling a treat.

I finished my meal and walked back into the main bar.

'So how d'ya like the red, gang?'

It had gone down well. One good ol' boy was a particular fan.

'It tastes kinda like Victoria's Secrets.'

There was an eruption of laughter. The sommelier was the first to regain his composure.

'Good for you, man. I'm gonna use that myself.'

I wasn't sure this experience mirrored that imagined by the Tour Divide organisers for those foolish enough to participate in their race, but it was fine with me.

....

CHAPTER 9

A RIVER RUNS THROUGH IT

DAY 6

I was determined that those following my progress from home would have no excuse to accuse me of another lie-in. Abdicating paternal responsibilities in the noble name of adventure was one thing, I reasoned; doing so merely to catch up on nearly seven years of interrupted sleep was quite another. I conveniently overlooked the fact that the end result of my absence was exactly the same.

I was equally determined to start early enough to have no excuses for not completing at least 100 miles by day's end. Yesterday's early stop might have temporarily saved my sanity, but not making a decent fist of getting to Mexico would cause longer-lasting psychological harm.

By 5.20 a.m. I was back on the bike. Once again the morning was cold, though not quite freezing. The deserted main road led silently to the fire track, which in turn led back to yesterday's green prison. The steely morning light of the sun's weak rays filtered through a veil of high clouds and emphasised the feeling of incarceration. Or maybe being cast adrift at sea was a better metaphor, given the oceanic scale of the forests around me. Still, unlike Captain Bligh, at least it was voluntary. And I did know where I was planning to stop for lunch.

I was also comforted, somewhat perversely, by more immediate obstacles, such as staving off the chill and overcoming the inevitable bad humour of the hour. I was contentedly grumpy until nearly 8 a.m., at which point I had something of an arboreal epiphany; I was almost enjoying the forest.

It was a reluctant sort of enjoyment that was distinctly uncomfortable to admit to, and I would have been quite prepared to deny it in a court of law. Yet its existence was all-pervasive. Even the forest's vast scale was no longer so discomfiting. It was strangely thrilling to be quite so overwhelmed, so completely alone. I made several unsuccessful attempts to count to 1,000 trees without missing any. The process was doomed from the start by the inevitability of distraction, either by terrain or navigation, but there was virtue in futility: by the time I conceded inevitable defeat the best part of another hour had passed.

There was also, it turned out, some variety in the trees themselves. Western larch I could positively identify, resembling the European larch of plantations at home; lodgepole pine and Douglas fir were harder to distinguish. Height might have been a determining factor had I stopped to look more closely, although they all seemed rather tall to me. A Douglas fir in Washington state had a claim to being the tallest tree ever recorded, having been measured at 120 metres in 1924. Even coast redwoods only rarely exceed 110 metres, and the largest recorded specimen registered 115 metres, though with four times the volume of wood due to its wider girth. Lodgepoles were pygmies in comparison, with a maximum height of around 50 metres.

This was plenty sufficient to obscure any view of my surroundings, however. I was apparently riding between the Mission Mountains on my right and the Swan Mountains to my left, but even recognising that I was in a valley was a challenge, and this in spite of the fact it was quite an important north–south artery: State Highway 83 was no more than a few impenetrable miles away. The avalanche chutes and areas of felled trees promised by the guidebook to offer splendid views of my surroundings were notable only by their absence. Although much of the riding was on good ground, the endless traversing of stream beds flowing off the Mission range created a convoluted and undulating route, twisting this way and that as it tried in vain to follow the contours. Even the route description seemed confused: 'Mile 26.3: Turn Left. The route is blocked and closed.' Only the absence of alternatives confirmed that I should not interpret 'blocked and closed', nor even the barely passable barrier across the track, as impediments to my progress.

If the rumoured magnificence of the mountains could not be appreciated, at least there was beauty closer to hand. The forest might have seemed superficially homogenous, but clearly there was sufficient variety of habitat to accommodate a wealth of butterflies and myriad other flying insects, mercifully few of which were mosquitoes. Each fleeting glimpse of colour inspired hope of recognition, but my fluttering friends remained steadfastly beyond the limited scope of my powers of identification.

I had more success with flowering plants. One flower in particular seemed to thrive in the otherwise unpromising shade of the forest floor. Having long had a love–hate relationship with cultivated lupins – their beauty not always outweighing the battle to keep the slugs and snails off them – it was something of a surprise to see great clumps of their wild cousins doing quite well enough without any human help. They were smaller and finer than those in the garden at home, and there was a greater number of flowering stems to each plant, sometimes a dozen or more. There was also no variety in flower colour, every plant the same lavender blue haze. But they were unmistakably lupins and their delicate charm was quite a tonic in such an ostentatiously rugged environment.

Finally, after nearly 50 miles of trees, I emerged onto the main valley road. It was almost as bereft of traffic as it had been five hours earlier in Swan Lake. A couple of miles further and I arrived at Holland Lodge, where I had initially intended to spend the previous night. A sign on a barn before the main lodge proudly proclaimed that it was a 'semi-dude ranch', dude-ranching being the unique brand of cowboy-themed hospitality offered by working ranches to soft easterners – dudes – in search of a 'genuine' western experience. 'Horses, hats and hospitality' was the aphorism of the Dude Ranchers' Association. Maybe a semi-dude ranch skipped the hats. Or maybe you had to already have lost some of your 'dude-ness' to be able to cope with the rigours of the horses and hospitality on offer, I thought, temporarily concerned about what I might be letting myself in for.

I need not have worried. The harsh realities of cowboy life were clearly not the lodge's speciality; demonstrating how refined a log cabin could be was the aim, even if the presence of large, stuffed animal heads on the walls might have left some wincing at such a notion of refinement. It was 11 a.m., and the kitchen didn't open for another hour. Nevertheless, the lodge owners lived up to the hospitality part of the Dude Ranchers' Association motto and rustled up crisps, salad and a toasted ham and cheese sandwich. They didn't even blink when I requested the same again. As I ate, I drank in the panorama across the still lake over the surrounding mountains. It was all the more impressive for its rarity. Two large, black and white swallow-tailed butterflies amused themselves in a nearby lilac tree, oblivious to the persistent chill of an overcast day.

By noon I was ready to resume my journey, although the prospect of abandoning the comfort of the lodge and its open vistas for another 30 miles of trees held only limited appeal. As promised by the map, the eminently cycleable forest road soon turned into a much rougher trail. Downed trees and grassed-over tracks slowed progress noticeably. Navigation became something of a vague concept as both the official route and unofficial alternatives seemed equally unfeasible. After several anxious moments I emerged surprised and surprisingly unscathed onto another gravel road, blinking like a rabbit released from a bag. I felt like I had won the lottery, and scampered off down the road lest I be recaptured.

Next on the agenda was the day's only noteworthy ascent. I had borrowed the phone at Holland Lodge to call home, and had been told, among other things, of messages from racers further along the trail warning how tough certain sections were.

'They said Richmond Pass, or something like that, was particularly tough, all covered in mud and snow and fallen trees,' Catherine had advised.

As the obstacle to which she referred meant nothing to me, I reassured her that I'd look it up on the map that night so as to be better prepared. Blinded by the obvious, I was incapable of making the link between the Richmond Pass of my phone conversation and the Richmond Peak I was about to ascend. Blissfully ignorant, therefore, of my impending tribulations, and still fuelled by my comfortable lunch, I waved heartily at two gun-toting quad bikers. They didn't flinch, continuing instead to chew the cud in a bovine stupor.

The trail once more vanished into the heart of the surrounding darkness. My enthusiasm didn't last long. At first, the simple effort required to ensure forward momentum on a rough, relentless incline sufficed to keep my predicament to the back of my mind. When the track eventually became too rough to pedal, however, the folly of disappearing into the undergrowth, towing what had effectively become a giant anchor behind me as I squirmed my way past adolescent Christmas trees, assumed greater prominence (I knew the trees were adolescent because of the way they congregated like feckless youths on street corners to intimidate passers-by, every now and then plucking up the courage for a sly physical assault – a trip, maybe, or an unexpected grab of an arm). The fact that the roughness of the terrain had miniaturised my assailants compared to the lofty jailers of the morning, and that I now had breathtaking views to at least one side, was little more than an ironic consolation. A golden eagle soared effortlessly, mockingly, above me, confirming the scale of the cliffs I could see across the valley.

Worse than the trees, though, were the bears. Not that there were any, as far as I could tell. The problem was that I couldn't tell very far at all. In places, visibility ahead was reduced to a few yards. I became convinced I was about to grope my way straight into the arms of a welcoming grizzly. My frazzled, frantic efforts to surmount the physical obstacles of mud and snow and fallen trees betrayed, not inner tranquillity, but equally frazzled and frantic psychological efforts to surmount the demons of the mind. At least I would be mauled to death in an area of great beauty, I reasoned.

The summit came slowly, after maybe an hour, but when it arrived it had the decency to be sufficiently denuded of trees to allow a moment's contemplation. I was astride a saddle between two great mountain arenas, the one through which I had just laboured aptly called Grizzly Basin. On both sides, mountains and valleys stretched away to infinity. It was terrifying. It was magnificent. Like Nina Simone, I sang just to know I was alive. More significantly, I sang to let the bears know I enjoyed being alive.

The descent of the south side of the peak was more open, but fear of the unknown was soon replaced with fear of the all-too-real. What passed for the trail traversed a precipitous hillside, where a slippery emulsion of snow and mud made lateral progress all but impossible. I became inordinately and hypocritically grateful for my bicycle-anchor.

Eventually, I reached safer ground and, after another mile or so of bushwhacking, a forest road. It had taken nearly four hours to cover less than 30 miles.

After consulting the map I concluded that a similar distance remained to be covered if I wanted to reach my intended destination of Ovando.

'Camping is allowed on the museum lawn, contact Barb McNally', the map notes advised.

I hadn't contacted Barb to ascertain whether she (in the case of it being 'Barb' as in Barbara) or he (in the case of 'Barb' as in a localised phonetic spelling of Bob) had any space, but it sounded perfect. Besides, competition for pitches didn't seem likely to be fierce. Apart from at Holland Lodge, I had seen no one all day.

The early start meant time was still on my side but, after 11 hours of riding, I was beginning to flag. Fortunately, the cycling was now much smoother. What's more, although I was still riding through mile after mile of forest, the nature of the tree cover had changed definitively since crossing the watershed on Richmond Peak. The canopy was less dense and the trees had a far greater respect for the personal space of their neighbours.

By the time I was enjoying the day's last descent, the countryside had become, to my starved imagination, almost Mediterranean. The grey skies of earlier in the day had dissipated and I was now bathed in early evening sun. The gentle warmth was all-enveloping. Wild lupins had been superseded by a variety of wild sunflower.

I was transported back to an earlier life, cycling through scented pine groves in southern France. I pictured myself descending to a French port, Cassis perhaps. It wouldn't be long before I would be enjoying *moules frites* and a glass of wine . . .

Not surprisingly, Ovando came as something of a shock. In fact, I was jolted from my reverie by the traffic on the main road on the edge of town; I had to stop for a lorry to pass by before the more habitual emptiness returned. Then I encountered the Ovando town sign, an accurate portent of what lay ahead.

'Town of Ovando, MT. Jewel of the Blackfoot Valley. Pop: About 50. Elev: 4,100. Dogs: Over 100.'

Two hundred yards further on and I was in the town itself. Rather than having been transported to a different continent, I had been transported back in time. I was now in the early twentieth century, around the time when one of the West's finest chroniclers, Norman Maclean, had been raised in this same valley and had lived the life he would later recount in book and film as *A River Runs Through It*.

So convincing was the scene that it could have been Maclean and his pals, or his brother Paul, standing outside the timber barn by which I stopped. Instead, it was three members of the volunteer fire department preparing for their annual test of fitness.

'What does that involve?' I asked, trying to reconcile the scene before me – three ever-so-relaxed but not-quite-so-trim middle-aged men – with what I anticipated to be a rigorous challenge.

The reason for their confidence soon became clear.

'We've got 3 pounds of weights on our belts and we have to walk 3 miles in 45 minutes,' they smiled as they ambled off.

That left Skip, Mayor of Ovando. His name and stature were immediately apparent, not thanks to any mayoral bearing on his part but to the crumpled, pencil-written note identifying him as such tucked in the band of his equally crumpled straw hat. I hoped such exalted company would be able to resolve the conundrum of where to stay. The lawn outside the museum had turned out to be little more than 10 foot by 20 foot of wispy grass in the middle of a dusty square (though the teepee opposite did suggest itself as a last resort). Any visiting tent also had to share the limited space with three trees, a flag pole, a bench, four boulders and half a set of wagon wheels. Of greater concern, Barb the proprietor – whether he or she Skip never did reveal – was as absent as the facilities I had associated with such an idyllic-sounding campsite. Having coped with 13 hours of cycling and 100 years of time travel, I decided I was in the mood for a smattering of luxury.

As hoped, Skip indeed came to the rescue, in spite of my being able to decipher only half of the words he spoke. The gist of his proposed solution was for me to knock on the door of a house a few yards away. I duly complied, and a beaming face soon appeared.

'Hi, I'm Nord – N-O-R-D,' said the owner of the face, pumping my hand energetically.

I explained my predicament.

'Well, I'll just open up the store and the guest house and you can make yourself at home.'

We returned past the camping lawn to the timber building of the Blackfoot Inn and Commercial Company where N-O-R-D was as good as his word.

'There's rooms upstairs but I can open the store too if you need any provisions.'

I certainly did, having virtually run out of cycling food and having nothing for tomorrow's breakfast. While I browsed, N-O-R-D told me that I wasn't the first cyclist to stop by. Alan and John had stayed the night two days previously, with the Petervarys' 'Love Shack' tandem also having called in.

'Seen any bears?' asked N-O-R-D.

'Just one.'

N-O-R-D sounded disappointed.

'One of the riders had seen 13 by the time he got here. And a mountain lion just as he was coming into town.'

My fear of bears, whether real or perceived (the bears, that is, not the fear – that was very real), had been so all-consuming that I had neglected to worry about mountain lions. This was clearly an error.

'How big is a mountain lion?' I asked, trying to gauge the prominence to give them in my informal animal-anxiety ranking.

'Oh, plenty big enough,' said N-O-R-D, pointing to a skin on the wall of the stairwell. It was 5 foot long, excluding the tail. I didn't fancy trying to grapple with it, even if it was only a rug. Nevertheless, it was significantly smaller than the grizzly skin next to it that had belonged to an animal shot in 1948.

After settling in, I followed N-O-R-D's advice to head another 200 yards to the other edge of town for dinner at Trixie's (truth be told, competition was strictly limited). It had previously occupied centre stage in the middle of the town, but the coming of the state highway had inspired a move to catch the trade from passing motorists. As a result, the original Trixie's had become the museum, while the restaurant itself was now housed in a former barracks imported from Helena. The eponymous founder had apparently been a daredevil horsewoman famous for her bareback tricks (the horse was bareback, that is, not the rider – had it been the other way round her fame might have been even more widespread).

The atmosphere was convivial. I sat at the bar and un-comprehendingly watched baseball on the TV. A few locals played pool while some more itinerant guests quietly ate their burgers to a country soundtrack.

The lady behind the bar took my order. Having now seen all that Ovando had to offer, I asked her what it was about the town that justified a museum.

'Not much,' she replied. 'It just tells you about the history, the logging and ranching, that sort of thing. There are a lot of old pictures.'

It used to be quite a bit bigger, she continued, pointing out that at Ovando's height there had been more than 200 inhabitants, before adding, a touch wistfully: 'And we had our own dance hall. They also thought about bringing the railroad through the valley but then they decided against it.'

My history lesson was disturbed by the arrival of another visitor to the bar who started talking embarrassingly at cross-purposes with a much younger female acquaintance about his relationship concerns. I devoured my excellent burger listening intently but discreetly to this real-life soap opera. Any lingering yearning for *moules frites* and the Mediterranean had by now been completely dispelled.

....

CHAPTER 10

THREE KINDS OF PSYCHOPATH

DAY 7

Leaving Ovando the next morning was a chore. It was another frigid, pre-dawn start. My gloves had proved themselves to be singularly inadequate for sub-zero temperatures, and holding onto the handlebars with unfeeling hands took a conscious effort. The air was dead still, but the unavoidable wind chill generated by riding at 15 mph froze my gritted teeth into a malevolent grin. As I rode across the broad valley bottom, through pockets of icy patches, I disturbed a herd of female whitetail deer. They cantered away across the surrounding farmland, and I lamented my departure. I would gladly have swapped yesterday's time travel for the ability to beam up my family to share the experience of such a delightful relic from a different age. The town sign had been right: it was genuinely a 'Jewel of the Blackfoot Valley'.

The farmland came to an end after an hour, but not before I had to answer a call of nature. Up to this point in the ride, the need for discretion had not been great and cover had been readily available. Now, in the middle of a wide, open valley, I was confounded by not only a complete absence of trees but also a passing farm truck that materialised from nowhere just after I had concluded I was safe to proceed. The look on the driver's face was as cold as the morning.

The wooded climb of Huckleberry Pass at last began to provide an antidote to the chill. The forest retained the appealing, open character of yesterday evening. There was none of the accompanying Mediterranean warmth, however; I was heading east, and the sun was yet to rise over the crest of the pass. Nothing stirred. The only sound came from my wheels as they crunched over the gravel.

I worked my way up to a small tarn in which the surrounding trees were perfectly mirrored. Then came the top of the pass, a narrow defile between the rocky peaks to either side. I paused to take in the altered view. Lower-lying ground had now taken the upper hand in its tussle with the mountains. Rather than the topography being dominated by endless mountain ranges and the corresponding valleys in between, such mountains as there were now stood like islands in a patchwork sea. Big, rocky islands, it should be emphasised, and there were still plenty of them, but they were no longer linked together in the succession of ridges that had dominated the scenery since Banff.

The descent to Lincoln was straightforward, and I was looking forward to a second breakfast in what I had anticipated would be a charming town of a reasonable size and with plenty of services. The reality was rather different. For a start, Lincoln had a rather dubious claim to fame, having been the home of Theodore Kaczynski, the psychopathic Unabomber, who lived alone in a nearby cabin without electricity or running water. It was an uncomfortable irony that I was now appreciating the same wilderness in which he had once lived and the protection of which from industrialisation had inspired him to three murders through his near twenty-year campaign of letter bombs.

On closer inspection the town consisted of no more than a crossroads, the branches of which were populated by half a dozen motels, a couple of diners, a post office and two gas stations with convenience stores attached. And JR's Taxidermy Studios ('Mounts on Show!'); just as long as they hadn't taken to stuffing cyclists. It ill behoves a rider on the Tour Divide to moan about such a broad array, but somehow Lincoln's practical benefits were outweighed by its sombre ambience. The forest seemed to have thickened again and its tentacles had enveloped the town.

Or maybe it was just me. Progress had been good and the scenery stunning, but I felt listless. Glum, even. Maybe Ovando had been too welcoming. Maybe I needed to avoid such creature comforts in order to better endure the rigours of the ride. I used the payphone at a gas station to call home and relay how much fun I had been having. Clearly I was not very convincing.

'But you're doing so well,' said Catherine, unprompted.

'Am I? I mean, I am?'

'Yes! You're not far from catching a group ahead of you, and there are still people behind you. Benjamin's very proud – you're not last.'

'Oh,' I said.

It seemed churlish to take offence at the surprise that had accompanied this last remark. I, too, had come to the conclusion that all those further back would have had the good sense to give up and go home. I had assumed the *Lanterne Rouge* was mine for the taking.

'And everybody here is addicted to watching your blue dot on the website, so you'd better keep moving.'

People outside my immediate family were watching li'l ol' me? Almost instantly I was transformed, in my own perception at least, from lonely wanderer to mountain bike racer with a global fan club, an ambassador for adventurers the world over. Did the good people of Lincoln – which by now seemed a much more charming place – know who I was, I wondered, as the gas station complemented my spiritual nourishment with more practical sustenance. Fortunately the question remained rhetorical.

I breakfasted on the porch: two pies, two pastries, two chocolate bars, two cups of coffee but only one banana.

'That sure saves on fuel,' said a man, motioning to my bike, not what I was consuming. 'It's costing me a fortune these days.'

I noticed that the truck to which he returned after buying his groceries had been left with its throbbing V8 engine running all the time he'd been inside. It seemed wise not to say anything.

Replenished, I resumed my journey. It was just after 10 a.m. High clouds obscured half the sky, but the weather seemed set fair. The aim of the day was to reach Helena, Montana's state capital and one of the biggest settlements on the entire route. In the intervening 65 miles there were two major climbs, not to mention the first three US crossings of the Continental Divide itself. There were also several sections of route described on the map as 'rough'.

The first of these materialised after less than an hour.

'Next 4.4 miles are extremely steep uphill, but they lead through fascinating country with several stream crossings,' read the description.

'Extremely steep' turned out to be an understatement. It was also stretching a point to suggest the admittedly delightful woodland, though perhaps not fascinating, was sufficient distraction. Previously, with the exception of the connector, all stints of bike-pushing had been brought on by seasonal modifications to the underlying terrain: snow; mud; overflowing streams; fallen trees. Here, it was necessary to push because of the underlying terrain. Not only was it steep, but the trail consisted almost exclusively of a succession of boulders, some fixed, most not. It was tiring work.

At the top, the reward was to traverse a flower-strewn meadow to the east side of the Continental Divide for the first time since before crossing Elk Pass in Canada. I staged a photo of relief masquerading as joyous celebration. Then came a freewheeling descent, through a noticeably more arid landscape, that immediately paralleled the nascent Marsh Creek. It seemed quite feasible, and almost equally appealing, to swap the bike for a canoe and continue downhill all the way to the Mississippi delta. At the junction with Little Prickly Pear Creek, however, our routes diverged. Huckleberry Finn would have to be left for another day.

It was nearing midday. I treated myself to an apple pie. Quite why such a simple dish required a list of ingredients that covered the entire back of the packet was a mystery, not least because most of the ingredients were either unidentifiable or unpronounceable, or both. It was delicious.

What goes down must go back up. Another hour-long climb, rideable this time, returned me to the western side of the Divide. It also heralded another change in scenery. I was now in mining country. Or, to be more accurate, I was in what had once been mining country.

So far every habitation on the route had been predicated on exploiting the area's natural resources. Most owed their existence to primary industries, mainly logging and agriculture; only Banff and Whitefish had transcended this reliance, though being service centres for visiting tourists ensured the essential link with their surroundings was unbroken.

Here it was mineral wealth. The precariousness of such a dependence was abundantly clear. Remnants of mining camps and the mines themselves dotted the scarred landscape. Not all of Montana was so fortunate in its abandonment as Ovando. I rode alongside a giant, crumbling lime kiln. It was as if a modern Ozymandias had briefly passed this way, but his legacy was no longer lasting than that of his ancient counterpart.

'Look on my works, ye mighty, and despair.'

Here, the despair was not just the dilapidation wrought on such mighty constructions in scarcely 100 years. It was also the despoliation of the surrounding landscape that would take much longer to heal.

The day's final crossing of the Divide was a simple affair, the route for once having deigned to remain near the crest of the ridge between passes. The roughness of the trail persisted, however. Boulders vied with ruts and roots to cause havoc to passing cyclists. It came as something of a surprise, therefore, to turn a corner and find a man ostensibly mending the track ahead. Alone, and bereft of such modern conveniences as a digger, I suggested he had his work cut out; an Ozymandias for straitened times.

'Oh, I'll just keep doing a bit here and a bit there.'

He may not have been much of a road builder but he was a considerable mountain-bike enthusiast. Although appearing to be well into his 60s, he had recently ridden more than 300 miles off-road across Iowa, and warmed visibly to my description of events so far.

'Say, when I get this ol' rock moved you could come and stay at my house. I've plenty of room and you could give the bike a once-over.'

It was a kind offer, but his house was 7 miles off-route, which seemed too high a price to pay. More importantly, an innate fear, fuelled by Hollywood, of psychopaths haunting just such locations to lure unsuspecting passers-by to meet a gruesome end, possibly later to be featured on an extreme reality TV show, was another factor in my decision to decline. He took it well, and showed no ill-feeling by recommending I stop at Van's Thriftway supermarket on the way into town for supplies.

The rest of the descent into Helena passed almost too rapidly, dropping 2,000 feet in 15 miles and half an hour, most on the smooth tarmac of US Highway 12. It seemed like a cruel taxation on the day's efforts thus far, though no doubt I would have plenty of opportunity to earn it again tomorrow.

The outskirts of town marked the beginning of 2 miles of hideous strip development – a procession of prefabricated showrooms selling everything from air-conditioning to real estate, interrupted only by parking lots and the streets of the town's grid layout. Weeds grew in the cracks in the sidewalk. The sun, up till now a benign presence, began to beat a tattoo on the bleached, dusty concrete. And on my head.

I came to Van's. Like its neighbours, it appeared cheap and not overly cheerful. A boy scout standing at the entrance selling popcorn to raise funds to attend a jamboree agreed to watch over my bike while I went inside. The first priority was to replenish my depleted stock of elastic bands, which I used to hold various bits of kit together. I asked a passing shop worker where I might find some.

'D'ya mean, like, hair bands?'

I checked to see if I was still wearing my helmet and it was obscuring my balding pate. I wasn't. In spite of the overwhelming evidence to the contrary and my mute incredulity, the shop worker had clearly already come to her own conclusion and led me down the feminine hygiene aisle to a surprisingly extensive selection of hair accessories. I wondered if she was going to recommend a style as well, but instead she left me to my own devices. Too tired to try again, I chose a multi-coloured selection pack. They lasted all the way to Mexico.

Still bemused, I was about to leave when I passed the store's deli. It was not like the cold meat and cheese counters at home. I stared in amazement at the array of hot food being served and tried not to salivate too openly. Eventually, a large lady completed her order and I was inadvertently propelled to the front of the queue.

'Whaddaya want?' came the question – though it was more like a command – from behind the counter.

I still hadn't identified the various deep-fried objects in front of me and wasn't sure I could face an explanation.

'I'll have what she had.'

After a short while I was presented with a bag containing two chicken wings and a 2-pound tub of mashed potato, all smothered in gravy.

I rejoined the boy scout. He seemed impressed by my selection. I settled on a nearby bench and was entertained while I dined by the comings and goings of Helenans on their shopping trips. It was not a particularly uplifting spectacle.

At the end of the nineteenth century Helena, still only a few decades old, was home to the highest concentration of millionaires in the US (or possibly the world, depending on which account you believe) thanks to the concentration of gold found in the city's famous Last Chance Gulch. Now, in spite of being the state capital and having outlived its erstwhile gold rush rivals long enough to be on the verge of celebrating its hundred and fiftieth anniversary, it had a median household income that was more than 15 per cent lower than the national average. A similar proportion of the population was deemed to live below the poverty line. It showed, and the boy scout's decision to sell his popcorn at $15 a box seemed a questionable marketing strategy.

I headed downtown to find a room for the night. Up on the hill stood the imposing State Capitol and the equally imposing though rather incongruous cathedral; below, the civic centre had a distinctly mosque-like appearance. I rode slowly, like a scruffy tourist, through the elegant mansion district. It was full of impressive Victorian villas from the city's heyday that now provided suitably grand homes for public officials, or suave guest houses for wealthy visitors.

Falling into neither of these categories, I continued my search elsewhere. At a traffic lights I was assailed by a fellow cyclist. He clearly wasn't a Tour Divide racer, as I had initially hoped, but I was nevertheless tempted by his suggestion of accompanying me to an informal camping spot he claimed to know on the outskirts of town. With motels in short supply, and such two-wheeled companionship on offer, I was about to set off when I noticed a large knife embedded up to the hilt in one end of his handlebars; I had assumed he just had bar extensions, but the carved wooden handle was a clear giveaway. Closer, though I hoped discreet, inspection of my new companion also revealed that his clothing was not what might be expected of a cycle tourist – worn out brogues, jeans held up by a string belt and a holey shirt with missing buttons. What I had taken to be camping gear lashed to his bike was in fact no more than a motley assortment of straps and ropes. His eyes, of course, had by now assumed a characteristic psychopathic glint.

'I'm a millionaire sailor,' he said in answer to my unspoken question. 'I own two boats in the Caribbean. I'm just here on holiday.'

I struggled to find a convincing reason to change my mind about camping, then decided it need not necessarily be that convincing.

'I've just got to pop to the laundry.'

Surprisingly, given his own malodorous state, evidence of which had now reached my nostrils, he understood the urgency of this requirement. We parted company on amicable terms. I turned a corner and, to my considerable relief, discovered the Bargain Motel. They had one room left for the night. I had a bath and went to bed. It was 8 p.m.

....

CHAPTER 11

SIGNS OF LIFE

DAY 8

Following the success of the past two days, in both of which I had covered more than the requisite 100 miles, I needed little persuasion to limit my aspirations to making it as far as Butte. It was only 70 miles distant, but those 70 miles were described on the map as containing some of the toughest riding on the whole Tour Divide. They also preceded another long stretch bereft of services and, in my imagination at least, inhabited by thousands of hungry bears. Stopping in Butte seemed tactically astute. And it rhymed.

The alarm sounded at the luxurious hour of 6 a.m. The lady in reception made good on her promise from the previous night and provided freshly brewed coffee. Combined with Danish pastries and yesterday's squashed bananas, it was as enjoyable a breakfast as I had had since Banff. Something about Helena clearly lent itself to comfort eating.

The route out of town was along Last Chance Gulch. The name alone was enough to reassure me that I had decided correctly not to venture forth with last night's knife-wielding companion. The eponymous warning signs increased as Last Chance Gulch turned into Grizzly Gulch.

'Don't worry, it was named because of the bear that used to live there when the town was still a mining camp,' yesterday's road mender had told me.

Here, in the grey morning light, was the story of Helena laid bare. The gravel road up the gulch passed between the scars of more old mine workings, the lime kilns here judged important enough to have been placed on the National Register of Historic Places. Interspersed with these relics were modern executive houses. Manicured lawns and double garages were the very manifestation of the American dream, the fruit of the pioneering spirit that was so clearly still evident. More striking yet, however, were the residents still apparently emulating their predecessors by eking a living from miniature excavations in the valley floor. Shacks little more substantial than those of the original shanty town emitted smoke from crooked chimneys between flooded pits. The logic seemed sound. The area had yielded placer-mined gold – pay dirt – to the value of $5,000,000 in its first five years and an estimated $30,000,000 all told. Nuggets were still said to be found in the gutters of downtown after a cloudburst. Yet the surrounding bone yards of decomposing cranes and redundant diggers suggested current pickings were more meagre. Rich and poor lived cheek by jowl but in all other senses the distance between them was infinite.

The climb up the gulch was not too taxing; the forest agreeably open between the dwindling number of houses; the sky two-thirds grey. Things continued in the same vein for another hour, until the right turn onto the north fork of Quartz Creek, 'a rough four-wheel drive track; next two miles are steep and rough'.

The only distinction from yesterday's hike-a-bike section was the added frisson of getting lost at the end of it. Although I had nagging doubts quite early into my unscheduled diversion, I pressed on with an obstinate determination not to accept the obvious for a good half-hour. Even banks of snow with no signs of the tyre tracks I had happily been following all day were insufficient warning. After all, there wasn't really anything to complain about. In fact, it was very pleasant. I had emerged from the trees into an area of broad, open meadows on top of a ridge. I was at well over 7,000 feet, and the nearby peaks rose higher still. The views to each side were seductive. I was just in the wrong place, something I later learned that Catherine and my other virtual supporters had become aware of long before I had.

Even the consequences of this temporary navigational error didn't seem unduly perturbing. It was not yet midday, and I could see routes down into both main valleys and some form of civilisation. One of them was bound to lead to the town of Basin, my next staging post. The only question was which one.

On my own, this stark choice might not have deterred me from chancing my arm. A natural aversion to retracing hard won ground was sure to bring out my inner gambler. The big brother nature of my SPOT tracker meant I was not alone, however; I had my fan club to consider. This invisible conscience then reminded me of one of the few rules of the Tour Divide that decreed a rider would be disqualified if they didn't cover the entire route, even if a diversion was considerably longer, and even if it meant retracing their steps. I finally yielded to the reality of my situation. The only solution was to return to the last point at which I was certain I was on the correct route.

That was easier said than done. If I'd noticed where I'd gone wrong, I was fairly certain I wouldn't have gone wrong in the first place. What's more, all route directions were based on having an accurately calibrated odometer (the maps themselves were too large-scale to be anything more than visual guidance). I had two, but the operative word was 'had'. Both were now out of tune with the elapsed mileage of the route by an unknowable margin. Even assuming I found the route again, it was uncertain that my sketchy mental arithmetic would be able to cope with the modifications necessary to follow subsequent directions.

Buoyed by such a cheering prospect, I performed a reluctant *volte face*. Halfway back up the first long, bouldery climb, I saw an optical illusion: a saloon car parked at the top of the hill. Then the optical illusion started to move, bouncing alarmingly over the stones and ruts. Recognising potential salvation, I started sprinting towards it. Progress was hampered, however, by trying to wave and blow my whistle at the same time. One-handed, uphill sprinting over rocky ground, on a mountain bike while trying to whistle Dixie as loudly as possible is not as easy as it might seem.

Rather surprisingly, the occupants of the car eventually became aware of my presence. Even more surprisingly, they had the courage to stop. It was something of a disappointment to discover they were as lost as I was, though on reflection it was the only reasonable explanation for such an inappropriate vehicle being found in the current surroundings. My own baffling presence suddenly seemed harder to explain.

I clambered back over the banks of snow marked by my solitary tyre tracks. Each pedal stroke was a further reminder of my folly. Surely I should be back on the route by now? I read and re-read the route description. It could just as well have been written in Chinese.

Then the silence of the forest was broken by a noise. It was the rhythmic throb of a rescue helicopter. Clearly, somebody back home had observed my plight and sent a message to the powers that be that I needed a little assistance. Oh, the wonders of modern technology.

The noise grew louder. I scanned the skies above but to no avail. Distracted, I was suddenly alarmed to be nearly run over. It turned out not to be a virtual rescue, but a typical Montana family on a quad bike outing. I tried to conceal my disappointment.

Once stopped, my new potential saviours unwittingly did a passable impression of the Three Bears of nursery rhyme fame: great big papa bear; equally great big mama bear; and surly, be-hooded adolescent bear.

'How ya doing?' said papa bear.

'I'm fine, but I'm a bit lost,' I replied.

'Where ya headed?'

I managed to stop myself saying Mexico.

'Basin, but I need to make sure I go past the old Hattie Ferguson and Morning Glory mines.'

I couldn't have fallen upon better guides. Surly, be-hooded adolescent bear obligingly unfolded the map and papa bear did the explaining. Mama bear nodded approvingly.

'We've just moved out to the country from Helena and we're out exploring ourselves. Last time we came up this way we got lost too, it's a maze of tracks and trails. Anyways, let's see.'

On his immensely detailed map he quickly determined where we were. I was about quarter of a mile short of my original route, where it would be a simple question of turning left to get back on track. I thanked them profusely. They insisted it was nothing worthy of praise. I persisted embarrassingly – a week in the wilderness does nothing for social etiquette.

Surly, be-hooded adolescent bear asked where I was headed after Basin. I said Butte, then added, rather hesitantly, Mexico. If I managed to stop getting lost, that was.

'Wow, that's some trip,' he replied, his face lighting up.

I explained about the race. His enthusiasm was contagious. I vowed to stop judging youthful Montanans by their dress sense.

'It sure is nice to see ya here in Montana,' said papa bear as our ways parted.

The rest of the descent to Basin was straightforward. After a welcome lunch at the town's only restaurant, I enjoyed the dubious pleasure of riding roughly parallel to Interstate 15 on a 'non-maintained cattle access trail' for the next hour. The sky had turned a menacing, uniform grey. An old, unlit railway tunnel dated 1911 offered fleeting intrigue, but the landscape scars of mine works were as nothing compared to the despolation created by miles upon miles of motorway.

Next came a paved road that ran right alongside the Interstate. Eight-axle trucks thundered past a mere stone's throw away. At least I had a headwind to distract me; at least I wasn't on the Interstate.

I had spoken too soon. It was there, in the route description, in black and white, and not in Chinese: the last 6 miles of the day would be the other side of the barrier on the Interstate itself. I pictured myself riding down the M23 at home. It was ridiculous; there was no choice.

Mercifully, only the first third of a mile was uphill. After that I began to pick up speed. And more speed. The descent was straight and long. I adopted an aerodynamic tuck and freewheeled down the hard shoulder at 40 mph. Lorries found it difficult to overtake. I toyed with the idea of playing chicken into the intersection with Interstate 90. It was quite thrilling; thrilling enough to distract me from the view of distant snow-clad mountains to my right and Our Lady of the Rockies, a 90-foot statue of the Virgin Mary, to my left.

At last the fun was over. I had scarcely turned off when I saw the sign I had been looking for: 'The Outdoorsman'.

Butte's pre-eminent bike shop, The Outdoorsman had further enhanced its reputation among Tour Divide racers by tracking participants' progress on the website and affording moral as well as practical support. It was also owned and run by Rob Leipheimer, the brother of Levi Leipheimer, the second most famous and successful of current US cyclists.

'You must be Paul from England,' said Rob.

'You must be the famous Mr Leipheimer,' I replied, instantly cursing my sieve-like memory. For much of the previous three hours I had contentedly distracted myself from the monotony of my surroundings by pretending to be Henry Stanley, the culmination of which artifice was going to be my uttering the immortal line: 'Mr Leipheimer, I presume.' Now I had blown my big moment. Still, Rob didn't seem to mind the slip.

'Are you staying here the night? We own the hotel next door, and there's a discounted rate for Tour Dividers.'

It was an easy decision.

'Have you seen anyone else today?' I asked, with little hope of a positive response.

'Sure, we've had a few groups through.'

My heart leapt.

'There were a few through this morning, and then two guys who left about an hour ago . . .'

'They've gone already?'

I silently cursed this morning's navigational lapse.

'. . . and one guy who's in the hotel.'

I might not have actually given Rob a hug, but it's difficult to be entirely sure. While he continued to clean and service my bike, I hastily checked in.

'Apparently you've got a guy by the name of Steve McGuire staying with you,' I said. 'You'll have noticed him – he'll have been as smelly and funnily dressed as I am. Could you tell me his room number?'

'I'm afraid I couldn't do that, sir,' smiled the receptionist.

Why not? Had I forgotten to say please?

'We can't give out room numbers of guests,' she explained, still smiling.

I was allowed – obliged – to cycle down the motorway, but privacy laws were seemingly going to prevent me from preserving my sanity. Then I had a brilliant idea (in ordinary circumstances it probably wouldn't have merited the description 'brilliant', but context was everything).

'Please could you let Steve know which room I'm in?'

I repeated the 'please', just in case.

'Sure thing!'

I had hardly entered my room when the phone rang. It was Steve. He was in a room three doors away. A few seconds later there was a knock at the door.

'Paul?'

'Steve! Come in. Boy, am I glad to see you!'

After more than 100 hours of solitude, I had a riding companion.

....

CHAPTER 12

SINGING IN THE RAIN

DAY 9

Steve McGuire proved the perfect cycling companion. In some ways that came as little surprise as he had already proved himself the perfect post-ride conversation companion and the perfect breakfast companion.

The previous night, as befitted his status as a professor of contemporary story-telling, Steve had entertained me royally with a brief account of his adventures thus far. These included not only getting lost in the same place as I had yesterday, but also having to spend the night camping rough as a result. Getting lost around midday had been one thing; getting lost at midnight with only an inadequate sleeping bag to provide protection from the cold and the critters alike had been quite another.

After that, neither of us had had the energy to be particularly sociable, but it mattered not. The simple presence of another Tour Divide rider in the same hotel was sufficient. It was like the desire to ensure the continuing presence of endangered species – tigers and lions, for example. You didn't need to be able to see them; just knowing they were still around was enough. Having said that, I realised that I used to feel the same way about bears. For the past week, not being able to see them but knowing they were around had become the problem.

There were no bears in the outskirts of Butte. Instead, there were miserable car drivers and antagonistic youths. The sight of a Lycra-clad cyclist clip-clopping his way to the Safeway over the road from the hotel was too much to resist. In less than 100 yards I was greeted with various manifestations of contemptuous indifference and a volley of insults hurled from a car window. It looked for one slightly alarming moment that the car's occupants were about to disembark en masse, but no doubt my menacing demeanour dissuaded them. That or the fact the traffic lights turned to green and they went from antagonists to objects of opprobrium from other drivers in short order.

Safeway had nothing to compare to the deli section of Van's, so I resorted to the neighbouring sandwich shop. I thought my luck was in when I found them selling family portions of lasagne the size of a tabloid newspaper.

'I'll take one of those, please,' I requested.

'You have to heat them up at home.'

Something about my attire, or possibly my accent, must have suggested this was unlikely. I was grateful for the warning.

'Could you not heat one up for me?' I asked.

After all, there was a microwave on the back wall.

'I'm not from round here so I can't heat one up myself,' I added, a touch unnecessarily.

'We're not allowed to do that.'

It was clear there was little point in pursuing the argument.

'And I suppose your pizzas are the same?'

'Yep.'

At least there was no ambiguity. I settled for sandwiches instead. Heated sandwiches, as it turned out. It started to rain. Back at the hotel I walked past a microwave on the way to my room.

At five the next morning Steve and I helped ourselves to waffles at the self-service breakfast counter. Not long after 5.30 a.m. we were en route. In an encouraging start, particularly in the light of our recent track record, we then managed to get lost within sight of the hotel. This time, however, it only took five minutes – and the help of the hotel concierge – to rectify the situation. We skirted downtown Butte with no further mishap, and headed through the skeleton suburbs of a town that less than a century ago had had more than 100,000 occupants but now was home to only just over 30,000.

It was a cold and grey morning. Rain threatened, then arrived. We stopped to don overgarments. Alone it would have been miserable, but the conversation was as easy as the riding along paved roads.

Steve, I discovered, was a youthful-looking quinquagenarian, married with two boys and living in Iowa, of which he was quite proud.

'How do you like our new president?' he asked.

Aware of the deeply divisive nature of US politics, and unwilling to aggravate a companion with whom I hoped to spend the next few weeks, I ventured that he was widely perceived as an improvement on his predecessor. I need not have been so coy. Steve was an enthusiast. It was the Iowa caucuses, he reminded me, that had turned Barack Obama from a possible to probable presidential candidate.

Steve also had some considerable pedigree as a cyclist and adventurer. He was a veteran of the Iditabike, the cycling equivalent of the great Alaskan winter husky-sled adventure, the Iditarod. He had also ridden to Iowa from Alaska, ridden the Trans-Iowa mountain bike race, and ridden around Iceland on a tandem, offering the stoker seat to anyone capable of telling a decent story.

As a devotee of winter cycling, he had also had the misfortune to encounter, on three separate occasions, unfortunate souls in peril in the frozen Iowa River; more impressively still he had had the courage to dive in and rescue them, the latest occasion being the previous winter when he had come across a car crash. I felt I was in safe hands.

After an hour we left the metalled roads behind and began climbing on familiar gravel. We passed under an imposing trestle bridge, another reminder of the area's past links with extractive industries.

To our right should have been views across Butte to Berkeley Pit, the erstwhile 'richest hill on earth', an open pit mine from which sufficient copper had been extracted to leave a hole 1 mile wide and 1,600 foot deep. In fact, the hole didn't last long for as soon as the mining stopped, the pumps were switched off and it began to fill with water. Or rather, what passes for water when it has a pH of 2.5 and is laced with arsenic, cadmium and zinc, among other contaminants.

Instead, there were neither views nor any other distractions to occupy us on the climb up to another crossing of the Continental Divide. Only rain and trees. And a slippery road surface that was the cycling equivalent of walking on snow sufficiently frozen on the surface to bear your weight 90 per cent of the time but which, one random step in every ten, gave way, plunging you into the powder beneath and depriving you of any momentum.

In spite of the effort required to maintain forward progress, a deep chill had begun to set in. At the top, we stopped to don more layers. It was raining heavily enough to make it essential to find shelter before overclothes could be removed safely; being wet inside as well as out would have been a serious mistake. We spotted a forest service toilet block.

'Welcome to the Montana Hilton,' said Steve.

The title seemed a touch grand. We were confronted with nothing more spectacular than a prefabricated outhouse, consisting of a small porch and a 5 foot by 5 foot cubicle, all sitting over a pungent faecal broth. I expressed my reservations.

'You obviously haven't had the pleasure of sleeping in one of them,' Steve explained.

It turned out that the previous night had not been Steve's only rough sleeping experience. He had also been caught out in a storm of such severity that the only way to survive the night with any degree of comfort, or indeed at all, had been to seek shelter inside just such a cubicle.

'All the "activity" below meant I was nice and warm.'

I was glad it was still early enough in the morning for such an eventuality to seem unlikely today.

The rain came down more heavily still. It was like a bad day in the Lake District. I said as much to Steve. His enthusiasm for a riding trip in the UK dropped visibly. Mud splashed everywhere, penetrating eyes and nose and mouth and ears. Tyres gripped less and less, adding an extra frisson of excitement. With visibility already impaired by the meteorological conditions, progress was treacherous.

The long descent counteracted the warming effect of our extra layers. Our feet and hands had the good fortune to succumb early to the cold and turned numb; the rest of our bodies could still feel the discomfort. Eventually, as the gradient eased, we realised the route was going to pass under the Interstate. The resultant tunnel was full of muddy puddles and noise and detritus from the cars passing overhead. It was delightful.

We shivered convivially and took stock. The good news was that we were now confronted with another major climb on which we could reasonably hope to generate some heat. The bad news was that it took us up to nearly 8,000 feet on the exposed upper reaches of Mount Fleecer. Worse, the subsequent descent had grown to assume legendary status on the Tour Divide.

'This will be difficult to comprehend until you confront it, but it's true that the descent from Fleecer is the toughest hill to negotiate on the entire Great Divide – and that includes the uphills,' said Michael McCoy in *Cycling the Great Divide*, the official guidebook of the route.

It also suggested that abandoning the trail and zigzagging through the scrub might be the better option, an assessment that had presumably been made in favourable conditions.

Accordingly, it was with some trepidation that we ventured once more into the wind and rain. For an hour the gradient maintained a satisfactory balance between effort expended and heat generated. Then we came out of the woods onto the broad, exposed shoulder of the mountain. The wind and rain were windier and rainier, though they now had the decency to be driving us in the right direction across the sodden moonscape. It would no doubt have seemed a charming flower meadow in more clement conditions. As it was, attempting to avoid the bogs with bike or feet was a wholly gratuitous effort.

After 20 minutes of uphill bike-dragging we turned a corner and started, tentatively, to descend. Half a mile of cautious weaving between shrubs later and we were beginning to wonder what all the fuss had been about. But that was to reckon without the fact we were on a convex slope. Slowly, ever so slowly, the true, precipitous nature of the descent still to come revealed itself. By the time we fully realised what we were in for it was impossible to do anything but continue. So continue we did, slithering and sliding our way down the muddy, shaley, shrubby hillside. The few bits of bike and body that had not already become damp or covered in mud gave up their rearguard effort. Clumps of sage offered temporary anchor holds. Clods of earth and stone disappeared down the slope below. Yet, miraculously, neither bicycles nor riders followed suit.

Eventually the gradient became such that we could first walk with our bikes, then ride them. We grinned maniacally at each other and cycled at a furious pace down the ensuing trail as if recently escaped from prison. Near hysteria at our survival had induced recklessness. Foot-deep puddles and rocky stream crossings were treated with disdain.

The rain and wind continued their assault. We ignored them. We had no choice. Some time later, it was impossible to tell exactly how long, we arrived where we knew we would have to arrive as long as we managed to keep pedalling. We later learned that this minuscule collection of buildings at the roadside, the only settlement for miles around, was called Wise River, but at the time the name was irrelevant. Only the fact that it had a restaurant with an open door was important. It had taken six and a half hours to cover 52 miles, 11 of which had been on paved roads.

No sooner had we prised open the doors of the Wise River Club with hands frozen into claws than we were greeted like long-lost friends. It turned out that the owner, Tom, an escapee from Scotland, thought we *were* long-lost friends. The fact that we were not, readily verifiable once we had peeled off our outer layers and wiped the mud from our faces, did not seem to concern him.

'There was an English lad came through on the same race last year, I thought you were him,' he explained.

I asked if it had been Alan. He said yes. Apparently, Alan and his then riding companion had turned up first thing in the morning, famished after spending the night somewhere on Mount Fleecer, only to find the restaurant closed. Tom's wife met them in the shop and had taken them home, where Tom had cooked them a splendid pancake breakfast. Whether inspired by this particular bout of hospitality, or a long-held desire to cater for passing cyclists, he had subsequently bought the very same restaurant-cum-hotel. For us, the outcome could not have been better.

We were given free run of the covered veranda to remove and hang out sodden clothes, as well as access to the tumble dryer (an inebriated woman wobbled off after we had started the machine, vowing to set her husband on us for having had the temerity to remove her dried laundry; when the husband duly arrived he asked politely if he might put the few damp items back in once we had finished; it was briefly tempting to say 'no' to see what happened, but common sense prevailed). We were then positively encouraged to steam and pong to our hearts' content in the diner as we demolished the finest burgers tasted to date. We also discovered we were not the only cyclists in the village.

'Hey, Tour Divide racers,' said a voice.

It belonged to a mop of blond hair above a lined and stubbled face (more lined and stubbled than it had been in Banff, at least). It was Dallas resident Ray. He had arrived earlier that morning, having spent the previous night in the very same Montana Hilton Steve and I had passed earlier that day. He had been asleep in a room upstairs for several hours, but still looked as if he were trying to warm up. He joined us to eat.

After more burgers and more coffee, Steve and I began to plan our next move. It was only 4 p.m., but it was still raining. Ray looked aghast.

'I ain't goin' out there again today,' he said.

Undeterred, or at least unwilling to admit it to each other, Steve and I resolved to ride another 33 miles to Elkhorn Hot Springs. It was not far, we reasoned, and it was all on tarmac. What's more, the famous Mr Leipheimer had said the scenery along the Pioneer Mountains National Scenic Byway made it one of his favourite road rides in the whole state, a real gem.

Clearly, the unlikely outcome of the morning's tribulations had been an unhealthy dose of bravado. We chose to ignore the impact of our earlier exertions; we conveniently overlooked the fact that it was uphill almost all the way and that it culminated in the highest point of the trip so far. More bone-headed still, and in spite of the overwhelming evidence to the contrary – it was still raining – we told ourselves the sky was brightening. The fact that we were likely to see nothing of the area's fabled beauty was also disregarded.

'It's bound to stop raining soon,' I enthused, irrationally.

Ray wished us good luck in a tone that indicated just how much he thought we would need it. He also said he would think about setting off again the next morning if the weather had improved.

By 5 p.m. we were on the road again. We didn't arrive until nearly 9 p.m. For the first hour or so we managed to find sufficient Dunkirk spirit to keep ourselves entertained. Conversation ranged widely from children to more politics via flooding in Iowa city and the contemporary relevance of ancient story-telling techniques. Then conversation waned. I sang tunelessly. Morale dropped ever lower. After that we each sank into silent worlds of mutual recrimination. At least, I did, and uncharitably I transposed my own sentiments to Steve. For two more hours we plodded upwards, accompanied by malevolent thoughts and monstrous trees. We may have been on a paved road, but civilisation was a distant prospect.

Just as all hope seemed lost (it really seemed that bad), we reached the plateau that signalled an end to the day's climbing. The land lay open in all directions. In the gloaming of impending dusk and lowering cloud it had an ethereal beauty that raised even our sodden spirits. Infinite shades of green faded into infinite shades of grey. Herds of elk sheltered at the woods' edge. They considered us pityingly, yet so inured had we become to the cold and damp and so lovely was the land that it seemed almost a shame to leave.

The realisation that we might already be too late for food and a bed for the night brought a quick end to such nonsense. We staggered up the steps into the timber lodge. Once again we were greeted with enormous warmth and enormous portions. The wind howled and the rain poured but we were warm and dry. It was the perfect end to an imperfect day.

....

CHAPTER 13

HERE'S MUD IN YOUR EYE

DAY 10

I had a dream in the middle of the night. A drunken man was wandering around the upper floor of the lodge, opening and closing doors loudly, and shouting.

'Hello. Hello. Where ish everybody? I've got a reshervation.'

I woke up to find it wasn't a dream. It was a real-life nightmare. There really was a drunken man doing exactly as I thought I had dreamt. As I finally slid back into consciousness, I realised Steve, clad only in a towel, was on his way to the door. It didn't need an ice-frozen Iowa River to inspire his inner hero. I stayed in bed. It was 2 a.m.

Steve went into the corridor.

'What are you doing shouting and waking everybody up?' he asked in a very conciliatory tone given the circumstances.

'I need a room for the night.'

Judging by the crashing and banging that had just taken place, he had already discovered for himself that half a dozen of the rooms upstairs were empty, but inebriation seemed to have compromised his short-term memory.

'And I've got a reshervation,' he slurred, drawing a piece of paper from a pocket.

Steve clearly had several reservations about this unwelcome interloper, but considered the evidence proffered to him.

'But that's not here, that's somewhere else,' explained Steve.

'But it shays I've got a reshervation,' the drunkard insisted.

'You have got a reservation. It's at another hotel. Now you must leave,' said Steve calmly.

It took several more minutes for the incontrovertible force of Steve's syllogism to register, but eventually the gatecrasher could be heard trying to open the external door. Then, alarmingly, a car door also opened and children's voices could be heard. The door slammed and the engine fired before the car and its occupants disappeared to an uncertain fate in a flurry of revs and wheelspin.

We woke again at 7 a.m. After yesterday's exertions and the nighttime disruptions it was too early, yet it was already too late for what lay ahead. The permanent closure of a shop – the shop – in Grant 40 miles ahead meant there were now no services of any kind until Lima, more than 100 miles away. No food was one thing. The prospect of spending a night on a bare mountain, or possibly a bear mountain, in weather like we had just experienced, was quite another.

The lodge owner had promised breakfast at 8 a.m. With no opportunity for re-supply en route, there seemed little option but to wait. I packed my belongings, separating wet from not-so-wet, and tried not to draw the obvious conclusion from the fact that Steve was not doing the same. In our reduced state last night we had both talked about the possibility of holing up for a day if yesterday's conditions were going to persist. Peering through the curtains, it was not raining outside yet, but the volume and colour of the clouds suggested it was only a temporary truce.

We went downstairs. As we waited for breakfast to appear, Steve confirmed what had already become apparent. He wasn't going to continue the race. I was devastated. I didn't think my singing the previous day had been that bad.

I asked if waiting a day with him would make a difference, trying to disguise my ulterior motives. After all, there were worse places to pass the time, and the eponymous hot springs would do wonders for chilled and aching limbs.

'No, I think that's me done.'

It turned out a nagging reduction in his enjoyment levels over the past few days had been exacerbated by the cold and rain and had turned a challenge into a chore. There was no doubt the conditions were atypical for the area and time of year.

'I just don't want to put myself through another soaking.'

The decision had obviously been a difficult one, but Steve's previous exploits made it clear he had nothing to prove in terms of resilience or courage. A lack of satisfaction in the task at hand was now the determining factor. In contrast, it was to a large degree a lack of imagination that compelled me to keep going; stubbornness and the ensuing ignorance of often much more appealing alternatives had always been in my nature. It also appeared that being brought up in Yorkshire had its benefits when it came to dealing with inclement weather.

Even without the imagination to stop, I wavered. Wet socks and gloves and shoes did little for morale. Finally, encouraged by Steve and too fearful of the distance still to come to prevaricate further, I set off again on my own.

Twenty minutes later Steve was bemused and concerned to see me reappear in the dining room.

'Don't worry. I made it five minutes down the road when I realised I didn't have my SPOT tracker. It took me quarter of an hour to climb back up again.'

The effort was worth it, though. If I was to be alone in the real world, I at least wanted to be sure of virtual company.

It was 8.40 a.m. by the time I was definitively under way. The sky was filled by ragged grey clouds, interspersed with just enough blue to patch a pair of Dutchman's trousers, as my grandma would have said. There was a strong, cold wind, but it was still dry.

In little time the road spilled out of its narrow gorge onto a much broader valley. In the confines of the canyon it had been possible to ignore the fact that I was on my own. Here, the scale of the land served to increase my solitude. Vast acres of cattle ranches and sage scrub spread left and right, stopping only at distant mountains, their tops covered in fresh snow. Buildings were scarce. The road was long and straight.

After nearly an hour I came to a junction where there was a sign for 'Wisdom'. Fittingly, it was 32 miles in the wrong direction. Another straight, empty road followed until the route turned off to Bannack State Park. The ghost town of Bannack had been the site of Montana's first gold rush in 1862 and, in 1864, it had become the then Montana

Territory's first capital. Then, almost as quickly, it had been abandoned as the gold dried up and new, richer veins were discovered elsewhere. A mile off-route, 50 preserved buildings were all that remained. Helena, the chief beneficiary of Bannack's demise, was clearly a success in comparison.

Thereafter, evidence of human activity was at a new premium, except for an incongruous information board to the side of the trail. It bore witness to the passage of Lewis and Clark, who had travelled this way in 1806 on their return from having been the first white men to traverse the United States overland to reach the Pacific. There was a diary entry made by Clark on 6 July:

> The Country through which we passed today was diversified high dry and uneaven Stoney open plains and low bottoms very boggy with high mountains on the tops and North sides of which there was Snow, great quantities of the species Hysoap [sagebrush] & shrubs common to the Missouri plains are Scattered in those Valleys and hill Sides.

The trail was now clearly in the 'low bottoms very boggy' rather than the 'high dry and uneaven Stoney open plains'. No sooner had the metalled road ceased than progress did too. The recent rain had turned the surface into mush through which it was impossible to cycle. Soon it became almost impossible to walk. I cursed the fat tyres I had fitted to the bike especially for the ride. Balled up with mud, the clearance between tyres and forks was soon exceeded. Rotation stopped.

I broke a sweet-smelling branch from a nearby sage bush and disconsolately poked at the congealed mass. Having succeeded in temporarily clearing the blockage, I stood up and surveyed the situation. The sun was now shining, but it was not encouraging.

I started to push again. Then, out of the corner of my eye, I caught sight of something moving. It disappeared, then reappeared an indeterminate distance ahead of me on the trail. Aware of the risk of hallucinations, I spent some time denying its resemblance to a cyclist. Eventually, however, the temptation became impossible to resist.

Inspired by the prospect of company, however unlikely, I redoubled my efforts. I shouted, I waved, I blew my bear whistle, all to no avail. Nevertheless, with no thought to saving energy for what was still to come, I closed in on my prey. At last, almost spent, I discerned it was Ray. One last effort brought me to within hailing distance.

'Ray! Ray! Ray!'

He stopped his own laborious attempts at progress.

'Ray, what are you doing here?'

'I keep asking myself the same question.'

Although having seemed on the verge of abandoning the race the previous day at Wise River, he was clearly made of sterner stuff. Finally thawed out, he had set off before dawn and already covered nearly 60 miles on his single-speed bike. It was impressive stuff.

After a brief pause for refreshment we resumed our battle with the terrain. Gradually, after another couple of miles, things improved and we were able to ride again, short stretches at first, then a whole mile in one go. With the gradient now also on our side we had just picked up some much needed momentum when we found another reason to come to a halt. Four more cyclists were gathered in a farmyard.

We stopped, as much out of amazement as anything else. Tour Divide racers were obviously like London buses – there were none for an age, then several came along at once. We knew them all. There was Jacob from Manitowoc, whose phantom I had chased on the day out of Whitefish. With him were Per, Trevor from Montreal and Stephen from Mississippi. Resplendent in mud-spattered overgarments, they were a motley crew.

They were also downhearted. Rain had slowed their progress considerably for the past two days now. Worse, Jacob's rear derailleur had snapped in the mud and he was having to effect running repairs. From his demeanour, it seemed he didn't think they would last long. Still, he had nearly finished and had no option but to continue.

The road after the farm was cycleable again, apart from when it was covered in small lakes a foot deep. Then came a short section of metalled road before the gravel resumed. We were now on the old route to Corinne, 300 miles and two states away in Utah, and which had developed to service the gold camps at Bannack and elsewhere in nascent Montana. It was one of the first roads into Montana, and clearly hadn't seen much maintenance in the intervening 150 years.

Ray's single gear and, perhaps, the fact he had started the day so early, saw him drop back. So, too, did Jacob, nursing his repairs, and Stephen, keeping him company. I rode with Per and Trevor. The trail was slimy but passable. After an hour we consulted the map. 'Next 47 miles are very remote' it said, followed shortly after by 'road can be potentially mucky when wet'. That much we knew already. The tautology of the description was only a small crumb of comfort.

At 2 p.m. we stopped for lunch. We had been climbing since the road junction some 10 miles beforehand. Another 15 uphill miles remained. After that, to our disbelieving eyes, there appeared to be a 30-mile descent followed by 8 miles on tarmac. Fifty-three miles to go, most of them downhill. It didn't seem too bad if you said it quickly enough.

Neither Ray nor Jacob nor Stephen caught us as we ate. The blue sky had all but disappeared. With menacing clouds beginning to obscure the tops of the nearby mountains, and rain squalls visible ahead, we decided to press on.

The valley swept on before us, its exposed, barren flanks rising to graceful ridges 2,000 feet above our heads. Medicine Lodge Peak stood proudly to our right. It was magnificent scenery. Which was just as well. Several new bouts of mud wrestling ensured we had plenty of time to appreciate it.

During one such period of enforced reflection, I noticed that Trevor had old-fashioned V-brakes rather than the disc brakes Per and I had.

'Don't they just clog up even more?' I asked thoughtlessly.

The answer was evident from Trevor's creased brow. He had one considerable advantage over me, however. He was strong enough to raise his bike onto his shoulder and carry it through the sage scrub. Per and I, meanwhile, had to persist in quite literally ploughing a lonely furrow up the road. A large four-wheel drive pick-up fish-tailed past on its way to a ranch. We were uncertain whether to be gratified or concerned that even with its weight and power it could scarcely maintain progress in the desired direction.

As promised by the map, the gradient increased sharply two miles before the crest of the evocatively named Medicine Lodge-Sheep Creek Divide and the road surface improved. The weather deteriorated, however. Grey clouds were massing upwind, and the temperature had plummeted.

All of a sudden, Stephen arrived. He had ridden like an express train since Jacob had succumbed to the inevitability of his mechanical situation and been forced to accept a lift back to civilisation from a passing ranch hand. He had passed Ray at the beginning of the worst of the mud more than 10 miles back. Now he was intent on getting to Lima before the weather broke.

It was a false hope. Hardly had we begun to descend than the first raindrops fell. Soon they were not alone. If yesterday had been like a bad day in the Lake District, what ensued next was Scottish weather at its most foul, a sage-covered Rannoch Moor in a deluge. To add to the excitement, the mud now had the temerity to stop us from even being able to cycle downhill. It sucked greedily at our wheels, at our feet, at our morale. Five miles of only intermittent cycling followed. If you didn't mind not being able to see what you were riding on, often the best route was through the deepest puddles. It was gruelling, and not only because the road surface resembled porridge.

I tried to lift spirits with Flanders and Swann's hippopotamus song, but no self-respecting hippo would have been seen dead in mud like this. In fact, there was a complete absence of wildlife. It no doubt said something about our folly that 'dumb' animals knew better than to be out in such conditions.

At 6 p.m. there were still 25 miles ahead of us before we even made it to the road. Nightfall under clear skies was 10 p.m., but it already felt dark. Time was of the essence. Fortunately, the intensity of the rain seemed to help, creating rivulets through the mud down which we could ride. Perfumed by earlier trips into the sage scrub, and sweating profusely with the effort in spite of the driving rain, I felt like a stuffed chicken. All that was missing was the onion and breadcrumbs.

At last the scenery began to change. We were now in what one might call 'injun' country: a limestone gorge, the flanks of which were replete with prominent bluffs and caves carved by an ancient river. Apart from the lamentable absence of native tribes it could scarcely have changed much since they were formed.

As we finally spilled out of the gorge onto the paved road that would take us to Lima, I looked behind to read a sign we had just passed.

'Road impassable when wet.'

The pace had taken its toll. Even the prospect of eight smooth, flat miles seemed too much. No amount of effort could now compensate for the bone-deep chill. A handful of cars and lorries, headlights already blazing, sped past, oblivious. Motivation finally came through salivation. 'Think of the food' was our rallying cry.

It can be a dangerous thing to seek incentive in the realm of the possible rather than the certain. Having relied on the prospect of something appealing, subsequent disappointment at its absence is all the more acute. There was no guarantee that anything in Lima would be open at such a late hour on a Sunday night to meet our needs. With a population of only 242, there was no guarantee that there would be anything there at all.

We were in luck. Tucked in a crook of the Interstate, Lima was still buzzing – relatively speaking – when we finally arrived at 9 p.m. More importantly, Jan's Café and Cabins was open. Yet, famished as we were, we hesitated on the threshold. We really weren't very presentable. How best could we exploit our plight to ensure a warm reception? I was elected spokesman.

'Use that charming English accent of yours,' said Stephen in his Deep South drawl.

With unjust trepidation after the warmth of all the hospitality received thus far, I sploshed into the diner, followed by a trail of mud. I need not have worried.

We were not the only cyclists to have passed this way that day. Seated at the bar, considerably cleaner than when she had arrived earlier in the afternoon, was Cricket, for whom this whole adventure was a 'Mommy holiday' (some holiday, some Mom, I had thought at the time in Banff).

'Boy, am I glad to see you guys,' she beamed.

Then, shortly after Cricket's display of enthusiasm, a lady with nearly as much makeup as I had mud on my face – though hers was considerably more flattering – batted nary an eyelid as she offered both food and accommodation. She then made all four of us swoon by leading us on stilettos through the yard to a hosepipe where we could clean body and bike.

'You can order food up to 10 p.m.,' she said once she had demonstrated how to operate the manual pump.

The work of a woman in rural Montana was nothing if not varied. Cleaned and as presentable as possible, we returned to the diner. We ordered five burgers.

'Are you expecting someone else?' asked the waitress.

'No,' said 6-foot-6-inches Per. 'Two are for me.'

CHAPTER 14

....

THIS IS NOT PERU

DAY 11

At 7 a.m. it was raining. Half an hour later it was still raining, which was encouraging. At 8 a.m., with no let-up yet in sight, we admitted defeat. We were delighted. It was just the excuse we needed to go nowhere.

'I'm not riding through any more of that mud today,' said Trevor emphatically. Murmurs of approval came from under piles of bedclothes. We had already decided the previous night that only brilliant sunshine and Hawaiian temperatures would tempt us to depart again in the morning. Our luck was in – such an unlikely improvement in meteorological conditions had been avoided.

This turned out to be just as well. Even getting out of bed to go to the café for breakfast was something of a reluctant pleasure but, as with the night before, an empty stomach was a powerful motivator. In the café, Cricket was still nursing a cup of coffee. Her plan for an early start had also been stymied by the rain. Yet she remained intent on sallying forth, alone if necessary, as soon as the rain abated (surely it couldn't go on much longer); attempts to persuade us to accompany her fell on deaf ears.

To try to make myself feel better for such a lack of gallantry, I tactlessly listed the reasons why waiting for a day would be a better idea.

'One of the messages on the website from a rider ahead said there were 80 miles of mud after Lima,' I pointed out.

The road had also apparently been closed less than a week ago due to flooding. But, like Margaret Thatcher, the lady was not for turning.

'I have to keep moving. I've had two short days already.'

In fact, she had been caught in the worst of the mud in the worst of the weather and for the past two days had struggled to cover less than 100 miles through the quagmire. The days may have been short, but they had not been easy.

Nevertheless, Cricket's experiences thus far seemed to have inured her to such difficulties. She had already had a face-off with a bear that had charged her after being spooked by her arrival, and which then sat in the middle of the trail in front of her for an hour, refusing to move.

'When it got dark and I couldn't see him any more it was a little frightening,' she admitted.

As we were still devouring breakfast, she seized on a break in the clouds and rode off. She had been chivalrous enough to save us from guilt at letting her venture forth on her own. Yet guilt there still was, not least because there remained so far to go. How could we conceive of a day off? Only an atavistic urge for food and sleep – and the timely arrival of another round of toast – saved us from succumbing to the perverse temptation to continue. Within seconds, however, Per, Stephen, Trevor and I were lazily and gluttonously justifying our inertia. Even though the clouds were continuing to disperse and sunshine was a real possibility, it wasn't difficult.

Shortly after we had finished breakfast we were mightily relieved to be rejoined by Ray. Our relief was as nothing compared to his, however. If he had looked only semi-thawed when Steve and I had met him in Wise River, he now looked to have only recently climbed out of a deep freeze.

'I'm done with this thing,' he said.

Having tried to dissuade Cricket from continuing, we now found ourselves trying to persuade Ray to keep going.

'Hey, have some breakfast, man, you'll feel better,' said Stephen.

'We're not going anywhere until tomorrow,' added Per.

But it was to no avail. It was easy to understand why. While we had spent the previous night warming ourselves in Jan's Café, Ray had had to chase a herd of elk from a derelict barn high on the pass to find somewhere to shelter from the storm through which we had cycled. It had been a long and cold night for a man from Dallas, and it had not been his first. The cumulative effect of the chill and having only one gear had clearly taken a heavy toll.

'My knees are just shot,' he confirmed.

Shortly after Ray had left to search out a box to put his bike in for the long journey home there was a knock on the door. It was one of the chefs from the café.

'Could one of you guys come and help out the other cyclist? He's cut himself real bad.'

Simply because I was nearest the door I traipsed with some curiosity but no particular urgency to the porch.

'Hi, Ray. Oh . . . what happened?'

A grey-faced Ray was sitting with a large pool of blood at his feet. One hand was clasping the other in a blood-stained towel.

'I just cut my hand when I was trying to box up my bike,' he said with some understatement.

He had done the same thing while un-boxing his bike in Banff, though clearly not to the same degree. An ambulance had been called, and Ray asked if I would mind tidying up his stuff and locking it into his motel room so it would still be there when he got back from hospital.

'That's quite an extreme thing to do just to make sure you don't change your mind about keeping going,' I pointed out as he was bundled into the ambulance to be taken to Dillon, 45 miles away.

Ray smiled. At least I thought he smiled; it might have been a grimace. After he had left, I followed the splatters of blood across the drying car park to his motel room. It wasn't a pretty sight. I sorted Ray's belongings and made a half-hearted attempt at tidying up before I was saved from such a noble act by the cleaner.

'Leave that to me, I'll do it later,' she said.

I decided not to argue.

The rest of the day was spent on more mundane activities. Bikes and clothes were cleaned. The sun came out and a strong, drying wind came from the east.

'It's a headwind for Cricket,' said Trevor.

I rang home to try and find out some more about the state of the race and conditions to come.

'Everybody's suffering from the weather and the mud,' said Catherine.

She meant it as a reassurance but, given the geographical spread of the participants, it was also alarming. There was a lot of mud still to come. We were not out of Montana yet but, in spite of conditions every bit as bad as we had experienced, Matthew Lee at the front of the race was nearly into Colorado. I didn't want to work out how many miles ahead that meant he was. Chris Plesko and Kurt Refsnider weren't far behind, and neither was the Petervarys' tandem. After that came a group of riders at least three days ahead of us, with a few more stragglers in between. Behind us, it was a relief to hear that Deanna was still plugging away on her fixed-gear bike, but 12 riders had now dropped out. We were guaranteed a place in the top 30, assuming we finished.

I also checked the Tour Divide website. There was a message from Tim, my brother-in-law, and his wife Lisa. Lisa had been remarkably prescient.

'Lisa's view on the mud problem (getting stuck, pushing your bike, cleaning your bike, pushing some more) is: don't bother. Find a nice little café somewhere, cup of tea, piece of malt loaf, read a book, and soon enough it will be time for dinner. Mmm, yummy pizza, perhaps a piece of cheesecake and then go to bed nice and early. Wake up for a lovely cup of tea, and then some more malt loaf a bit later. Stuff the mud and biking nonsense.'

Tim, on the other hand, was made of sterner stuff.

'I view your noble endeavour with the utmost admiration and approval. I'd almost like to be there myself. It's just the mud and cycling bit that puts me off.'

More food was consumed. In fact, the day's theme was food, and the food at Jan's was excellent. This was just as well, as the more I ate, the hungrier I became.

Breakfast had been a fry-up preceded by porridge and followed by several rounds of toast. The aching hours between finishing that feast and lunch had been filled by a meagre snack – a slab of chocolate cake and a banana. Lunch itself was a main-meal salad followed by fish and chips and apple pie with ice cream. Afternoon snack was more pie.

By dinner time – we could scarcely make it past 5 p.m. – this conspicuous consumption provided an opportunity to learn some more about the peculiar vocabulary of US cuisine.

'What exactly is a chicken-fried steak?' asked Per.

Stephen, being the only native in our group, took it upon himself to explain.

'Basically, it's nothing to do with chicken, it's just a steak covered in breadcrumbs and fried in a pan. That's what it is in Mississippi, anyway. And you sometimes get brown gravy with it.'

'Sounds good, I'll try one of those,' Per decided.

It was something of a surprise he didn't ask for two. Bereft of imagination I ordered the same as at lunch time.

In between meals I read the mighty *Lima Ledger*, subtitled *The Preservation of News in the Red Rock River Valley*.

Preservation had obviously been something of a recent concern – this was only issue 34 of Volume Two – but the headline suggested 'news' was something of a rare commodity.

'Come enjoy 4th July in Lima! "Celebrate Small Town America".'

The events to be enjoyed were still nearly two weeks away, and the edition I was reading was dated a week earlier. Yet it sounded promising.

'Start your day with a pancake breakfast sponsored by the Lima Voluntary Fire Department. Pancakes, sausage, eggs and coffee or juice $5.'

Thereafter, an eclectic range of activities would be on offer: bed races; a horseshoe tournament; half a beef at 2 p.m. (to benefit the Springhill Assisted Living centre); and FREE swimming at the Lima Community Pool between 3 p.m. and 6 p.m. The day's festivities were to be rounded off by a 'Patriotic Community Sing-A-Long Karaoke' and a firework display. If my race came to an end before the 4th of July, I knew where to come.

There was also some real 'news' in the form of an article about the hospital in Dillon to which Ray had been taken and which had signed a deal to purchase land for its expansion. Construction was not due to be finished until the end of 2011, however, so Ray would have to make do with the existing services.

Further diversion came in the form of the brief history of Lima provided on the back of the café's menu. I learned that 'in former days, Lima flourished as a railroad town'. Its principal attributes had been a spring providing water for passing steam engines and a location ideal for crew changes on the route between Pocatello and Butte. The tracks still passed through the town, but not many trains.

After the demise of the railroad, ranching had become the biggest business in the area.

'The rest of us are hanging in here, proud of our community and making it with hard work, diligence and social security,' the menu continued.

Clearly a sense of humour was an important attribute too. Then came the somewhat vexed origin and pronunciation of the town's name.

'If you want to know how Lima acquired its name, ask the waitress, she can probably make up as good a story as any.'

I asked the waitress.

'Oh, you mean the lime in the water that fouled up the trains' boilers?'

I said that sounded plausible.

'But nobody really knows,' she added.

And the pronunciation?

'Lyme-ah – like the bean.'

'Not Leema like the city in Peru, then?'

'No.'

Perhaps that explained the absence of Paddington Bear souvenirs.

There was even the chance to explore Lima. It didn't take long. Apart from Jan's, the town's services consisted of the Mountain View Motel, a sports bar, an Exxon gas station and store, a post office, a surprisingly well-stocked hardware store that had provided Ray with a cardboard box big enough for his bike, a school (home to the Lima Bears basketball team), an antiques and curios shop, a church and a swimming pool.

Of more interest, however, than the current meagre existence scraped from a rump population and passing traffic were the remnants of Lima's busier past. This included a timber-and-brick building seemingly on the verge of collapse that had been the original stage wagon stop and mercantile. A lean-to porch proudly bore a sign that read 'Lima Historical Society', but the door was closed.

Further evidence of the obsession to legitimise the tenuous present by celebrating fragments of a not particularly glorious history was found nearby. In a small display cabinet, under a handwritten heading

'Parts of Our Past', were a dozen or so black and white photos with explanatory notes. Perhaps the most intriguing had no accompanying photo, however.

'In 1904 a fellow named Walter P. Chrysler was working as a machinist in the machine shops in Lima. He went on to build his Chrysler car and form his own corporation.'

Across the railway that bisected the town was a small grid of residential streets. All were fetchingly tree-lined, and the gravel roads faded pleasingly into informal lawns outside each plot. Pick-up trucks, preferably old and slightly battered, were the vehicle of choice. One bumper sticker read 'I love Ronald Reagan'. The houses themselves were mostly low and detached, with well-tended gardens. As if to prove the point, a large woman in a flowery nylon frock, blue slippers and pink rubber gloves mulched her rockery in front of a US flag.

'It's a lovely evening now,' she said as I ambled past.

In the warm glow and long shadows of the lowering sun, still just above the imposing flanks of the Tendoy Mountains, I couldn't help but agree. With the wind temporarily concealing the noise of the Interstate it was a delightful spot.

I returned to the diner for one last feed before bed.

'A piece of your delicious pie, please.'

After having already sampled three varieties (apple, pear and apricot), I needed only pecan to complete the set.

'They really are good,' I enthused to nobody in particular.

The still heavily made-up proprietor, who had further won our hearts by mopping up Ray's blood and uncomplainingly sweeping away the mud that inevitably accumulated after each of our visits, pointed to her husband.

'It's the big guy who makes the pies.'

His size suggested he was a keen advocate of tasting his wares, too. A fellow diner asked where I was headed. I said down the Centennial Valley into Idaho.

'Jeez, I wouldn't even take a goddam' horse down that trail.'

On that much, at least, we were agreed. Another visitor, a huge man who could not be described accurately without descending into a caricature of lumberjacks past, joined the conversation. I explained we were then headed to Mexico.

'I sure admire your intestinal fortitude,' said the newcomer.

I wasn't sure if he meant the food I was eating or the route I was taking. Nevertheless, given the size of his own waistline, this was praise indeed. We watched the weather forecast on the TV.

'It's exceptional rainfall for the area and for the time of year. We've had two inches in the past week,' said the presenter.

Two inches might not have sounded a lot, but it was nearly a quarter of the yearly average.

'It's been very cold too. Yesterday there was a high of only 28°F in West Yellowstone, and it's mostly been in the low 40s.'

'Yep, it's the worst weather in 30 years, probably longer,' confirmed the man-mountain. 'My grandpa homesteaded down here so I've been coming here for ever – he was in his 60s – and I've never known it so cold and wet.'

....

CHAPTER 15

LEAVING MONTANA

DAY 12

Tuesday, 23 June dawned clear and bitterly cold. There was frost on the cars as we bade something of a sad farewell to Lima. Hands, ears, nose and feet froze almost immediately.

To begin with the road passed through the low canyon of the Red Rock River Valley above where it spilled out into the broader surroundings of Lima. The early morning sunlight ahead of us was brightening the hills to each side, but we rode in shadow. We had been warned the trail would be gumbo, but in fact we were now reaping the benefit of yesterday's fine weather and drying wind. Treacherous sticky patches remained but could by and large be avoided.

After about an hour we passed the dam at the head of Lima Reservoir. A pair of pelicans huddled together on the water. The sun shone from a faultless blue sky and the land broadened again considerably. It was easy to see why Montana was known as 'Big Sky Country'.

Though still loosely following the eastward track of the Red Rock River, we were now in the Centennial Valley. This time, however, the pleasure of the mountains was indirect, in the great, isolated upland basin they created ahead of us rather than the immediacy of their presence. Some distance to the north was a gentle range, dusted with fresh snow. To the south, nearly 10 miles away, was a more crenellated ridge that marked the frontier between Montana and Idaho. In between was a vast sweep of grassland and sagebrush interspersed with wetlands. I spotted my first pronghorn antelope of the trip.

After two days of purgatory we were elated to find ourselves in cycling heaven. The valley was flat, the sun was out and the wind was helpful. Progress was good. Then Per drew to an abrupt halt. Trevor and Stephen, by now accustomed to his various mechanical issues and the speed with which he could resolve them, carried on.

I stopped, as much out of curiosity and a desire to inspire such companionable behaviour should I ever find my progress stalled as out of concern. I could not offer any help – and not just because of my limited mechanical skills. One of the handful of rules of the Tour Divide was that every rider must be entirely self-sufficient.

'What's the problem?'

'It's just the bolt that holds the panniers on that needs tightening.'

Nothing serious, then.

'I thought you'd tightened them all up yesterday.'

'I did.'

It turned out Per's preparation for the race and his choice of equipment had been even more haphazard than mine. He had only bought his mountain bike a few weeks before the start and had built it up himself. His pannier rack had been the cheapest he could find, and the bolts clearly weren't up to the jolting they had received. To reduce the weight it had to carry, he had used an old leather belt to strap his sleeping bag under his saddle. He'd also had to extend the bottom of the rack with brackets from a hardware store to accommodate his extra large wheels.

'I've got two spare brackets with me as they keep wearing out. I've had to replace one already,' he explained breezily.

'Most people have spent the past year carefully selecting the best kit and testing it to destruction,' I pointed out.

'Where's the fun in that?'

We were quickly on our way again. The cycling might have been good, but it was still likely to be a long day. After Lima, there were nearly 90 miles with no services. This time we were motivated by more than simple necessity, however. We wanted to cover sufficient ground to convince ourselves that making it all the way to Mexico was still a possibility. Yesterday's rest had been entirely beneficial, but the fact we needed a rest at all was a cause for some concern.

We had also discovered an extra reason to start moving more quickly. Per's limited holiday entitlement meant he had been constrained to book his return flight to the UK on 11 July. Allowing a day to travel to the airport in Phoenix, that gave us seventeen days including the current one to reach Antelope Wells.

'Plenty of time,' said Per.

Buoyed by the morning's success, we readily agreed, at least until the atrophied cogs of our mental calculators began slowly to turn. So far, we reckoned, we had covered little more than 800 miles. It had taken us 11 days, which gave an average of not much more than 70 miles per day. Even discounting the rest day, on the tempting but fallacious premise that it obscured an accurate assessment of the speed at which we had cycled, we had only covered 80 miles each day.

By a long-winded process of deduction we eventually worked out that ahead of us lay the best part of 2,000 miles. More alarmingly still, that left us with the daunting task of now covering an average of nearly 120 miles per day.

'No problem,' insisted Per.

Those of us who didn't have a plane to catch felt inclined to demur.

Light relief from such challenging arithmetic came from playing cowboys. Not, as fortune would have it, in the form of fending off hostile natives. Rather, it was the slightly, though only slightly, less disconcerting sight ahead of a Montana traffic jam. The trail was blocked by a vast herd of cows which stretched way beyond the confines of the dirt road itself, across the grass to each side, right up to the ranch fences that were mini-versions of those Steve McQueen failed to jump on his motorbike in the Great Escape. Our chances of success, should push come to shove, seemed similarly low.

For those, like me, used to encountering similar blockages on the lanes of Yorkshire, cycling past massed ranks of cattle should not have been a problem. But that would have been to overlook the skittishness of US bovines. And their very sharp-looking horns. Recent experience had made it clear that even the passing shadow of a cyclist was enough to spook them into kamikaze flight. Nobody mentioned the word 'stampede'; nobody needed to.

Fortunately, a genuine expert was on hand to offer us some advice – our first bona fide cowboy of the trip, complete with boots, hat and lasso. And a horse, of course.

'Hey, fellas, where ya headed?' he asked, oblivious to our concerns and paying us the compliment of appearing as interested in us as we were in him.

We explained our route for today and afterwards.

'Wow, that's some ride.'

The same could be said for him. With the aid of a couple of dogs he was escorting several hundred head of cattle a dozen miles down the valley to new pasture.

'How do we get through the cows?' I enquired.

'Just ride right through 'em. Just tell 'em you're a comin' and keep goin'.'

It seemed no time to stand on ceremony. It sounded deceptively easy. And it was. Adopting a close formation down the right edge of the road and unabashedly making as many guttural, cow-herding-type noises as we could muster (a surprisingly imaginative collection, it transpired), the cows parted before us like the Red Sea before Moses. In only a couple of minutes we were through to the promised land, bearing only cowpat-stained tyres as evidence of our escapade.

'I wonder if there's any scope for the development of bicycle-mounted cowboys? We could then get paid to ride the Tour Divide by offering our services on the way,' suggested Trevor.

We rode on for another 10 miles, then stopped for lunch at a place identified on the map as a village called Lakeview. It was not so much a village as a small collection of houses and barns. The focal point was the headquarters of the Red Rock Lakes national wildlife refuge, established in 1935. This provided flushing toilets, drinking water, and a wonderful source of information about Trumpeter Swans. Some 300–500 of these huge birds – up to 4 foot long, with 8 foot wingspans and weighing up to 30 pounds – now lived on the reserve, with several thousand more migratory visitors. This was a distinct improvement on the situation in the early twentieth century, when fewer than 75 birds remained in the whole of the US, having once ranged as far east as the Mississippi and as far south as Arkansas.

'Plume hunters and ladies' fashion wreaked havoc on the population. Birds were shot, plucked, and thousands of skins were shipped to the East Coast and Europe,' read a sign.

For every 'Ying' there is a 'Yang', however. While the population of Trumpeter Swans stabilised and then grew, in a rare victory for the animal kingdom the human (and cattle) populations plummeted through the removal of access to the valley's prime grazing lands; the cows from earlier in the day had clearly been part of the 'rump' population. It was too little, too late for the bison that used to roam in the area, but moose, elk and antelope were now all making the most of the swan-inspired tranquillity.

We dined on mince and slices of quince, or slices of salami wrapped in tortillas, at least. Following the cold and rain of the past few days it was something of a shock to be seeking refuge from the sun.

After a brief respite, the riding continued to be as agreeable as the weather. Ten miles further on and we began the climb to Red Rock Pass, where the mountains to our south at last turned north and crossed our path, requiring another traverse of the Continental Divide. At the summit we encountered a major landmark – the border between Montana and Idaho. The amount of Tour Divide lore that has managed to accumulate in the few years since the route became a reality is limited. But one recurring theme is that if you make it out of Montana, the state with the highest mileage on the whole route, you stand a good chance of making it all the way. We celebrated with more cowboy impersonations.

'Yeehah,' said Trevor convincingly.

'Yahoo,' echoed Stephen to great effect.

'Wey-hey,' I added, revealing my imitative inadequacies.

Per, wisely, stayed quiet.

Once more the scenery ahead of us changed markedly. We descended steeply into much more wooded country, and promptly got slightly lost in our own, private Idaho. This time the confusion was only minor, however. Not long after 3 p.m. we emerged back into civilisation, if that's an appropriate description for the small collection of fast food joints and gas stations at the intersection between our route and US Highway 20.

Per's considerable appetite came once again to the fore and he insisted we precede our planned meal at the restaurant over the road with a trip to the Subway sandwich shop.

'It's for breakfast,' he reassured me, waving a large baguette. 'Or maybe a second tea.'

Over at the restaurant we were greeted by a rather overly effusive waiter. His bonhomie seemed contrived, and largely inspired by a financial motive. For once, my cynical, English view of platitudinous North American hospitality seemed justified.

We asked if he had seen Cricket. We assumed she would have made it this far yesterday, or this morning at the latest.

'There was a woman came through? Jeez, and I missed her? Was she hot?'

Stephen chivalrously dismissed the question. The waiter seemed unimpressed.

'Jeez, she came through on my day off, I can't believe it . . .' he lamented as he trailed off into the kitchen.

Functional quantities of food were consumed rapidly. When Trevor announced it was his birthday, we toasted him with Pepsi and root beer. He was, it turned out, 32. Although originally hailing not far from Banff, Alberta, he now lived in Montreal, where he worked as an illustrator and designer as well as sometime bicycle courier. He had by far the best beard of the four of us.

We didn't tarry. Ahead lay one of the most deceptively difficult sections of the entire route. We hoped to complete it before nightfall.

After 3 miles of road, the next 30 miles ran along the old railbed of a spur of the Union Pacific Railroad, developed in the early 1900s specifically to bring tourists into the fledgling Yellowstone National Park. It sounded idyllic, but that was without reckoning for the soft, volcanic soils across which the railway had travelled and which now sucked energy from passing cyclists like mosquitoes suck blood. It was a tough call, in fact, whether the sandy terrain or the mosquitoes, which had been blissfully absent from most of the route thus far but which we now encountered with a vengeance, were more trying.

For Per, however, the answer was clear. It was neither. Instead, it was the relentless undulations of the route, caused by the erstwhile presence of sleepers exacerbated by the modern curse of quad bikes.

The result was not unlike riding over giant sheets of corrugated metal (covered in sand, of course). Having struggled in silence thus far, Per could no longer conceal the pain in his right knee and thigh. The day off had not been as kind to him as it had to the rest of us.

Even for those of us still with two working legs it was tough going. I was moved to suggest we call the Fat Controller and request urgent repairs. Stephen seemed nonplussed.

'Thomas the Tank Engine. It's very popular with the children at home,' I explained.

I volunteered myself as Thomas. With some persuasion, Stephen assumed the role of Henry, Trevor of James and Per of Percy.

Eventually we came to the end of the line. There was a minimalist campsite, and there was space for our four weary bodies among the super-sized motorhomes. The requisite 120 miles had been covered. It was time to stop.

IDAHO AND WYOMING

IDAHO & WYOMING

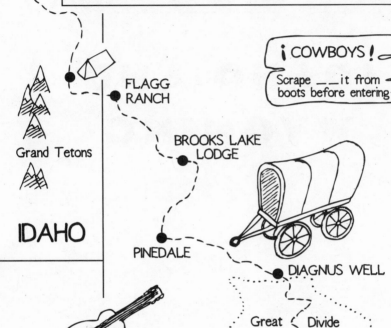

¡ COWBOYS !
Scrape ___ it from
boots before entering

Grand Tetons

FLAGG
RANCH

BROOKS LAKE
LODGE

IDAHO

PINEDALE

DIAGNUS WELL

Great   Divide
Basin

WYOMING

RAWLINS

Calamity
Jane
woz 'ere

COLORADO

....

CHAPTER 16

NO ROOM AT THE INN

DAY 13

For some reason we made a slow start to the day. It certainly wasn't the peace and tranquillity of the campsite that induced us to lie in. Just as dawn was breaking, a large motorhome had arrived and promptly performed the popular campsite slapstick routine of 'how do we park this thing?' Very loudly. As a result of this funny-were-it-not-so-painful performance, no prolonged sleeping had been possible.

Yet we were lucky to leave before 7.30 a.m. Maybe it was untangling the cord with which I had insisted we suspend all our odoriferous belongings to reduce their appeal to passing bears. With everyone else secure in the metal carapaces of their vehicular homes from home, the campsite (obviously the designation was a relic of the days when people actually camped) contained no bear bins.

Still, we had survived unmolested and, late as we were, we were soon rewarded with fine views of the western flanks of the famous Teton mountains. This, apparently, was their less flattering side, but it still showed up pretty well across the Idaho arable land through which we cycled.

'My mom used to say that Tetons is actually the French word for breast,' confided Stephen.

'It's true,' I said, shamelessly implying a European linguistic superiority over my American host.

'Yeah, she was a French teacher,' Stephen added.

We both agreed that we had never seen quite such jagged breasts, but it was better than the original Anglophone alternative: Pilot Knobs.

After several miles of tarmac we turned onto the Ashton–Flagg Ranch road, also known as the Reclamation Road, though what it was reclaiming and from whom was unclear. Initially it was quiet but broad and straight and covered in dusty gravel. It felt as though progress should have been easy, but the gradient was deceptive. It was also hot. For the sun, though, we were still prepared to be thankful.

Another hour or so later and we departed our second state in two days. We left Idaho with considerably less fanfare than we had left Montana – partly because it had not required undue exertion to pass through, but mainly because of the volume of mosquitoes. They were so prolific that even stopping for a call of nature was hazardous. In fact, I suffered the indignity of being bitten in a very sensitive area while watering the last flowers in Idaho. Otherwise we would quite happily have celebrated our departure over-enthusiastically.

Our entry into Wyoming saw the road turn into a trail and become much tougher going. It was both rougher and steeper, and Per in particular struggled. It was clear that the pain in his knee meant he could no longer stand up to pedal when the gradient required. In fact, though he tried to hide it, he could scarcely tolerate sitting down and was forced to walk not by gradient or terrain but by the pain.

I was concerned I was becoming something of a curse. First Steve McGuire, then Jacob, then Ray – all had been constrained to stop shortly after I had caught them. I explained my concerns to Per.

'I might have to take steps to stop you instead,' he said grimly.

I assumed he was joking.

I asked what he did when he wasn't voluntarily causing himself considerable discomfort in such unlikely surroundings. He said he had come to the UK from Sweden to study at university in London ten years ago and hadn't returned. He was now 29 and worked for F&C Management doing something with derivatives and spreadsheets. I say doing something. Per wasn't secretive about it. He did explain exactly what it was, but having almost as complete an aversion to financial markets as to the terrifying ubiquity of Excel, it fell on deaf ears. Instead, I resorted to caricature.

'Ah, you're to blame for the credit crunch,' I said, using provocation to distract Per from his pain and the possibility that he might really take it upon himself to exorcise the curse that I apparently inflicted on my riding companions.

'No, I'm the one who can make the money to get us out of it.'

Given my state of ignorance, I felt in no position to argue.

We plodded on. The going might have been challenging but the scenery was beautiful. We were once more in thick tree cover, interspersed this time with water meadows and gently flowing streams. This beauty should not have come as a great surprise. After all, we were sandwiched between two of North America's most famous and popular national parks – Grand Teton to the south, and Yellowstone, the granddaddy of them all, to the north.

Even if its main attractions were to remain elusive, passing this close to Yellowstone was a highlight of the trip. It needed little introduction: it was the world's first national park; it was estimated to contain half of the world's active hydrothermal features, including 300 geysers; it had recently been worthy of its own BBC documentary, complete with an awed voiceover in hushed, reverential tones. Fittingly, an impromptu, David Attenborough-style commentary came into my head.

'Here, now, is a strange species, not believed to be native to Yellowstone but one of the few remaining large, nomadic creatures to still roam across the whole of the continent. The cyclist. Long thought to be related to humans, the antipathy evident in some of their interactions with us, particularly with motorists, has led scientists to conclude that they are in fact a completely separate species. But no one knows for sure where they have come from, nor even where they are going.'

In the short term our aspirations were no greater than to reach Flagg Ranch for lunch. We weren't sure what to expect when we got there, Flagg Ranch having assumed a far greater importance on the Tour Divide route map than its size appeared to justify, but we felt confident of a hot meal and warm welcome. We received the hot meal at least, though at a price far beyond anything paid on the trip so far. The welcome was less convivial.

This seemed to have a lot to do with the fact Flagg Ranch was nothing more than a glorified service station designed to exploit the myriad tourists passing through. With miles of nothing in all directions, and a prime location on US Highway 89, the main route between the two big national park honeypots, the simple economics of supply and demand determined that prices would be elevated. Why it was necessary to be quite so disdainful of impecunious cyclists was less obvious, unless we were perceived as a deterrent to more lucrative custom. Or maybe it was the constant, mosquito-induced itching in my nether regions which Lycra did a very poor job of disguising.

After eating our fill, the descent from the sublime beauty and tranquillity of the morning to the ridiculous omnipresence and incompetence of motorhome-driving holiday-makers was soon completed. It was then exacerbated by roadworks. As a result, we had to deal not only with the inevitable post-prandial torpor but also blazing sunshine and a mile-and-a-half-long queue of cars and trucks.

At the front of the queue was a man holding a 'stop/go' sign. He had just turned it to 'stop'. With frustration at progress already slowed by squeezing past static traffic and discomfort in the heat growing in equal measure, I tried to sneak past and keep riding along the section of the road that was cordoned off; of course, no work was actually being undertaken. It was to no avail.

'Hey, you can't ride through yet.'

Worse was to follow.

'You've got to put your bikes in the pilot car. We're not insured to let cyclists ride through the roadwork zone.'

Ignorant of the concept of a pilot car, I was uncertain what to expect. It turned out to be a woman in a small, beaten-up pick-up whose job was to drive ahead of each wave of cars, a modern equivalent of the man with the red flag in the early days of motoring. She clearly had little experience of accommodating cyclists, certainly not those as laden as we were.

'I guess we'll have to put your bikes in the back, but I can't do more than two at a time,' she suggested.

Per and I being the two closest, we inelegantly hauled our bikes onto the back of the truck and tried in vain to make them secure. The irony of this being the greatest threat to their and our well-being was not lost on us; nor was it lost on our driver.

'I don't have insurance that covers damage to bikes on my truck,' she said, rather pointedly.

Had we realised we were uninsured either way it would have been preferable to take our chances on the road, but it was now too late. I couldn't help but contrast our current fate with the distinctly laissez-faire approach of Montana, where cycling down motorways and riding motorbikes without helmets was not only allowed but *de rigueur*. This, on the other hand, seemed symptomatic of the pettifogging bureaucracy that suggests the US is doomed to be a failed experiment in individual freedom: a rampant fear of central government, but a similar phobia of placing sufficient trust in personal responsibility to avoid regulatory micro-management. Except in Montana, perhaps.

After three miles of sporadic road-mending activity we were allowed to disembark. The flood of cars behind us had dissipated, and the next few miles were blissfully car-free, on our side of the road at least. Then the next wave came, and so it continued for the next 30 miles, the longest paved section of the ride so far.

Relief was provided by expanding views to our right of the eastern, more photographed flank of the Tetons. Seen reflected in the calm waters of Jackson Lake under a cloudless sky, they were spectacular indeed. They were also the most 'mountain-like' of all the mountains encountered in the past thousand or so miles, at least to the eyes of a European brought up on Alpine vistas. They had sharp edges befitting their imposing stature – up to nearly 14,000 feet at Grand Teton – as well as permanent snow and glaciers. They also had the distinction of rising a clear 7,000 feet above the valley below them, with nothing in between.

This notable difference from all that had preceded them, even the serried ranks of snow-clad peaks in Canada, was due to their considerable youth, having only been thrust upwards in the past ten million years or so. Much of the rest of the Rockies is 70 million years old, and the topography of even the highest peaks has been modified and softened by prolonged exposure to weathering and erosion. Indeed, thus far, the only common thread that had run through the journey was the diversity of the mountains encountered. The Rockies, it appeared, were far from the homogenous chain envisaged in childhood hours spent poring over maps and dreaming of adventure.

The sun continued to beat down. Even on the valley floor we were more than 7,000 feet above sea level, but there was no respite from the heat and the still, claustrophobic air. The sun's rays seemed to be intensified by the bleached concrete of the road. Per and I stopped to wait for Trevor and Stephen. Once reunited, we continued our eastward progress.

Eventually we came to a junction with a quieter road, and were greatly relieved to be directed down it. We were even happier to find, soon afterwards, an unheralded café on our left. The decision to stop for cooling refreshments was unspoken but unanimous. It was also inspired.

The Buffalo Valley Café was as charming and welcoming as Flagg Ranch had been cold and soulless. We set up camp on the veranda, then went inside to peruse the menu. We passed under a handmade sign:

'Cowboys! Scrape __it from boots before entering.'

It was clear what __it was.

'You've got to have a body fat test before you can order anything here,' said a typically well-built cowboy propping up the bar on his day off.

We explained our route and told him that we could eat with the best of them. He seemed reassured by our credentials. A minute later, however, he came out to the veranda to inspect us further. He was, it transpired, retired rather than resting, having been thrown from a horse once too often and broken his neck. He nevertheless sported the most immaculate pair of lilac cowboy boots. This was cowboy bling.

He also wore a T-shirt emblazoned with a slogan that was hard to decipher due to the lumberjack shirt that partially obscured it.

'This Vietnam Vet is heavily . . . ated.'

Was 'decorated' the missing word? An unfolding of the arms revealed the truth.

'This Vietnam Vet is heavily medicated for your protection.'

That was all right then.

The somewhat eccentric cross-examination continued while we waited for our order to arrive. We had been persuaded to ask for 'ice-cream shakes', a somewhat unconventional nourishment for elite endurance athletes (was it possible they hadn't recognised us for what we clearly were?). No sooner had we ordered four, in coffee-caramel flavour, however, than it became apparent the café had run out of ice cream. Not that this was a deterrent. A golf-cart trip to the neighbours later and they were on their way. When they finally arrived, in foot-high glasses, they were well worth the wait. All they had to do now was fuel us up the last climb of the day.

Togwotee Pass represented another crossing of the Continental Divide as well as a new high-point. Eighteen miles of climbing would take us from 7,000 feet to more than 9,500 feet. Fortunately, a large chunk of the climb was on metalled roads. But first, we had to climb steeply through rough country at the bottom of the pass. The intensity of the sun had begun to wane – it was now after 5 p.m. – but was more than compensated for by the effort required. Occasional trail-engulfing puddles served as a reminder of the rain of previous days, but in the main the route was dry.

Gradually, after more than an hour, the gradient eased and the main road was rejoined. The last nine miles were easy by comparison and the road largely traffic-free. At the top we reconvened and admired the view. At 9,658 feet we were above the treeline, among meadows. Close to hand were buttresses of ancient sedimentary rocks rising well above 10,000 feet. Further afield, the Tetons were still visible behind us, silhouetted against the lowering sun.

We congratulated ourselves on the progress made, and looked forward to the imminence of our overnight accommodation.

'The lodge is less than 5 miles away and it's all downhill. We should be there in 20 minutes, by half past eight hopefully,' I said.

My description was accurate, but my ETA was out by an hour. I had overlooked the most pertinent section of the route description:

'It is impassable when wet.'

The western side of the mountain had had sufficient time to dry; the eastern slope clearly had not. No sooner had we left the main road and returned to the darkening woods than it became impossible to cycle. We were up to our axles in mud. Worse, the mud was compounded by remnant snow patches several feet deep and several hundred yards long.

I reacted with unconcealed rage, charging into each obstacle in a fury of cursing and shouting. I stumbled and bludgeoned my way forward. It was not an edifying spectacle, but it was the only alternative to sitting down at the side of the track and crying.

Further behind, and once again handicapped by his sore knee, Per had apparently adopted the same philosophy, only with more colourful language.

'Ride. Stop. Fall over. Swear loudly in Swedish. Repeat,' was his subsequent description.

I asked what was the appropriate Swedish swear word for the occasion.

'Fan!'

The feeling with which Per said it rendered a request for translation irrelevant.

Not surprisingly, it was in a slightly harassed state that we arrived at our intended accommodation for the night. Stephen and I were there first, and we decided to ignore the sign on the gate that read 'Reservations Only'. After all, there was nothing on the map to suggest Brooks Lake Lodge was any different from all the other suggested overnight stops we had already encountered.

This changed when we asked a girl drinking beer on a porch outside one of the log cabins if we could stay for the night.

'Well, the answer's no if you haven't reserved in advance,' she said apologetically.

Covered in mud and grime and barely able to talk coherently, we didn't need to explain that we hadn't booked.

'I guess I could go and ask the boss, but I'm pretty sure he'll say no.'

It was a chance we were prepared to take. The sun had long since set, and the clear sky meant temperatures had plummeted. With the warming effect of the adrenalin of our latest escapade now having worn off, the prospect of a night under canvas with inadequate insulation was less than appealing.

'Hi, I'm Adam, how can I help?' said the boss, not looking particularly intent on being helpful.

I began to plead for somewhere to stay for the night.

'Even a barn we could pitch our tents in would be great . . .' I trailed off.

Adam appeared pensive.

'I think we've got a couple of rooms that housekeeping hasn't yet cleaned up, let me go and see.'

He disappeared. We fretted. He returned.

'Yep, you can have the rooms if you don't mind sharing them between you.'

Mind? We were delighted. In spite of our filthy state, we were shown in through a magnificent, timbered living room with vast open fireplace to two of the plushest bedrooms I'd had the pleasure to see.

'Er, perhaps I should just ask how much it will cost,' I whispered to Stephen.

He nodded.

'Oh, you're not really supposed to stay but you seem like nice guys, so just leave twenty bucks for housekeeping,' said Adam.

Our joy knew no bounds. Per and Trevor arrived and could scarcely disguise their astonishment.

'I thought he was gonna be a real hard ass when he first came out, but Paul's English accent did the trick,' said Stephen.

In fact, it seemed Adam had little need of external motivation to be hospitable. He just needed the lodge to be empty of paying guests – those who paid more than $300 per night for exclusive access to its services, that is. Looking at the state of us, it was not an unreasonable viewpoint.

'Would you guys like something to eat? The chef is off duty, but I've got plenty of stuff in the fridge.'

We didn't need asking twice. Cold meat, salads, bread and glasses of milk appeared and then rapidly disappeared. The *pièce de résistance* was birthday cake.

'Go on, eat as much as you can. It'll only get thrown away otherwise. The person whose birthday it was has gone.'

Ours, it appeared, had come early.

....

CHAPTER 17

DOWN THE GREEN RIVER

DAY 14

It might have been a reaction to the previous morning's tardiness, or it might have been so as not to abuse Adam's hospitality; either way, we started early. Just after 5.30 a.m., in fact. Within less than a minute, we had begun to regret being so bold.

It was freezing, by far the coldest morning of the ride thus far. We were all wearing every layer of clothing we possessed, though it seemed to make little difference. To make matters worse, the day's riding began with a 15-mile descent. Of course, this would normally have been a cause for celebration, not consternation. But then, equally normally, there would not be the imminent danger of losing all – and I mean all – appendages to frostbite.

We were in a classic Catch-22. The faster we went, the more the discomfort increased; the slower we went, the longer it lasted. Stephen seized the initiative and plumped firmly for a swift end to our suffering. He had the added benefit of being able to keep at least his hands warm by cycling downhill non-handed on a laden bike at 40 miles an hour. I was not entirely confident this wouldn't bring an end to our current brand of suffering by creating another – a mess of limbs and bike wheels on the road in front of me – but it was a spectacular sight.

At the end of the descent we resisted the mild temptation to continue nine miles to the bright lights and certain coffee of Dubois (pronounced Do-Boys, of course). Instead, we turned right on the prescribed route towards Union Pass. Having just lost nearly 2,500 feet in altitude in 15 miles, we had now to regain it in less than 10 miles. With a 2-mile downhill section in the middle, that effectively meant two 4-mile climbs at a gradient of nearly 10 per cent, as steep and prolonged as anything we had encountered thus far. At least it would keep us warm.

Not that such a relative luxury deterred us from dreaming of breakfast at a café marked on our maps in between the two sections of climbing. It promised more than just psychological succour. Last night's meal at Brooks Lake Lodge had been far better than nothing, but it was considerably less than we could have eaten. Having also used some of our dwindling food supplies for a pre-departure snack, we were beginning to run a bit low. Most of the climb was spent silently salivating and collectively speculating.

'I fancy pancakes,' said Trevor, after waiting for the rest of us at the top.

'I'll take anything as long as they have some coffee to keep me awake.'

Two minutes later, after a short descent, we spotted the café we had been fantasising about. It was closed. Not just for an hour or two, but indefinitely.

'Due to a death in the family,' read a handwritten sign on the door.

In the circumstances it was hard to feel bitter, but I tried my best. Now there was no guarantee of any services until the town of Pinedale, 80 miles away. There was the possibility of a café after 50 miles, but our faith in its continued existence was waning. We consumed more of our meagre stockpile in the weak morning sun, then set off again. There was little else we could do.

The next climb was as gruelling as the first, without the carrot of a café at the top. Still, our growing appetites matched and even heightened the growing sense of isolation. We were high, exposed and alone. It was thrilling and, without the smothering trees of Montana and with two weeks' worth of habituation, not too intimidating.

After the top, the terrain eased. We were in a broad saddle, right on top of the Continental Divide, the wetlands around us destined to feed rivers running to both Atlantic and Pacific oceans. We rode peacefully, almost reverentially, through wild, open pastures. In fact, our eventual arrival at the 9,210-foot Union Pass had the peculiar distinction of being at the end of a gradual, 5-mile descent from our earlier high-point.

The pass marks the meeting point of three mountain ranges, hence its name. To the north is the Absaroka range. To the west are the Gros Ventre Mountains, which merit a less flattering translation from the French than the breasts of the Tetons: fat stomach, or big belly if you prefer the vernacular. Finally, to the south and east, and our near companions for the next 150 miles, is the Wind River Range. This includes the highest point in the whole of Wyoming – Gannett Peak, 13,804 feet high and a whole 33 feet above the biggest bosom itself, Grand Teton – yet its presence seemed far more muted than its more celebrated neighbour. Instead of a photogenic arête bereft of foothills, the Wind Rivers, almost as broad as they are long, keep their mystique a more closely guarded secret. It felt a privilege to be experiencing them, even if only tangentially.

The privilege of such proximity was brief as our highland odyssey continued on a westerly track before curving back south down a steep, rough descent into the headwaters of the Green River. Just before the descent started, Trevor and I came across a large, brown, hairy animal ambling around in a stand of birch saplings. We had just passed a sign that read 'Grizzly Bear Area: Special Rules Apply', though it hadn't deigned to explain what those special rules might be. Fortunately, we didn't need an impromptu lesson. It was a moose. It considered us briefly with sublime indifference, then continued ambling.

Ahead, Stephen rode as if he were still trying to warm up. In fact, he was intent on ensuring his arrival in Pinedale before the anticipated closing time of the bicycle shop in order to re-true his increasingly buckled rear wheel. In spite of this apparent handicap, he disappeared down the hill like a bat out of hell and then kept going along the valley bottom until he was well out of sight.

For the rest of us laggards, however, the upper reaches of the valley seemed to defy gravity. The route map indicated we should be heading downhill, and the logic of having a river flowing in the same direction as we were cycling seemed incontrovertible. Yet the effort required for each pedal stroke seemed far more than that necessitated by the constant headwind.

I could only presume those involved in the early tie drives along this very same stretch of river were not similarly confounded. Tie drives – where timber from the surrounding mountains was harvested in vast quantities before being driven or floated downriver to be used as ties or sleepers on the ever-expanding railway network – came to the Green River in 1867. Under the impetus of Charles DeLoney, described as a 'youthful Civil War veteran from Michigan', the timber harvested that season by 30 men was then driven 130 miles downstream on the flood waters of the following spring to the railhead at Green River City.

The quantity of timber involved in this particular drive, and that of the following year, was lost in the mists of time, but similar drives in Utah provided up to 350,000 ties in a year. Perhaps repentant at the scale of denudation he had caused, DeLoney went on to become Wyoming's first forest supervisor.

The Green River's other claim to fame is as the starting point for Major John Wesley Powell's first descent of the Colorado River through the then uncharted lands around the Grand Canyon. Powell, another Civil War veteran and by this point reduced to only one arm, took it as an affront that, while the country had now been explored from coast to coast, there was still such a vast, unmapped area. Almost completely ignorant of the terrain ahead, and equipped with what were effectively no more than wooden rowing boats, it took Powell and his nine fellow explorers more than three months and innumerable near drownings to reach civilisation again 1,000 miles away in modern-day Arizona. It put our travails into appropriate perspective.

Humbled and subdued, it came as a considerable surprise to find the apparently randomly located 'The Place Café' was still alive and kicking. So too, thankfully, were its staff. Stephen had already ordered a late lunch. This was no time for him to demonstrate his otherwise impeccable table manners: it was after 2 p.m. and he still had another 30 miles to cover before he would reach the sanctuary of the bike shop.

Clearly suffering from delusions as much as hunger, I ordered, to universal surprise, a salad. I was sure I had intended to ask for a large bacon-cheeseburger and chips, but both Trevor and Stephen confirmed that the salad that soon arrived was exactly as I had requested. Per arrived and Stephen, having already finished, took his leave. I made unconvincing noises of gustative appreciation; Per and Trevor tucked into their vast burgers with carnivorous relish.

Still bemused, we saddled up once more. Almost immediately, I felt a changed man. Gone was the lethargy of previous days. In its stead I found a renewed, if unfathomable, *joie de vivre*. I fairly sprinted up the hill after the café. Then came a glorious, sweeping series of gentle descents on smooth tarmac that took us halfway to Pinedale. I couldn't go fast enough. It was plain, open country and the skies were thick with threatening, leaden clouds. Yet I was in heaven.

This unlikely, salad-fuelled state of grace continued on the gravel trails that ran into town. Given the apparent downturn in the weather, the continued evidence of the impact of recent rains in the slick, gooey surface and overflowing drainage channels should have seemed ominous. But I was carefree. I communed silently with the nearby ranchland and the now-distant Wind River Mountains until I found myself, to my considerable surprise, on the outskirts of Pinedale.

Suddenly aware of my obnoxious state and, more particularly, that of my bike, I stopped at a car wash. A pair of youthful cowboys with a huge pick-up belied their brash, overbearing exteriors and offered me the remnants of the time they had already paid for. They asked where I was from.

'England. And you?'

'Pinedale born and raised,' they said in a way that made it clear they had neither been required nor desired to venture much further afield.

Yet opinions of Pinedale were divergent. After locating Per, Trevor and Stephen, who had succeeded in fixing his wheel but only through the expedient of doing it himself, it being too complex a task for the hardware store-cum-bike shop, we headed along the main drag to find somewhere to eat. It could never be called a charming town, though it possessed the answers to all our immediate needs.

As if to prove the point, we settled on a Chinese restaurant, though we could have chosen Indian (as in the country of that name, rather than original natives of Pinedale), Mexican or burgers from any number of diners. The couple at the next table were travelling retirees. They had come to Pinedale to assess its merits for relatives who were also intent on perpetuating the American tradition of relocating when drawing a pension.

'We won't recommend they come here. It's too open and windy and there are no trees.'

From our brief experience to date, it was difficult to argue. Certainly, our route into town could not have been called picturesque. The town itself had an unfinished air, perhaps associated with recent expansion on the back of the discovery of substantial oil deposits in the vicinity; we had passed several dowdy motels, disreputable-looking even, and had in the end been thankful that they were full, block-booked by rig workers.

Then the waiter added his implied denunciation of his adopted home town, or perhaps just of his current employment in the family business. In a strong Chinese accent and in very broken English he expressed a powerful yearning to join us on our journey (or at least undertake a similar trip – it was the adventure he sought, not necessarily our company). To have travelled so far from his native land yet still seem so unsatisfied was disturbing to see.

Nevertheless, an after-dinner exploration of the town gave a different, homelier impression. I had no qualms leaving my bike unlocked outside the municipal library. Access to computers and the Internet was free. I read more welcome messages of support from home, including a suggestion that a group rendition of 'Chitty Chitty Bang Bang' might nicely complement our Thomas the Tank Engine misadventures.

The residential streets nearby were tidy and green, with well-kept lawns and immaculate yards. Buoyed by this discovery, I returned to the hotel to find the others in thrall to the television. Michael Jackson had died. I sought solace – from the intrusion of MTV rather than Wacko's untimely demise – in my copy of the *Western Wyoming Penny Pincher*. Along with adverts for drive-thru' liquor stores and an open house for alpacas, one particular request caught my eye.

'WANTED. 12-ga pump or semi-auto shotgun, ugly condition preferred.'

Perhaps Pinedale wasn't quite so homely after all.

....

CHAPTER 18

ENCOUNTER WITH A COWBOY

DAY 15

U nsurprisingly, our accommodation in Pinedale was not a patch on that at Brooks Lake. It had the great benefit, however, of a kitchen. We made the most of the facilities. Between us we had assembled quite a feast: cereals; toast with a variety of spreads; porridge; yoghurt; and fresh fruit. There was also fruit juice and coffee. All that was missing was Radio 4. Instead we had MTV still blaring away in the other room.

Our motivations for such excess – to save money and time compared to eating elsewhere – had been legitimate. But neither goal was fulfilled. We had each bought more food than was needed and as a result we remained rooted to the spot, indulgently gluttonous, for far longer than was strictly necessary to set us up for a day's riding. After half an hour, even the excuse that we needed to build up our reserves as we were once again heading into a vast area of nothingness – there was no grocery guaranteed to provide anything useful for the next 220 miles – was running a bit thin.

Finally, we summoned the courage to depart. As we did, it started to rain. Heavily. Stephen passed up the chance to purchase a pair of waterproof overtrousers. In spite of the weather and our previous experience, Stephen's reluctance didn't seem unreasonable. It was inspired in part by budgetary constraints created by having left his previous job (something to do with IT in the car industry) and not yet having started his new one (something else to do with IT in the power industry). It was also inspired by a near-pathological aversion to carrying superfluous gear – he had the lightest load of all of us – and a dogged belief that things would come right in the end. What's more, by the end of the day we hoped to be in the Great Divide Basin, the first desert of the trip.

It was more of a surprise that a shop selling such items was open before 7 a.m. in an otherwise still somnolent Pinedale, a town of below average annual precipitation in one of the driest states in the US. Clearly the proprietor was either a fool or an opportunist: in the same way as an ice-cream seller in the Arctic would have only a short season, he had deduced that the most had to be made of such infrequent windows of good fortune.

The first 35 miles of the day were on paved roads, the first 17 on US Highway 191. The rain intensified from heavy to diluvian. It was now on a par with our descent into Lima. The road was covered in standing water. It was like riding through a cold shower. We were assailed by rain from above, spray from below and splashes to our sides from passing vehicles.

By the time we turned off the main road, the situation was grim. In full kit, I was uncomfortably cold. Stephen was in a far worse condition. At 26 he was the youngest in our group, but was already toughened by considerable experience: he had hiked the complete Appalachian Trail, the world's longest footpath, without a break, and was more of a mountain biker than the other three of us put together. What's more, his incredible energy levels had been amply illustrated by the speed at which he had cycled the previous day and his aversion to a television-free motel room. Yet he still had no waterproof trousers, and what passed for his waterproof top was really in breach of the trades descriptions act – it was a top, but that was it.

Imagining how I would have felt in Stephen's shoes – and, more pertinently, shorts and top – hypothermia seemed a distinct possibility. The few ranches passed early in the day had now dissipated into nothingness. Self-sufficiency would be the only option, yet for one still just warm enough to pedal the prospect of stopping in such vile conditions seemed anathema. I cursed the waterproof-clothing salesman in Pinedale for not having been more persuasive.

More selfishly, having lugged a full set of waterproofs with me for over 1,000 miles to avoid just such an eventuality, the thought of having to stop and prolong my own discomfort to accommodate somebody else's oversight seemed to be asking a lot of my generosity of spirit. What's more, no self-respecting Yorkshireman would let a drop of rain catch them out; they'd never venture outside if they did. Then again, Stephen wasn't from Yorkshire. He hailed instead from the much balmier climes of Mississippi. It crossed my mind that it could well be the case that no self-respecting Mississippian would be caught out in quite such conditions anywhere other than on the Tour Divide; or in hurricane season.

Besides, Stephen was doing a confoundingly good job of demonstrating that all my suppositions about hypothermia were hypothetical, or a vicarious projection of my own hypochondria, or both. Although manifestly cold and damp, he continued to ride uncomplainingly. The history of exposure to rain might not be shared, but his commitment to the old Yorkshire dictum 'mustn't grumble' was to the manner born.

Then, as if to put all such debate to an end, after three hours of incessant downpour, the rain came to an abrupt halt. The sky was still battleship grey, the road was still made of brown glue, but it was dry. We were grateful for small mercies.

In fact, the dirt roads were not impassable, just unpleasant. It looked like we were riding through a thick layer of peanut butter. I imagined it felt pretty similar too. This proved to be a useful analogy. By applying my natural sandwich preference for smooth, rather than crunchy, to the road surface, I found progress was improved. The 'smooth peanut butter' tracks tended to look slippery and treacherous but were in fact watery in nature and often concealed a hard-packed base on which reasonable progress could be made. In contrast, the 'crunchy' areas looked outwardly appealing because of the traction hinted at by the nuts (sorry, stones) in the general gooiness, but were in fact too stodgy to be palatable; I mean, cycleable.

A moderate climb led to a slightly higher plateau than the land through which we had been cycling and provided, according to the guidebook, 'some of the emptiest, biggest, most dramatic views imaginable'. Just imagining the area ever experiencing sunshine, let alone views, was sufficient challenge. The ascent also signalled the first of three back-to-back crossings of the Continental Divide, the last of which presaged our entry into the Great Divide Basin proper. It was an intimidating prospect.

The basin was effectively a great hole in the Continental Divide, which split into two at the end of the Wind River Range before reconvening not far north of the Colorado border. What little surface water there was in the area drained into the basin, where it then either percolated into the parched soil or evaporated, rather than ending up in either the Pacific or Atlantic oceans. In an area with so little rainfall it had become a desert. In wetter climes it could well have been a lake with no outlet; it was not difficult to see why. It covered 4,000 square miles, and had a human population of 500, who were comfortably outnumbered by wild horses and pronghorn antelope.

Fortunately, we had the rest of the afternoon to acclimatise ourselves to its unique charms before having to take the plunge and bisect it. First came another section of paved road as we headed through the famous South Pass, symbolic heart of the westward expansion of the United States, though our gentle descent to it out of broad plains rendered its geographical pre-eminence less obvious. A small visitor centre and several informative signs were all that marked the spot.

> The South Pass, in which you are now located, is perhaps the most significant transportation gateway in the Rocky Mountains. Indians, mountain men, Oregon Trail emigrants, Pony Express riders, and miners all recognized the value of this passageway straddling the Continental Divide. Bounded by the Wind River Range on the north and the Antelope Hills on the south, the pass offered overland travellers a broad, relatively level corridor between the Atlantic and Pacific watersheds.

Uncharacteristically, this rather undersold the erstwhile significance of the pass. Although discovered as long ago as 1811, South Pass was then 'lost' again to white men until 1824. In fact, it was not until 1832 that the first rag-tag caravan of settlers and missionaries, opportunists and proponents of the sordid doctrine of Manifest Destiny passed this way. After this slow start, however, the die was rapidly cast. In the next 37 years, until the opening of the first US transcontinental railroad in 1869 sounded its death knell, anything up to a staggering 500,000 people were estimated to have emigrated through South Pass and along the Oregon, California, Mormon and Bozeman Trails. More than 200,000 of these intrepid souls were in the 1860s alone. In a land which even now seemed remote and inaccessible, this was a veritable motorway of its day.

It was fascinating stuff, and I had an inkling of how so many US tourists must feel when visiting Europe and being confronted with so much 'history'. But we were not history snobs. Of equal import were the capacious and heated restrooms, complete with hot-air hand driers under which we could thaw our frozen extremities after another intemperate cloudburst had preceded our arrival.

Warmed and informed, we saddled up. The next goal was Atlantic City, 15 miles further on, for an early tea. First, though, we rode through South Pass City, a restored and preserved example of a frontier mining town. Like the pass itself, the city had seen more productive days, though not until the passage of emigrants had begun to wane. It was founded in 1867 after the discovery of gold in the area and gained fame and notoriety two years later when it passed the first legislation in the US allowing women to vote and hold office. Such prominence waxed only briefly, however, until the deposits began to dry up. Now it was little more than an outdoor museum. Nevertheless, it was an outdoor museum in its original setting, which should not be taken for granted. In the 1960s, the town only narrowly survived being purchased by a California theme park and shipped wholesale to the west coast.

Continuing the conservation theme, up the hill from the town were the restored remains of the Carissa goldmine, the site of the original gold strike. As recently as 1980 it had once again been considered for possible reopening, but was now the property of the State of Wyoming and was destined to mine tourist gold rather than more natural seams.

A few miles later we finally arrived in Atlantic City. Where South Pass City had been mummified and turned into an exhibit, Atlantic City was still clinging to life as a genuine ghost town. For the second time in the trip, we rode past a sign that said 'Population 50'.

It had a bar and, as the route maps might put it, 'non-full-service' grocery.

'We see you guys coming through on bikes and think "Is there anything you'd like or need?",' said the proprietor.

Looking at the barren shelves, the temptation was to reply 'something, anything'. I tried in vain to be more constructive. There was also Wild Bill's Gun Shop – 'Guns. Ammo. Gunsmithing. Customised Knives' – and the genuine Wild West feeling was confirmed by the only other commercial venture in town, the Atlantic City Mercantile – 'Steak house. Saloon. Cabins'. There were no drunken, brawling cowboys spilling onto the dirt high street as we leant our bikes against rails built originally for horses, but it seemed only a matter of time.

Inside, apart from a gregarious Italian family of tourists, this was the real deal. The timber-framed walls were clad in garish wallpaper and black and white photos; the stuffed moose head on the wall had a cigarette hanging from its mouth; there were bulls' balls, also variously known as Rocky Mountain oysters, cowboy caviar, Montana tendergroins and swinging beef, on the menu.

Our food choice was more conventional, varying the routine only by the additional request for four bowls of warming noodle soup. We were ready for such comfort. In spite of the flatness of the terrain, it had taken us nearly ten hours to cover 90 miles.

The soup arrived with some unexpected news.

'Do you guys know a woman cyclist? I can't remember her name,' asked the waitress.

'Do you mean Cricket?' asked Trevor.

'Yes, that was it. She only left a short while before you came in. She said she was planning on camping in the Basin somewhere . . .'

Apparently she had been deterred from leaving earlier by the rain. At just gone 6 p.m., after eating our fill, we set off in hot pursuit. Actually, the pursuit was far from hot. We grunted our way up an exceptionally steep but mercifully short climb out of town. There was intermittent sunshine between the bruised clouds. Only once the climb had been crested did we begin to pick up speed. As we did so, the map encouraged us to bid farewell to the last trees we were likely to encounter until Rawlins, 135 miles away. Shortly afterwards, while still riding through puddles from earlier downpours, we were alerted to the fact that the next potable water source close to the route was 69 miles away.

With the gradient and wind in our favour, we made good progress to our intended camp spot for the night. The water at Diagnus Well was not recommended for untreated consumption, but it would at least ensure that we embarked on the next day's riding with replenished bottles.

As we approached the well, we also became aware that the waning sun behind us was rapidly becoming obscured by an immense black wall of cloud with orange below and deepening purple above. Just in case such a visible storm warning wasn't enough, the wind began to rage in destabilising gusts. We arrived at the same time as the first raindrops; their companions could be seen sweeping across the plain to join them. It was eerily like the arrival of a plague of hungry locusts.

Trevor and I raced to pitch our tents before the storm became fully fledged. We were not entirely successful. The sandy soil refused to hold onto my pegs, while Trevor lost a pole, blown away into the gathering gloom. The only way to be sure they would stay in place was to lie in them.

Per and Stephen had bivvy bags, rather than tents, so were reluctant to bed down in the deluge that the wind brought. Instead, they sought shelter in the unlikely company not of Cricket, who had apparently been through but decided to continue, but of another bona fide cowboy who was also calling the well home for the night. In fact, as I discovered after the tempest had passed and it was finally safe to deprive the tent of my services as a counterweight, he was calling the well home for the best part of two months.

'I've been here since May and I'll be staying until the 4th of July. After that I'll move to another spot.'

He offered some of his whiskey. The evident loneliness of his job hadn't dampened his social skills. A thousand reasons to say no flashed instantly across my mind. What if the whiskey were really illicit moonshine and I ended up blinded, or worse, by alcohol poisoning? What if, by accepting, I rekindled the latent alcoholism that I unfairly assumed to be a prerequisite for all those with such isolated lives?

Or what if it was I who descended into inebriated discombobulation after three weeks of abstinence and considerable expenditure of effort? Drunken men and guns did not seem like a healthy combination.

Per and Stephen declined and took the opportunity of a break in the rain to retire for the night. I found myself saying yes. Chances to drink bourbon with cowboys come along only rarely. A bottle purporting to contain Jim Beam was passed my way. It looked like whiskey. It smelt like whiskey. I took a swig. To my considerable relief, it was whiskey.

The bottle owner's name was Jason and, like the Mercantile in Atlantic City, he was the real deal. He had a large gun, a broad knife and two horses – Joe and Tucker.

'Joe's the stayer, I could go all day on him, and Tucker's the strong one. Look at the width of his haunches. He's only small but he can pull a cow out of a ditch.'

I asked how many cows he looked after.

'I've got 1,500 head of cattle to look after in an area the size of Yellowstone.'

He said 'yeller' in the same way John Wayne would have said it to describe a coward.

'Why are they so much flightier than the cows in the UK? At home they're all really docile.'

The explanation was as simple as it was obvious.

'Well, they're prey animals, ain't they. I guess you ain't got too many bears and wolves and mountain lions over in England?'

The rain came again, so we took refuge inside his wagon. It had the classic, round-arched shape of wagons from the movies. The only concession to modernity was solid wheels and pneumatic tyres.

'They put them on last year but they still load it onto a truck for travelling or it would fall apart,' said Jason, somewhat wistfully.

Basic it might have been, but inside it was the height of domesticity. There was a bed across the end away from the door, under a little window on which was suspended a Native American dream catcher. There was a table and a chair, while Jason had added his own home comforts including several books and a guitar. Most important of all, given the current inclement conditions, was a solid fuel stove.

'I burn dried cow dung,' he pointed out with enthusiasm.

It worked a treat. It was as warming as the whiskey. As the wind continued to howl outside we compared notes about the merits of riding horses and mountain bikes. Jason was impressed by the distance we could cover, but reckoned a horse would have the edge in the mud. I was happy to agree. He also expressed a surprising desire to travel to the UK to see red deer.

'But you're surrounded by elk, which seem much more impressive to me,' I said.

The pile of antlers he used as extra currency on his return to civilisation proved the point. But even in Wyoming, the grass was always greener on the other side.

'That's why I'd like to see something different.'

It was properly dark when I returned to my tent. The clouds had disappeared to reveal a desert sky replete with diamonds. Jason picked up his guitar and sang a self-penned lament. The strumming was charming; the lyrics were tender; the tune was pursued with admirable enthusiasm if not always great accuracy.

....

CHAPTER 19

ACROSS THE BASIN

DAY 16

The sky was still clear as day dawned. The wind had abated, and the absence of clouds suggested the weather had changed definitively for the better. Indeed, things in general were looking up. Per and Stephen had not been attacked by snakes or insects in the night; neither Trevor's tent nor mine had been blown away. To complete the cheering picture, Jason popped his head out of his wagon and offered us fresh coffee. It seemed preferable to whiskey.

The coffee, brewed on the dried cow dung-powered stove, was excellent. It complemented very satisfactorily my factory-fresh Danish pastry and packet of crisps. We struck camp. Jason bade us farewell and repeated an earlier warning about the animals we would likely encounter once we hit New Mexico (he had already said we should not give too much credence to the assertion that grizzly bears didn't roam south of Pinedale – 'I seen 'em come across the Basin, and I seen 'em in the mountains in Colorado.' Whether he was right or not was impossible to tell, but he certainly had a point. How would a grizzly know if he was south of Pinedale?).

'I been all over the country and I worked two years down in New Mexico. You be careful of those tarantulas. And you might think rattlers are the problem. But they're not. It's the western diamond backs you want to be careful of. There's no negotiating with them.'

Then, almost apropos of nothing, he added, 'I'm through with sleeping rough in a camp blanket.'

Per and Stephen tried to look unconcerned. Trevor and I tried to disguise our smiles.

The first part of the day's riding began to take us into the desert and away from the Oregon Trail. It was something of a mixed blessing. We were heading into a vast unknown, but we were leaving behind what has been labelled the longest graveyard in the US. Over the same four decades that saw half a million travellers pass this way, an estimated 16,000 of them perished en route to the west coast. That equated to between 3 and 4 per cent of the total, or one in every 25–33 travellers. It was pretty certain every wagon train contained someone who didn't make it.

Diseases, particularly those associated with contaminated water such as cholera, typhoid and dysentery, accounted for more than half of those deaths, perhaps explaining the practical legacy of descriptive river names around the basin: West Alkali Creek, Sulphur Creek and, more promisingly, Sweetwater River.

Storms were another factor. Late last night, just before our own minor scrape with the wilder forces of nature, we had passed within a mile or two of the site of the Willie Handcart Company's disastrous encounter with an October snowstorm. The company of Mormon Pioneers, named after the carts on which they hauled their meagre belongings and the leader of the trip, was fresh from England that year, explaining their late crossing of such exposed terrain. Estimates of those who died as a direct result of the storm vary from 15 to 27. That was clearly neither the beginning nor the end of their tribulations: 68 of the original party of 404 failed to make it to Salt Lake City. It gave considerable pause for thought.

The terrain ahead was not entirely flat, but nor could it be described as undulating. No part of the Basin was more than 200 metres different in altitude from any other, a remarkable statistic for an area roughly 100 miles by 50 miles. It resembled a slightly rumpled tablecloth. We were the ants crawling among the crumbs.

The day's agenda consisted of the apparently straightforward task of covering the 112 miles to Rawlins. Initially it was as simple as it appeared. We rode around the edge of the Basin and the dusty road wormed its way along the contours, making for easy riding. It was a pleasant change. As was the presence of a strange, warming, gold-coloured object which rose inexorably into the cobalt sky.

'It's the sun,' Trevor reminded us.

All around was a sea of nothing. As the heat of the day began to grow, so did consumption of our precious water supplies. I told myself that five and a half litres of increasingly tepid water would be quite sufficient, but it didn't stop me feeling like the Ancient Mariner. I racked my brain for barbarous portents of doom akin to killing an albatross. I was reassured to find none.

The marine metaphor was reinforced by the sighting of an oil rig a mile or so to the south of the road. It was not just in and around Pinedale that the story of our seemingly insatiable appetite for the earth's mineral wealth was being repeated.

The rig aside, the likelihood of encountering anybody else in this sagebrush wilderness seemed vanishingly small. The route had already taken us to remote places. Yet there, the mountains that caused our solitude had also tempered it by restricting us to valleys and passes. These were the natural conduits for any human movement. With few alternatives, anybody else passing through such areas would likely be on the same trail.

Here, there were no topographical barriers to progress in any direction. Possibilities for travel, if you were so inclined, abounded through 360 degrees. It came as something of a surprise, then, to cycle past a man seemingly asleep in the scrub at the side of the dirt road. It was clearly not Cricket, yet it was surely a Tour Divide cyclist. Who else in their right mind would be sleeping on their own in the middle of the desert?

But there was no bike. Indeed, the strange figure seemed to be bereft of all useful belongings for such a tenuous existence, apart from a thin sleeping bag. The mystery man, clearly no longer asleep, sat up at the side of the road. He looked as surprised to see me as I was to see him. In fact, surprise seemed to have rendered both of us speechless. I didn't have the presence of mind to stop or say anything, but I freewheeled gently down the trail, looking over my shoulder. I waited expectantly for him to request assistance. I didn't know what I would be able to do, or what he might ask for, but he couldn't possibly be there by design. Nevertheless, after staring straight back at me for what seemed like an age, he shook his head and lay back down. He looked for all the world as if I had just had the temerity to cycle through his garden and disturb his siesta.

I caught up with the others.

'Did you see the guy in the sleeping bag?' I asked in astonishment.

'Yeah. He didn't say anything to us either.'

It was late morning and the heat was intensifying rapidly. As far as the weather was concerned it was either feast or famine. The sense of desiccation was exacerbated by the wind. According to the guidebook, Wyoming has a reputation for wind (and not one associated with baked bean-eating cowboys). Headwinds in the state are generally described as 'infamous', a widely recognised euphemism among cyclists for 'hideous' or 'purgatorial'.

We had been fortunate so far that the wind had been generally gentle and favourable. Now, however, it became stronger and more constant. What's more, the route began to ignore its curvy, symbiotic relationship with the minor differences in terrain and embarked instead on a series of large zigzags; a straight line to Rawlins would have halved the distance we had to cover.

The result was vexing. On any one zig the wind would be largely unfavourable. It followed, according to our logic at least, that the subsequent zag should provide us with wind-induced respite. It didn't work like that. The only relief came from the diverting presence of pronghorn antelope dashing hither and thither in considerable numbers. The absence of a natural predator seemed to inspire them to provoke whatever passed their way in a perverse bid to get their adrenalin flowing. They were an impressive sight, reaching speeds of up to 60 mph in short bursts, and maintaining 30–40 mph for several miles. There was also the less appealing scar of a distant uranium mine on Green Mountain at the Basin's edge.

For want of any more significant landmark, we stopped for lunch at a junction between a zig and a zag. It hardly needs saying, but it was an exposed spot. This time, however, we were exposed not to rain and cold but sun and heat. It was not a furnace, but it did a passable impression of a fan oven. Lunch itself was a feast. I washed down rubberised cheese wrapped in flaccid tortillas with as much of my lukewarm water as I dared consume. Per tried manfully to make his sweaty salami seem appetising. I decided to skip the sweet course.

Back on the bike, the slow-roasting continued. All that was missing was being basted. It was less than 24 hours after our brush with hypothermia yet I was now becoming anxious about overheating.

Stephen, on the other hand, was going from strength to strength. Surprisingly, he also seemed to be wearing more now than he had the previous day. From somewhere deep in his luggage he pulled an Arab or Bedouin-style shawl that he wrapped over his shoulders and around his head to keep the sun off. Apart from creating the disconcerting impression that we were now accompanied by Yasser Arafat on a bike, it seemed effective. By comparison, my gleaming, balding pate and green and black cycling outfit were considerably less so. In fact, the more I fidgeted and squirmed in the sun and wind, the more Stephen seemed conspicuously comfortable. It crossed my mind that he could now be in exactly the same position as I felt I had been the previous day, though extending my own uncharitable attitude to others might have been unfair.

Whether due to the effectiveness of his protective measures against the sun and wind, or simply because he was intent on making up for our slow progress yesterday, Stephen once again rode off into the distance. He was accompanied by Trevor, who seemed equally unperturbed by cold or heat, rain or sun. Per and I maintained our own lonely vigils.

Then I noticed Per having to rectify another minor mechanical mishap. Misanthropy abandoned, I decided to wait. It was a lonely place for any serious breakdown. It was also the perfect opportunity to administer some more suncream and self-pity. I stared aghast at the vastness of the panorama. Some horses chewed disconsolately at the scrub in the middle distance. For want of anybody to contradict me, I decided they were wild horses. It was a timely fillip.

Per caught up. It had been his front rack this time.

'I'm gonna get rid of it,' he said.

We rode together, talking little. The Basin's fan oven thermostat had kicked in and the temperature seemed to have stopped rising. I now no longer felt like I was cooking. I felt more like a joint left to 'rest' after cooking but before carving. I started looking for vultures.

An hour after lunch we turned left off the dirt onto a paved road. It was the most incongruous strip of tarmac we had yet come across. The map's description – 'more or less void of vehicle traffic' – was an understatement. Only the tumbleweed was missing from the classic image of desolation.

Still, it was an important landmark for us. A mere 26 miles along this road would bring us to the charms of US Highway 287, from where it was only another 16 miles to Rawlins. Neither section had much to recommend it. Eventually, both were completed and we entered the outskirts of Rawlins, a town with something of a reputation.

In Ovando I had come across an old newspaper cutting in which an even older woman recounted her younger days in Rawlins. As a child, she recalled, she had been out on the street one day tending her chickens when an outlaw on horseback rode up and shot one of the luckless hens.

'Make sure you tell your ma to pluck her and cook her when I return.'

Daughter and mother wisely obliged. The outlaw returned for his meal and, when satisfied, paid up with a gold coin.

It was also known as the haunt of one of the Wild West's iconic characters, Martha Canary, better known as Calamity Jane. Fittingly, we cycled past the Wyoming State Penitentiary in which she had once resided, the result of 'a disorderly drunken binge of legendary proportions' according to the guidebook. It was an episode conveniently overlooked by the saccharine musical version of her life story. The jail had closed to its inhabitants in 1982 and was now a museum.

More recent history was also less than flattering. While we had been riding the South Downs, Steve had said Rawlins was best avoided.

'I just didn't like the vibe of the place.'

Even though it was only just 5 p.m. and Steve's words were being borne out before our eyes, we had no desire to continue. Fortunately, Alan had been slightly more constructive.

'It's not so bad. Try Penny's Diner.'

We did. From the outside it looked great, a sleek silver trailer straight from the 1950s. The theme continued inside, with appropriately uniformed staff and booths into which the four of us could only just squeeze. The food was prompt and considerable, but the illusion of homespun charm was undone somewhat when we asked for dessert.

'I'll have a home-made apple pie, please.'

'It shouldn't say home-made 'cos it's not made here. It's all shipped in frozen,' said the waitress.

The look of disdain on her face meant I didn't dare tell her I hadn't really expected anything different.

....

CHAPTER 20

SAVED BY A SIREN

DAY 17

After eating our fill of non-home-made produce at Penny's, we had booked into a nearby motel. It turned out to be as cheap and cheerless as the rest of the town, though I was prepared to accept that two days of being exposed to biblical portions of first rain and then sunshine were liable to have coloured my perception.

Certainly, the stark beauty of last night's camp had been replaced by an ugly, prefabricated concrete block surrounded by highways and parking lots. Wide open spaces and fresh air had been swapped for a cramped hotel room filled by four sweaty, smelly bodies. Jason's off-key lament had once more become MTV. Michael Jackson was still dead.

To add to the sense of disorientation, we had been confronted with the bewildering choice afforded by a trip to the supermarket. I wandered round the store aping what I hoped were the carefully considered purchasing plans of the others. Not surprisingly, I ended up with far too much stuff. Nor was it nutritionally well balanced. Jamie Oliver would have been aghast, but I was content to settle for volume.

At the till, I found Stephen being surprisingly congratulated on his tomato-red cycling attire. Then it was my turn to receive the same complimentary reception.

'I just lurve your top, it's so cooool. Do you want some help packing?' said the super-size seller.

Encased in a sweat-stained, mud-spattered apology for a cycling jersey, it was an incongruity too far for me to be able to think of a response. Fortunately, no response was necessary.

'I just wish I could get one like that. Do you have a pointy helmet too? Hey, Janine, come and look at this cooool top. Do you think they do them in my size?'

I wasn't sure the question was being addressed at me or Janine. In fact, I wasn't entirely sure the whole episode was actually happening.

'I think I could almost take up biking to get hold of a top like that.'

Now I knew I was dreaming. The boy was clearly delusional. He must have lived in Rawlins too long. Stephen's top was far more appealing than mine.

For want of any better options, we returned to Penny's Diner for breakfast. It might not have had home-made pies, but it was open all hours. Ahead lay another day of uncertain food supplies. In fact, there were none available until the attractively named town of Steamboat Springs, some 135 miles away. With the route now returning to the mountains and a new high-point of nearly 10,000 feet ahead, it seemed too far to consider it our day's destination.

Nevertheless, in spite of the distance to cover, we left later than anticipated. The time it took to pack up and depart seemed to be directly proportional to the number of people involved in the process, even though there was no obvious connection between us. We each stowed our own luggage, ate our own breakfast and cleaned our own teeth. Yet what could be done in half an hour alone invariably took more than an hour as a foursome.

We rode out of town under the Interstate, passing a bench proudly bearing the logo of the Wyoming Gas Company. It conjured images of conversational, flatulent old men.

Next came a short hill, followed by more than 20 miles of rolling tarmac. We were on the edge of a broad valley. To our left the land fell imperceptibly away. To our right it rose gently until it shot vertically upwards in the form of the escarpment of the appropriately named Atlantic Rim.

Apart from Per, we were feeling fit. Having managed to avoid falling into the trap of pushing ourselves too hard too early in the ride, we were now reaping the benefit of having so many miles in our legs.

Yet for Per, even the rolling terrain was a real challenge. The flatness of the past two days had allowed him to disguise the obvious discomfort brought about by his sore knee. Now it could be disguised no longer. Already the previous night he had hinted heavily that he was coming to the end of his tether, and the terrain was about to become much more challenging. We would be in Colorado later in the day, a state containing innumerable high passes, three of which would see us climb above 11,000 feet.

Trevor, Stephen and I reached the crest of the day's first major climb after six miles of uphill some way ahead. I expressed my concerns.

'He's been talking about making it to Steamboat as if that were the end of the race. I'm not sure how much further he'll go.'

'I don't know there's much we can do,' said Trevor.

He was right. Nobody else could pedal for him. Besides, Per had neither complained nor requested any assistance. Instead, the growing legend of his indestructibility had been given more credence when I had asked him about his cycling history. He had none. Well, none as a mountain biker, at least. He commuted 15 miles a day in London, and had completed a couple of day-long road events, but had never ridden a mountain bike, let alone owned one, before deciding to undertake the Tour Divide.

'My longest ride on a mountain bike was the first day of the race,' he had revealed without bravado.

Prior to that, the longest he had managed was 50 miles on a tow path near London; ideal preparation.

We were now in the mountains once more. This time it was the Sierra Madre range. Initially it was open, high country, but slowly our surroundings became more wooded. We entered the Medicine Bow National Forest accompanied by another punishing succession of short, steep ups and downs.

At a clearing in the forest, just after a descent to another stream crossing, we stopped for lunch. It was hot and sunny and the perfect spot for a picnic, though last night's random approach to shopping meant my picnic was far from perfect. Stephen completed the Enid Blyton picture by heading off to the stream to refill his water bottles.

I had filled all my bottles in Rawlins. It seemed rash to me to rely on sporadic water sources of uncertain cleanliness along the route.

'Do you think the water is good enough to drink?'

'Yeah, it'll be fine.'

To Stephen it seemed wasteful not to make the most of nature's bounty. It also saved him several pounds in weight not to be loaded to the gunnels each day.

After lunch we came across a notable landscape feature known as Aspen Alley, a natural avenue of Aspen trees that ran along the trail for a good mile. Then came a sinuous, paved descent. As we lost height so we gained heat. The descent ended at the Colorado border.

This might have been an important landmark for us, but clearly the sign-makers in this part of the country were not of the same opinion. Not that we were particularly in the mood for celebration. It was 2 p.m. and the fan oven had been turned on again. The bleached road and rocks reflected the blinding sun. Even the trees seemed overwhelmed; most were little more than scrub versions of the impressive stands we had spent the morning riding through.

Ahead lay 30 miles of more or less uninterrupted climbing. I began to daydream, or possibly hallucinate. The road started out through a canyon, home to dozens of imaginary Indians sporting bows and arrows. Then I came round a corner to find Trevor gesticulating at me and shouting inaudibly. I was so distracted by his frantic waving that I ignored a strange pile on the road. Only after I had ridden right past it did I become aware of the peculiar rattling noise it was emitting. I reached Trevor, who was clearly relieved.

'I was shouting "snake!"'

I looked back. Sure enough, there was a rattler in the middle of the road. There was no time to ponder the possible consequences of my inattention, however. A battered pick-up truck came careering down the road ahead of us. It made little effort to accommodate our presence, then screeched to an abrupt halt. Four bare-chested bumpkins jumped out, beer cans in hand. They were clearly spoiling for a fight. Fortunately it was not with us. After a brief period of goading, one of them pulled a long-handled spade from the pick-up and proceeded to very ineffectually decapitate the snake.

'Welcome to Colorado,' said Trevor.

A short distance further up the road the heat enforced a drinks break. We cowered at the side of the road like convicts on a chain gang. Even Stephen seemed to be distracted. Nevertheless, the protection afforded by his Yasser Arafat shawl, and the fact that Trevor's impressive beard seemed to be having a similarly beneficial effect, saw the pair of them once again ride off into the distance.

Per and I were labouring after them when he had a puncture. I waited until it was fixed, then we carried on. The track was rough and progress was slow. I was moved to revoke my commitment not to enter into any more Faustian pacts about the weather; rain would have been welcome at any price. But it was to no avail. The only water evident anywhere were the drops of perspiration that stung my eyes and obscured my vision. Perhaps I shouldn't have had my eyebrows trimmed in Banff before the start.

Then I started hallucinating again. Ahead was a collection of buildings that gave every impression of being a lodge and bar. At the door was a woman, waving and beckoning me in. Even in my reduced state I was aware of the risk posed by such a siren. Yet the mirage was too alluring to ignore.

'Hi,' said the siren in a convincingly real voice. 'Come in, come in. You must be hot. I've got cold drinks and fresh fruit inside.'

Maybe I wasn't hallucinating, though anything more than monosyllabic conversation was still beyond me. Fortunately my host didn't seem to mind my incoherence. As I slowly returned to my senses it became apparent that I was in Brush Mountain Lodge being ministered to by an angel called Kirsten. In front of me was a can of Coke and an enormous fruit salad: melons, water melons, strawberries, grapes to name but a few of its ingredients.

'I know how you guys get by on gas station food so I always think you might appreciate a few vitamins.'

Kirsten, it turned out, was another Tour Divide junkie. Although, in my mind, we were a million miles from anywhere, she had been following our progress avidly on the Tour Divide website. We were far from the first racers to have stopped by this year, and only a moment's inattention had precluded her from accosting Trevor and Stephen.

Just then, I saw Per through the side window. I jumped up to hail him, then once again demonstrated the debilitating effect extreme heat had on my articulacy.

'Per! Per!' I yelled. 'Water melon! Water melon!'

Fortunately, Per had enough imagination to stop, even if he had also been lost in his own private world of suffering.

'I saw your bike but it didn't dawn on me that meant you would be here.'

He climbed in through the veranda, and let out an involuntary yelp of pain as he flexed his leg to stand up.

'Ooh, that sounds sore. Are you all right?' asked Kirsten.

'It's nothing,' said Per, tucking into the food in front of him with atavistic gusto.

Cooled and refreshed, we eventually managed to respond to Kirsten's hospitality. We discovered that Matthew Lee was within a day of the finish.

'That's all right, we're in Colorado now so we can say we were within one state of him,' I pointed out.

There was also a message from my sister-in-law and her family.

'We have no idea what the Tour Divide Basin is but think it's great that you've crossed it! Hope the weather has improved, but not too much because you wouldn't want to be cycling in the temperatures we're having in Sussex today (36 degrees!).'

What we wouldn't have given for only 36°.

Of most immediate import, though, was the fact that Cricket had been through earlier in the day.

'She said she'd spend the night in Steamboat. She's desperate for you boys to catch her up.'

Per's ears pricked up.

'Do you think we could get all the way to Steamboat tonight?'

'Sure, it's about 50 miles, but it's all downhill and most of it on paved roads once you get to the top of the pass.'

The pass itself was another 15 miles away. We had planned to camp at the top and roll into town in the morning to visit the bike shop before continuing. Now there was a more appealing option. If we carried on riding to Steamboat, we could have a lie-in until the bike shop opened. This was the clincher. Even a long day and some night riding would be comfortably paid for by such a prize.

Per, certainly, was a changed man. He set off again with renewed determination. It was 5 p.m. and the temperature had dropped appreciably. The countryside was also becoming more and more attractive. Trees grew taller. In between were lush meadows.

I was bitten by Per's bug and began to race along. The revivifying effect of Kirsten's fruit salad was palpable. I could not help but succumb to the temptation to ride as if there were no tomorrow; or at least no riding to be done tomorrow. It was liberating, if somewhat shortlived.

By the foot of the last, steep climb up to the pass I was spent. Fortunately the trail was by now far too rocky to ride so I could use my bike as a wheeled zimmer frame. Mosquitoes needed no second invitation to take advantage of such a slow-moving feast.

I found Stephen and Trevor waiting at the top, having a snack of dried biscuits. I tried and failed not to tell them of my earlier good fortune. Per arrived not long afterwards. We had a quorum. A council was called. The new plan was proposed, considered and approved.

The wisdom of our strategy was immediately called into question, however, by the first few miles of descent. They were as rocky as anything we had yet encountered. Stephen bounced his way down them like an escaped pingpong ball. I was still using my zimmer frame, metaphorically at least.

After 5 miles the trail levelled. Eight miles more and we were back on tarmac. Night was about to overtake us, so we rummaged in luggage for lights. Between us we had four front lights, of which only Stephen's was truly effective, and two poor rear lights that would have failed to impress a police officer. There was no way we were stopping now, though. The road was not heavily used at that time on a Sunday night. Yet street lights were noticeable only by their absence. At least we could discern the road ahead of us. Then we turned onto gravel, and even that crumb of comfort was removed.

We felt our way through the dark until we came at last to the outskirts of town. It was nearing 10 p.m. Kirsten had said Cricket was aiming for the Rabbit Ears Motel, which in other circumstances might have sounded surprising. We did likewise. The receptionist recognised us as fellow travellers, but Cricket's room was dark. We decided not to disturb her. We could hook up in the morning.

Back in our room we took stock. It had not been easy, but we had covered 135 miles in just under 16 hours. Trevor, Stephen and I joined Per in setting another record. None of us had ever cycled further on a mountain bike. Our satisfaction was complete when Stephen had a moment of genius.

'Let's order takeaway pizza.'

COLORADO

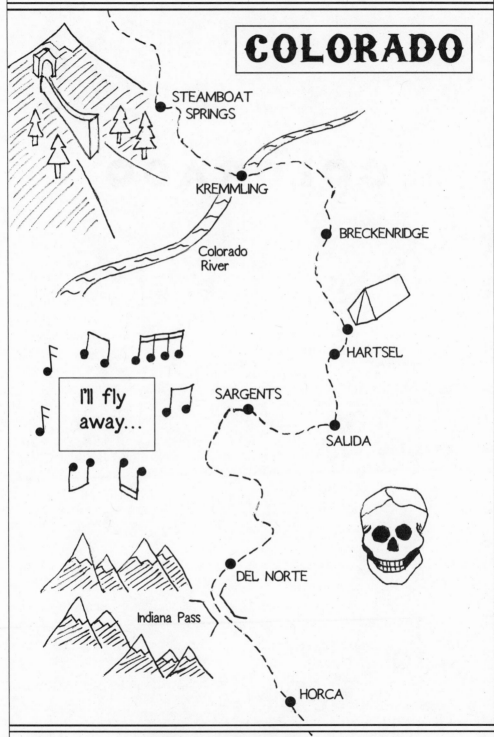

....

CHAPTER 21

MOSCOW CALLING

DAY 18

Even though the rationale behind pushing on to Steamboat the previous night had been to enjoy a long sleep and a lie-in, things didn't quite go to plan. Or not to my plan, anyway. The pizzas had been delivered promptly, and their consumption was as rapid as might be imagined, but the television was not finally extinguished until after midnight. Shows featured in the flurry of channel-hopping even extended to a recording of proceedings in the House of Lords, which at least had the merit of providing an air of tranquillity. For five minutes, that is, until the novelty wore off.

Then, in the morning, a mobile phone vibrated violently on a bedside table at 7.30 a.m. Lest anyone doubt the significance of this noisy disturbance, the television immediately resumed its pre-eminence. Quite why it had been deemed necessary to return to the conscious world so early I didn't understand. The bike shop that was the sole motivation for prolonging our stay in Steamboat didn't open until 9 a.m. Practised as I was in the early morning rush – try getting four children aged six and under out of the house on time and you'll see what I mean – an hour and a half preparation time seemed like unwarranted luxury, especially when sleep was the biggest luxury of all. The growing disparity in the ratio of my cranial hair to facial wrinkles served to emphasise the point.

I consoled myself by eating breakfast in bed, secure in the knowledge I would not be afflicted by crumb-induced discomfort for long. As I did so, I read an article in the *Steamboat Pilot* about Eric Lobeck, one of the two Steamboat residents who was participating in the Tour Divide (the other was Leighton White, who had already ridden the race last year and who had been a mine of information and reassurance in Banff). It was hardly a surprise to have it confirmed that he was significantly further down the trail than us – he had passed through on Wednesday; it was now Monday morning. Yet to find that there had been time to interview him, write the story and print it in a newspaper was something of an eye-opener.

All the more reason to press on, it seemed. Yet at the current rate of progress it was unlikely we would ever complete all the mandated tasks before lunchtime at the earliest. Just getting ready to go to the bike shop had become a logistical challenge of almost military scale.

At 8.30 a.m., with breakfast and newspaper devoured, I went to see if Cricket was awake. As if to emphasise our tardiness, she had already left. We seemed doomed to continue missing each other all the way to Mexico.

Trevor and I then rode to the bike shop to ensure our bikes could be serviced as promptly as possible. Orange Peel Bikes was every bit as welcoming and enthusiastic as we had been led to believe they would be.

'Hey, man, you guys are doing a great race.'

It was a sign of my weakening mental state that I was prepared to agree, adopting the convenient North American-cum-reality television trait of overlooking the facts. Doing a great ride, maybe; doing a great race, clearly not. To underline the point, it was confirmed that Matthew Lee had been through a week earlier and was indeed on the last stretch to the finish, more than 1,000 miles away in Antelope Wells. More pertinently, though there were just 26 of the initial 42 riders still going, only 5 of them were behind us; 2 of those had disqualified themselves for unintentional navigational mistakes that they had decided not to rectify. The *Lanterne Rouge* was still within our grasp. Maybe this morning's delay could be passed off as a cunning plan?

The owner appeared.

'How can I help you guys?'

Trevor recounted a carefully thought-out and observed list of ailments that needed tending. The mechanic nodded sagely, obviously recognising a kindred spirit in the accompanying detail. Then came my turn. I decided that the best way to conceal my comparative ignorance was to avoid direct comparison with Trevor's compendious knowledge and keep things straightforward.

'So far I've had no problems and I'd like to keep it that way, but maybe it could use a clean . . .'

Suddenly I was conscious of the incongruity of trying to ride 2,800 miles in the muddiest conditions in the history of the race while asking for no greater mechanical assistance than a bit of a tidy up. I tried to compensate; I overcompensated.

'Just do whatever's needed to keep her running smoothly until the Mexican border.'

The mechanic had the decency to smile encouragingly, though it could have been in anticipation of the blank cheque I appeared to have just signed. The bikes disappeared. There seemed nothing else to do, so Trevor and I went for a second breakfast.

Accidental tourists or not, we made a good fist of appreciating the holidaymaker appeal of Steamboat. It was better known as a winter resort, and owed its venerated status to the famous Howelsen Hill skiing area and ski jump, the longest continually running ski area in Colorado. The site, first developed in 1914, was named after Norwegian immigrant Carl Howelsen, a famed cross-country skier and ski-jumper. Howelsen himself built the ski jump.

Yet the town lost none of its charms on a sunny Monday morning in June. It was, like so many other US towns, laid out in a grid format, but it was softened by its location – on the banks of a fast-flowing river, in a valley between imposing peaks. There was also enough non-tourist-related activity along the main drag to give the town a sense of vigour and purpose, and sufficient watering holes to cater to the tastes of all visitors. Orange Peel Bikes had unanimously recommended the Creekside Café and Grill. We saw no reason to go against their advice.

Enjoying the temporary freedom of being bikeless we strolled to the café which, as its name suggested, was alongside a creek. We sat on the patio surrounded by fellow visitors and resident ladies-that-lunch (or brunch), listening to the babbling brook. All in all, Steamboat Springs was the perfect holiday location. It was just unfortunate we were not on holiday.

The menu was comprehensive and largely understandable, even if it did seem to consist of incongruous juxtapositions of everyday items. With some trepidation, I plumped for a croissant breakfast: sausages, eggs, cheese and fried potatoes, all with a croissant (the trepidation was caused by remembering the adverse reaction of a French friend on a visit to London when confronted with the admittedly unedifying spectacle of a ham-filled croissant: 'Why are you murdering a perfectly good croissant?').

I need not have worried. It looked and tasted delightful, though the compulsive need to consume calories coloured every culinary critique. Trevor and I had almost finished when Per and Stephen arrived. They were still en route to the bike shop.

I went to collect my bike. They had done exactly what I would have asked them to do had I had the presence of mind to be able to articulate it. They had cleaned and re-greased all moving parts, and replaced the chain.

'Yeah, it was pretty much about to wear through. You certainly wouldn't have got to Mexico without it snapping.'

They had also replaced the gear cables, which had become encased in gunk and had stopped moving freely.

'We had a look at your forks as well but we couldn't find anything wrong with them,' the mechanic explained.

For some days now I had not been able to lock out my suspension fork at the front of the bike. It was a minor issue. When riding on paved roads it was more efficient to be able to lock them out; on some climbs, even off-road, it was also beneficial. But the vast majority of the time it was much more comfortable to have the full effect of the suspension to cushion the unevenness of the terrain. In the past, racers had been compelled to quit due to the hand-numbing impact of the millions of daily vibrations. Not content with a damaged knee and a home-made bike, Per, of course, had fully rigid forks.

I did some more food shopping and went back to the motel to check out. I returned to the bike shop. Trevor's bike had been restored to full working order, but Stephen and Per were in the middle of major bike re-builds. Or that's what it seemed like to a mechanical novice like me. Of course, for them, installing a new drive train, whatever that was, was just a pleasant manifestation of a favourite hobby. Still, for all the practical assistance being rendered by the shop staff, I couldn't quite dispel the notion that this was akin to having a dog and barking yourself.

It was clear we weren't going anywhere soon. In spite of the two breakfasts, my stomach was also telling me it was nearly lunchtime. I went to buy another sandwich. I also went to the post office to send home some unwanted belongings. I didn't actually have anything that I felt was surplus to requirements, but one of the morning's principal activities for the others had been discarding weight. I was now paranoid that they would be able to ride much faster than me and would eventually leave me behind.

I selected a bag at random from inside my rucksack. It was my change of cycling shorts and top, along with a spare vest. That would have to do. Smelliness seemed a reasonable price to inflict on the others for my being able to keep up with them. Then, perversely, I stopped at a thrift store and bought a rather smart, light blue cotton shirt. Having seen the success of Stephen's approach to protection from the sun, something loose and made of natural materials seemed appealing. I returned once more to the bike shop. Everybody was now waiting for me, with varying degrees of patience.

We set off immediately. It was half past midday, and cycling further than the small town of Kremmling 80 miles away was now out of the question. Somehow it had taken five hours to complete routine bike maintenance and shopping, yet now we were in a rush. I had great difficulty riding out of town while trying to eat my recently purchased sandwich and drink a can of Coke. In no time at all my one remaining set of clothes had become saturated with sugary liquid and covered in mayonnaise. I could pass as a tourist no longer.

The first 10 miles or so of the day's ride took us along a stretch of road that could have been European. The vast, straight, highly engineered roads of the ride so far had provided compelling evidence why old-school road racing and riding has never taken off in the US. Here, though, was a strip of tarmac that wound and undulated its way through fields and between barns. It would not have looked out of place in the Alps. As we rode we were mobbed by red-winged blackbirds.

Buoyed by the terrain and the sunshine, we made good progress. Until Stephen disappeared. Initially we were not concerned. For all his meticulous preparation, he had developed an almost Pavlovian habit of having to respond to a call of nature within the first hour of starting each day's ride. When he still had not rejoined us after five minutes, though, I retraced our steps to see what could have gone wrong. I rode more than a mile back the way we came, yet found nothing. I was just about to break the alarming news to Per and Trevor when I saw that Stephen had already found them. Apparently his call of nature had necessitated drastic action.

'I found a Portaloo by the roadworks and I, er, couldn't resist.'

We rode along the Upper Yampa River Valley, then on a pleasant cycling trail round Stagecoach Reservoir. Next came the long climb up to Lynx Pass. It was warm work, but not overly demanding. The valley was dotted with expensive, exclusive ranches, though ranch-style condominiums might have been a better description. Several were for sale; a sign of the times, perhaps.

After the top of the pass we crossed a main road, then headed into high country that had managed to resist attempts to turn it into a private playground for the rich. Instead, the watery meadows dotted between the surrounding peaks had been little touched since the demise of a Wells Fargo mail service that had used the same route. We passed the well-preserved Rock Creek Stage Station, a smart, timber building. Shortly after we had to ford the deepest stream of the route so far.

'If this creek is too deep to safely cross, which it may be in May or June, backtrack to the highway and turn right,' advised the map.

It was not too deep to cross, but it was deep enough to warrant removing shoes and socks and also to necessitate the shouldering of bikes to prevent recently re-greased bearings from becoming sodden. It was also cold enough to merit a five-minute pause to restore circulation to chilled extremities.

The next noticeable feature came in the form of an unintentional rollercoaster. What was dismissed on the map as 3 miles of short ups and downs was, in reality, five near-suicidal descents, each followed by five lung-burning climbs. Then came the mother of all downhills, losing 1,500 feet in little more than 3 miles. It was exhilarating, but not as exhilarating as crossing the railroad at the bottom with only moments to spare between two converging freight trains. It was not any danger that caused such a frisson – the trains were far too slow-moving for that. It was the belated realisation that we had narrowly avoided having to wait for these juggernauts to trundle past before we could proceed. With a combined total in excess of 200 wagons it would have been a long wait. One train-jumping exploit was enough for any trip.

'Proceeding' was still a priority. It was nearly 6 p.m. Kremmling was a mere 20 miles away, but the profile was not encouraging. In fact, it was greatly discouraging. We were now in a great, rocky gorge, Gore canyon, carved by the nascent Colorado River, which we had crossed shortly after the railroad. The railroad had monopolised passage through the canyon, leaving the road to find a tortuous route over and around the fearsome granite bluffs.

The first climb was less demanding than anticipated; the second much more so. It had the temerity to lead straight past a great natural promontory called Inspiration Point. Even in the cold evening air of altitude, Perspiration Point would have been a more fitting title; or 'driven to distraction point', due to the thousands of voracious mosquitoes attracted to the sticky, sweet-and-salty mess that masqueraded for my cycling outfit.

Nevertheless, the views of the canyon were indeed inspirational. It had been named after the unlikely figure of an Anglo-Irish Baronet, Sir St George Gore, who had passed this way on a hunting expedition in 1854. During a hunting spree in which he lived up to his surname, he and his men were reported to have killed 2,000 buffalo, 1,600 elk and deer and 100 bears, 'a destruction that shocked and angered Indians and Whites alike', according to the roadside sign.

Eventually the climbing finished and we were rewarded with a 40 mph descent to the main road. Three miles more and we had made it to Kremmling. It was nearly 9 p.m. Unlike Steamboat, and in spite of the obvious opportunities for an ironic, Moscow-themed amusement park, tourism had passed it by.

As a result, options for food and accommodation were strictly limited. At a crossroads in what appeared to be the centre of town we found a solution: Shake 'n' Burger. Placing four orders at once, even though we were the only customers, seemed a challenging concept. The situation was aggravated when I ordered a takeaway ice cream sundae for dessert. While every other order was compiled inaccurately (no chips, too many onion rings, the wrong burger, that sort of thing), an assistant barely out of high-school spent an age creating my sundae, ensuring it was an exact replica of the picture on the menu. It was a work of art. He presented it proudly to me, only to be visibly crushed when I asked him to squash his towering creation into a plastic container so that I would be able to take it to the motel over the road.

'I did say takeaway,' I said sheepishly.

'He meant "to go",' explained Stephen.

At the motel, my misanthropy returned and I grumpily insisted on banning television for the night. As a result, endless speculation about Michael Jackson's demise was replaced by stunned silence. The sense of shock was exacerbated by the tiny room (to save money, we all shared a twin room, which came equipped with two double beds). Fitting four of us inside was enough of a challenge; adding four bikes was a recipe for chaos. Even bedtime afforded little comfort. The novelty of sharing a bed with a different cyclist each night was beginning to wear a bit thin.

....

CHAPTER 22

EAT, SLEEP AND BE GRUMPY

DAY 19

After the successful day into Steamboat, when we had covered 135 miles, yesterday had been something of a disappointment. We had, on reflection, made good progress in the time we had been cycling: 80 miles in eight hours. It was just that the time we had spent cycling had been limited.

This disappointment came as something of a surprise. But although we might have come to accept that we were no longer racing in the sense of competing against others – everyone else was either too far behind to catch us or, more commonly, too far ahead to be caught – we were, in spite of occasional appearances to the contrary, intent on making it to the finish as quickly as possible. We also had the imperative provided by Per's flight. It might have lacked the life-and-death urgency of the classic Western *3:10 to Yuma* – Per was certainly an unlikely Glenn Ford-style villain, and none of the rest of us had the nobility and desperation of Van Heflin's rancher – but it was an imperative all the same, and we had invested as much honour as is possible in completing such a self-indulgent frivolity as the race itself.

Accordingly, we had all resolved to start early. It had also been agreed that it should really take no more than an hour to be in the saddle. The only outstanding question was which hour that should be. Rising at 4.30 a.m. was mooted, but the likely shock to the system after yesterday's laxity was considered too great. Alarms set at 5 a.m. for departure at 6 a.m. was the compromise solution. It sounded like a half-hearted challenge to a duel, and the negotiations on which it was based recalled the nagging impositions of everyday life from which we had all sought refuge on the Tour Divide. Yet it was better than emulating the Tammy Wynette hit 'D-I-V-O-R-C-E'.

For once, and apart from the unanticipated distraction of an open gas station serving fresh coffee, we succeeded in our aims. In the morning light, and in a more philanthropic state of mind, Kremmling seemed a more welcoming place. Certainly, the icy-cold half an hour spent cycling alongside the youthful Colorado River was a delight. Then came another long Colorado ascent, gentle at first, then steeper, up to Ute Pass. The first few miles were through a wide, open side valley. Further up it narrowed and became more wooded.

We cycled past a series of signs at the side of the road that presaged another imminent change in scenery: 'Warning: Natural Gas Pipeline'. Written in large letters, this seemed clear enough. In smaller letters on a separate sign underneath, however, came some rather contradictory advice: 'Pipeline not under marker'. Which had come first? The sign that required the stake to be wrongly placed, or an inaccurate placement of the stakes that had required a modified sign?

Then the man-made scars of active mineral exploitation came once more to the fore. To our right was a huge earth dam straight from a Hollywood disaster movie. As we climbed higher it became clear that it contained a noxious mass of mine sediment. The nearby slopes, in stark contrast to those visible further afield, were conspicuously denuded of trees; those that did remain were mostly dead or dying. It was almost sad to admire the magnificence of the snow-clad peaks across the far side of the valley.

A fast, paved descent took us down the far side of the pass and onto a 13-mile stretch of main road to the large town of Silverthorne. On a road bike it would have been good riding. The fat tyres of a mountain bike merely added to the frustration of riding such an inefficient means of transport, however. In fact, the hotter it became – it was now late morning – and the longer I had to spend in the company of the vast trucks thundering past, the more I was inclined to revert to old prejudices about mountain bikes in general.

'They're no good. You can't really use them to get into the mountains and explore,' I moaned contentedly to myself, ignoring all the evidence to the contrary provided by the past three weeks. 'And then you get to some smooth road and they're just so mechanically inefficient they're a parody of what a good road bike should be,' I added, warming to my theme.

For once, my cantankerousness was not inflicted on the others. Surprisingly, Stephen was struggling. Trevor was at the front, setting a relentless pace, while Per and I ploughed our own lonely furrows in between.

On the outskirts of town we passed two more cyclists. They turned out to be a sexagenarian English couple from Nottingham who were partway through riding the Trans-America Cycle Trail. Running more than 4,000 miles from Astoria on the Oregon coast to Yorktown in Virginia, this was the granddaddy of all US bicycle trips.

'We're nearly halfway through. We're hoping to do it in two months,' said the wife in a pronounced East Midlands accent; it came as something of a surprise that she didn't conclude with 'me duck'. She asked what we were doing.

'Oh, that sounds fun. My husband would enjoy that,' she said, pointing up the road towards a fast-moving, silver-haired dot.

Perversely, this unintentional diminution of our endeavours cheered me no end; it invoked a long-overdue sense of perspective. I arrived in Silverthorne in fine spirits, which was just as well given the exasperating difficulties encountered when trying to call home from a gas station pay phone. It cost two phone cards and ten dollars to discover that the phone didn't work. It was clear much more immediately that the gas station manager was not interested in this malfunction.

'I can't give you a refund as it will mess up the till,' he explained with an insincere smile.

I pointed out that I'd just had my phone calls messed up and had paid for the privilege, but it fell on deaf ears. In fact, it was one of the most impressive and shameless defences of a completely untenable position that I'd ever had the misfortune to come across. In the end I almost felt like congratulating him. He was certainly wasted as a gas station manager – he should have been a politician.

From Silverthorne we climbed up to the impressive dam containing the waters of Dillon Reservoir. Although on the west side of the Continental Divide, it provided drinking water for Denver, on the east side. This odd arrangement succeeded through the creation of a 20-mile tunnel under the surrounding mountains. 'Go figure,' as the locals might have said.

In fact, the locals seemed disinclined to say anything. The next 20 miles were along a car-free bike path. Unsurprisingly, the good citizens of Silverthorne, Frisco, through which we passed, and Breckenridge, at the end of the trail, made good use of this fine resource. More surprisingly, they seemed intent on ignoring the cycling fraternity around them. Preoccupied by heart rate monitors or iPods, or their own importance, we could count on one hand those who returned the conventional greeting extended by those on two wheels.

'Some people take themselves way too seriously,' said Trevor.

In the midst of all this simmering animosity, Per demonstrated just how un-seriously he was taking things by nearly contriving to fall off his bike on the smoothest piece of tarmac experienced in the past three weeks. To be fair, we had provoked each other into something of a race through a winding, switchback section of the path. Also, keeping up with Stephen and Trevor was a significant challenge. What's more, Per's 6.5-foot frame meant he was disadvantaged by a centre of gravity somewhere near our heads. Yet how he managed to career perilously all over the trail until he finally succeeded in unclipping a foot and steadying himself was unclear.

'Don't quite know how I did that,' he said mildly.

It wasn't obvious whether he meant losing control or managing to regain it.

We arrived in Breckenridge in time for a late lunch. It was a place the like of which we had not previously encountered on the route. Even the guidebook saw fit to point out its somewhat plastic charms.

'Beware of getting splashed with cappuccino as you roll along the buffed and boutiqued Main Street.'

An Italian restaurant deigned to let us join the tourist throng. Cyclists at a neighbouring table ignored us. It was to be expected – their clothes were much cleaner than ours.

We ordered a combination of pizza and pasta dishes. I plumped for lasagne. Feeling strangely demob happy, I also ordered a bottle of beer. I hoped it would induce the siesta I planned to take.

The food was satisfactory, but not as voluminous as might have been desired. There was no option but to order dessert. Even then, the alcohol had its work cut out to induce anything more than a fitful sleep; there remained a nagging feeling that insufficient food had been consumed. Of course, it could have been that the bench I was reclining on was exceptionally uncomfortable.

Whatever the cause of my difficulties, I persisted with admirable stubbornness, aided by a pair of earplugs. Over an hour after I had unilaterally imposed a moratorium on leaving town, Stephen, Per and Trevor had exhausted all other forms of entertainment – fiddling with bikes, shopping – and were ready to leave. I woke with a start, even though I could have sworn I had not been asleep. A further delay was incurred as I still had to replenish my supplies. At the supermarket, I was unable to resist the siren charms of fast food. I hastily indulged in the unlikely combination of coffee and cake followed by ice cream and Pepsi. I knew it was likely to be a mistake, but I couldn't resist.

The mistake was confirmed immediately. The 10-mile climb to lofty Boreas Pass began as soon as we left town. So did my discomfort. I was in need of the kind of intestinal fortitude recommended by the homesteader in Lima. It was not forthcoming. I was racked with stomach cramps and nausea. My sloth in Breckenridge had initially been motivated by fear of tackling such a major climb in the heat of the day. Any concerns about the heat were now nothing more than a vague memory.

Trevor, unassailed by such gourmandise, steamed ahead; Stephen, in spite of his customary pause to answer a call of nature, rode out of sight; even Per, still effectively riding on only one leg, disappeared from view. Given the nature of my afflictions, it was probably best for all concerned that I was left to suffer on my own. Boreas Pass was fast becoming Laborious Pass.

After about an hour my intestinal discomfort began to fade. Shortly after, the slope began to ease near the summit. It had, on reflection, been a delightful climb. The gradient was constant and bearable, thanks to the road following the course of an erstwhile railway. The views from the top were breathtaking. We had ridden above the timber line and could see for miles to both north and south. Peaks above 13,000 feet abounded on all sides.

We stopped to don extra layers. A wooden house and a railway carriage provided in-situ evidence of the area's railway heritage. The Denver, South Park and Pacific Railroad had arrived at Boreas Pass in 1881, en route from Denver to the then mining boom town of Leadville. It was some feat, and it had functioned effectively in spite of the exposure of its route for more than 50 years. At one point, 150 people lived on top of the pass itself, justifying the installation of the US's highest post office for ten years from 1896.

Now it was blissfully peaceful after the hustle and bustle of Breckenridge. On a slope high to our left a snowboarder amused himself on a large, remnant snow patch. It was hard to know whether he or his dog was having more fun.

The fun, freewheeling descent from the summit rekindled my love affair with the mountain bike. I felt moved to apologise for my earlier expressions of disloyalty. The huge panorama ahead was captivating. This was what mountain biking was all about. I was hooked again. For now at least.

We stopped once more in 'historic' Como. The 'historic' tag seemed to allude to its significance in the early days of the railway. It had been named by Italian labourers after Lake Como, though any resemblance between the two must have seemed somewhat far-fetched even 130 years ago. Now it was another tiny collection of houses and a 'Mercantile'. Its only other distinguishing feature was a fine stone road house that could have come straight from the Highlands of Scotland, though the vastness of the landscape was beyond anything in the British Isles.

The Mercantile was closed, so I cycled to the road house to see if I could find some water as we planned to camp rough for the night. It, too, was closed, but a carpenter was busy restoring the reception.

'Are you looking for the other cyclist?'

I must have looked surprised.

'A woman on a bike.'

'You mean Cricket?'

'Yeah, that's her name. She's upstairs asleep.'

It turned out that she had arrived earlier in the afternoon in a state of considerable exhaustion. Although not yet officially reopened, the carpenter had kindly let her stay in one of the roadhouse guest rooms. I was torn between letting her know we were here and letting her sleep.

'Oh, I wouldn't wake her, she seemed pretty worn out,' advised the carpenter.

I settled for leaving a note on her saddle. We intended to ride until dusk – another couple of hours – then camp. We would stop for breakfast tomorrow morning in the small town of Hartsel. It was less than 30 miles away, and she could probably catch us there if she had an early start.

We rode off under the setting sun. This was South Park, a 1,000-square-mile grassland basin with an average height of 10,000 feet. Its scale left us transfixed and, not for the first time on the trip, slightly unsettled. For the first few miles we headed straight towards a huge thunderstorm raging on the basin's side. Just as it had begun to appear inescapable, we turned sharply right and rode once again into the twilight.

We rode silently between grazing cattle and more pronghorn antelope. The sky between the high clouds and the horizon assumed the colour of whiskey. Our reverie was interrupted first by the arrival of a pick-up truck, then by the fact that it stopped. The driver wound down her window to speak to us.

'Are you guys planning on camping for the night?' she asked.

It was not something we could convincingly deny.

'You do know that this is all private land?'

She didn't ask in an unfriendly way, but it was still a difficult question.

'Well, ma'am, we were just planning on finding a quiet spot and bedding down for the night,' said Stephen.

'We'll be off at daybreak,' I added.

It was not a winning hand, but our new inquisitor wasn't intent on exploiting our weakness.

'My cousins live a few miles down the road. They won't mind if you pitch your tents on their land. Just go and knock on the door and tell them Kirsten sent you. They're called Theresa, Dennis and Owen.'

She then concluded the encounter with a further surprise, conversing briefly in Swedish with Per.

'She said she was originally from Norway,' he explained after she had driven off.

The house Kirsten had described to us was not difficult to find; there were few to choose from. Yet there was nobody at home. We considered pitching our tents anyway and waiting for the owners' return, but this seemed an imposition too far. Instead we reverted to Plan A.

A mile further on, with both sun and temperature now plummeting, we discovered the abandoned baseball diamond and children's playground that had been marked on the map. The whole area had seemingly been pencilled in for housing development. The plans had been discarded, but the playground remained.

We hurriedly pitched camp. Stephen and Per struggled to decide which was the lesser of two evils: leaving their heads exposed to potential storms; or contending with the smell and disconcerting animal noises in the dilapidated toilet block with its cold, concrete floor. Stephen chose the latter, Per the former.

Secure in my tent, and once again ravenous, I delved into my goody bag. As an appetiser I had two packets of cheese biscuits and some mini Baby-Bel cheeses. Then came the main course: four waffles, remarkably still intact, smothered in mashed bananas and drizzled with honey. Dessert was two packets of chocolate chip cookies. It was all accompanied by a locally produced sweet wine known as Gatorade. This was the highest of haute cuisine.

Short of reading material, I totted up my calorific intake from the information plastered over the back of every food packet. With an estimate for the bananas, it worked out at just under 2,000 calories, or four-fifths of my recommended daily intake. Not bad for a light supper. I fell asleep before I could extend my calculations to include all that had already been consumed earlier in the day.

....

CHAPTER 23

I WANDERED LONELY
AS A CLOUD

DAY 20

We broke our fasts as planned in Hartsel. It was another tiny place, though this time without the 'historic' tag. The presence of US Highway 24, which passed straight through it, probably precluded such a prestigious label.

It was just after 7 a.m. when we arrived. There seemed to be only one place open, which at least made choosing easy. The HOB café and saloon was small town America writ large, though without the antique façade of the Atlantic City Mercantile. It had the same old-time wallpaper, however, and a magnificent copper ceiling. It also had a nice line in snappy aphorisms, of which the best was embroidered on the waitress's ample T-shirt: Never Trust a Skinny Cook.

Fortunately, skinny customers seemed to be OK, although the regulars were all of distinctly heavier build. They also seemed to share a political persuasion that could best be described as Palin-esque (as in Sarah, not Michael).

'Did you hear about that cap 'n' trade deal?' one of them asked his companions.

It was a rhetorical question.

'The Democrats added 300 extra pages at 3 a.m. When the Republicans got hold of it they found it was a load of rubbish. We're gonna pay billions of dollars to other countries to buy carbon credits, but I don't know how many other countries plant trees in the US.'

Murmurs of approval reverberated from the copper ceiling. Then it was someone else's turn.

'I heard one senator say he'd vote for the healthcare reform bill if all government officials were put on the state scheme.'

'That would be a good deal.'

Cue general guffaws. There followed an intense discussion about public finances that was partly obscured by the arrival of my blueberry pancakes and grapefruit juice. Tranquillity returned in time to catch the clinching argument.

'The government's not got any money and it's not designed to have any money,' said the first speaker definitively.

Then he contradicted himself with equal authority.

'There's only three ways it can get money. It can tax you, it can print money, or it can sell bombs to China.'

After the arrival of coffee, conversation shifted to Barack Obama himself. The opening gambit proved popular.

'He's gonna need to get a big chequebook.'

It was immediately trumped, however.

'He's gonna need to get in touch with reality.'

This was a real crowd-pleaser. In fact, it almost broke the ice sufficiently for the four of us to be engaged in the conversation, but we were saved by the unlikely arrival of another cyclist. It was not Cricket. Instead, it was the leader of a supported Trans-America Cycle Trail group ride organised by the Adventure Cycling Association. He was not actually riding his bike, but driving the support vehicle. His 'team' were expected through Hartsel in late morning. We explained that he might meet Cricket.

'Be sure to tell her we're just up the road,' said Stephen.

He offered us the use of the tools and provisions in the back of the van. Oranges were the only fruit, but we didn't complain about the lack of diversity, unlike some of the riders he was chaperoning.

'I prefer the self-guided tours where people are a bit more self-sufficient. These guys really need some nannying, and they get a bit arsey if there aren't the right kind of oranges at the right time or if it gets too hot or things we can do nothing about.'

I felt my by-now semi-permanent state of disgruntlement had slightly greater justification. We cycled out of town past the self-proclaimed 'Hartsel Jail and Sheriff's Office', which was in fact no more than a dilapidated, whitewashed former gas station with broken windows and hand-painted signs. Had we known of it 12 hours earlier we might have become the first people to knowingly break in to spend the night there. Then came a sign for a special service to be held that Sunday at the Gateway Church. 'Join us at the Boomerang Express. 3yrs to 6th Grade.'

'It's for repentant sinners who've now seen the error of their Godless ways. They just can't help coming back,' explained Trevor.

'Youthful, repentant sinners,' corrected Stephen.

'Youthful, repentant sinners in a hurry,' said Per with a degree of finality.

The countryside south of Hartsel was initially very similar to that through which we had ridden from Como the previous night. Yet the harsh, bright light of what seemed destined to be another hot day turned it into a more austere and arid landscape. What had appeared in soft twilight to be lush grazing was in fact meagre pickings. Yet away from the ranchlands, glorious wildflower meadows showed the fecundity of nature in even such exacting circumstances. Most of the plants were alien to me, but no less beautiful for their anonymity: red, iris-type flowers were the most common, accompanied by drifts of daisy white and buttercup yellow. Aromatic shrubs also abounded.

I came over all wistful. Why rush through such beauty? Why not stop and enjoy nature's bounty? I gave voice to my concerns. If the others heard me, they did not show it. I cursed them under my breath. Ignorant, soulless swines. How could they not want to pause and commune?

I silently cast myself as a frustrated Wordsworth of the Rockies.

'I wandered lonely as a cloud/That floats on high o'er vales and hills,/When all at once I saw a crowd,/A host of ruby-red, iris-type flowers . . .'

It was a work in progress.

I brooded petulantly at the back of the group, hoping to act as a brake on our speed. To no avail. It was my fault: I had kept my sensitive, romantic soul hidden for too long under a façade of brash ambition. The others assumed more prosaic explanations: fatigue, or laziness, or both.

We crested the watershed divide that was our route out of South Park and down into the town of Salida. The magnificent views over the 14,000-foot peaks of the Sawatch Range exacerbated the problem.

We stopped to take photos. It was not enough. I wanted to paint. I wanted to hike. I wanted to go all Julie Andrews and prance around among the edelweiss.

Actually, that might have been a bit too energetic. I was coming to realise that all I really wanted to do was stop this mad rush and rest for a while. I wanted, I acknowledged to myself, to stop. Full stop.

It was something of a relief to admit to such heresy, and also something of a surprise. Not since my solitary vigil in Montana's multitude of trees had I actually thought about stopping. Even then it was only because I was being driven mad with claustrophobia. Now, I had developed the imagination to understand where Steve McGuire had been coming from. Maybe it was just time for this bike ride to stop.

Per, Stephen and Trevor clearly didn't think so. They careered into Salida. I trailed in after them. I raised my concerns. They looked askance.

'I think I might stop here for the day,' I said, not willing to reveal the true extent of my affliction.

'What do you want to do that for?' asked Per in a way that seemed to exemplify thousands of years of restless, resilient Scandinavian adventurers' genes.

It was a good question. There were a million answers, but articulating any given one of them was all but impossible. I decided relying on my recently discovered enthusiasm for poetry and painting might sound implausible.

I was saved from my dilemma by Safeway. Trevor and Stephen had bilaterally decided that yesterday's luxuries of restaurant and siesta had been a step too far. Instead they headed to the supermarket deli section. Unlike the novelty charm of Helena, it was the very acme of soullessness. A true romantic would have struggled to find inspiration; all I could find was semi-frozen quiche and potato salad. It was not a place to end the adventure of a lifetime. In fact, it scarcely passed muster as a place to spend a lunchtime.

Even the debilitating heat of Salida – it was nudging 100° F (nearly 38° C) – was preferable to the air-conditioned atrophy of Safeway. The three amigos rode off. I accompanied them.

To lighten the mood, Trevor pointed out that it was Canada Day.

'Canada Day? What does it celebrate?' I asked.

'What do you mean?'

'Well, 4th of July is Independence Day in the US, so . . .'

'Oh, nothing special. Just Canada's "day", I guess.'

An hour later and I had my first puncture of the trip. It coincided with the ominous massing of cumulonimbus clouds above the high peaks ahead. As I fumbled with inner tubes and tyre irons, drops of sweat mingled with drops of rain.

'Bet you're glad you decided to keep going,' said Trevor.

The remainder of the climb to Marshall Pass, a mere bagatelle at 10,842 feet, was memorable for all the wrong reasons. It was long and steep. Navigation at the bottom was surprisingly awkward. And then there was the not inconsiderable matter of a terrific thunderstorm that accompanied us at far too close quarters for the best part of two hours. Lightning flashed incessantly. The sound of thunder was deafening. It was like riding in Thor's chariot itself. I blamed Per. I told him as much, but he couldn't hear above the surrounding din.

The rain, too, was interminable and torrential. It became so intense that, against all advice and logic, Per, Trevor and I sought shelter in the trees at the side of the road. Stephen was somewhere ahead, we hoped. It was too cold to stand still for long, however. Back on the bike, the deluge that ran over nose and mouth made breathing difficult.

We ploughed on and on through rivers of mud. Movement was the only protection against hypothermia. Finally, the top brought a refuge – of sorts. Leaning against a prefabricated toilet cubicle was Stephen's bike. Inside was a shivering, half-naked Stephen, trying desperately to find some non-sodden clothes to wear for the descent.

'Howdy! Come on in!' he said gallantly.

It was, on reflection, an unlikely invitation, but I accepted it with alacrity. The scene then repeated itself twice more as first Trevor and then Per arrived. It was something of a squash. I hung my coat on a hook and anxiously read the sign detailing the construction of the cubicle. It said the base was designed to withstand a force of 3,000 Newtons per square metre. My antipathy to physics lessons at school had not prevented me from remembering that a Newton was roughly one tenth of a kilogram (remembering useless facts was never a problem; understanding what they meant was). That equated to 300kg per square metre. I weighed about 70kg wet through, which I was.

'How much do you weigh?' I asked as nonchalantly as I could.

'What? Why do you want to know that?' asked Per.

'Oh, just curious.'

'185 pounds,' said Per.

'175 when I set out, but less now,' said Stephen.

'155 pounds,' said Trevor.

This was going to tax my arithmetical abilities more than I had anticipated. That was 525 pounds, divided by 2.2 . . . erm . . . er . . . a bit less than 250kg. Probably. Plus my own 70kg. Even assuming a safety margin in the construction process, that took us perilously close to breaking point. I eyed-up the size of the cubicle. Probably one and a half metres each way. That gave us two and a quarter square metres of floor space, minus the toilet itself.

'We should be all right as long as we don't all stand next to each other,' I concluded triumphantly.

I was surrounded by blank faces. Nobody had any intention of being closer to anyone else than they could possibly help.

'The strength of the floor. That sign up there tells you how strong the floor is. I've just worked it out. If we don't all stand next to each other, we won't end up in the shit.'

The others were delighted. Just in case I had been wrong, I opened the door and stepped outside. The weather was as foul as before. It could be said we were in the shit already.

Fortunately, the descent was long but easy. Desperately trying to reach the bottom before my slowly deflating rear tyre made another repair stop necessary, I even outdid Stephen's remarkable downhill skills. A large herd of elk, sheltering at the roadside, disdainfully ignored my sodden progress.

It was after 8 p.m. when we arrived in Sargents. It was not how I had pictured it. The map showed a wealth of services that still, in the mind of someone from a small, crowded island, implied a town. Or at least a village, with shops, houses, a small green, perhaps. Instead there was little more than a trailer park at the side of a main road with a gas station and bar-cum-restaurant. The gas station was closed. The bar, the Tomichi Creek Trading Post, was open, and extremely welcoming.

If Sargents had been something of a disappointment from the outside, once inside the bar we found it exceeded our expectations. There was, said the slightly tipsy bartender, a cabin for us to rent, and a grocery store that she would open up for us. There was a wholesome menu, and food was still being served. Most important of all, there was a karaoke birthday party.

After we had reserved a cabin and ordered our food, it became apparent that there was little to distinguish between staff and guests. Those propping up the bar reappeared behind it; those behind it were clearly not immune to the temptation to keep the customers company. Every now and then, all would rush to the backroom for a singalong. It didn't seem to make for a very sound business plan, but it certainly made for a convivial atmosphere.

In fact, the mood was so compelling, and our relief at having made it this far unscathed so overwhelming, that we celebrated by ordering only our second alcoholic drinks of the whole trip.

'I think I'd better have a bottle of Fat Tire beer,' said Trevor appropriately.

Seizing on this indication that we were not such killjoys as we appeared, we were corralled into participating in the karaoke.

'You've got to come and sing with us. It's the rules. Everyone in the bar has to sing when "I'll Fly Away" comes on,' the smiling waitress explained.

Per, Trevor and Stephen were disadvantaged by the fact they didn't know the song. I knew the song, but couldn't sing (not just couldn't sing – can't sing). We did our best; it wasn't very good, it certainly bore no resemblance to Alison Krauss's original, but it didn't seem to matter.

'I think we made them smile a bit,' said Trevor.

'I'm not sure they need much help in that direction,' said Stephen.

My enthusiasm for continuing the race had been restored.

CHAPTER 24

CANNIBAL ADVENTURE!

DAY 21

If it had taken for ever to reach Sargents, it took even longer to leave. Yet our attempts to depart started early enough. In fact, Stephen's mobile phone resounded balefully at 5 a.m., a full hour earlier than anticipated. Disbelieving, I checked the clock, but there was no escaping the early hour.

'Stephen, it's 5 a.m.,' I pointed out.

'I know,' came the muffled reply.

I shouldn't have been surprised; after all, it was his phone. Nevertheless, I thought it pertinent to remind Stephen that the intention had been to have a minor lie-in, this time until the luxurious hour of 6 a.m., so that we could make the most of the café and shop next to the bar in which we had caroused the night away. It did not open until 7 a.m., and we could not leave without going to the shop as ahead lay another 100 miles of nothing.

By the time I had completed my litany of complaint Stephen had wisely gone back to sleep. I did not. Instead, I lay fulminating as ill-humouredly as if my beauty sleep had been disturbed by one of the children at home. By the planned rising time of 6 a.m., however, my frustration had mellowed and I had put the intrusion into some sort of perspective. At least I hadn't had to change a nappy or mop up a pool of toddler vomit at the same time.

With little need for haste, an orderly queue formed for that rarest of luxuries: a morning shower. Then, just as it was my turn, I pushed

208

past my bike and realised the tyre that had been slowly deflating during the descent from Marshall Pass was now completely flat.

Relinquishing my place in the shower queue, I set about removing the tyre. At certain times – say a sunny evening at home, in the garden, with a glass of wine to hand – mending punctures is a pleasure; at others, as yesterday, it is a simple necessity; mostly, however, it is a pain in the backside. Nevertheless, with practice it can be accomplished quickly and painlessly. After ten minutes, I sat smugly looking at a job well done.

Then I remembered the two spare inner tubes that now had holes in them. If I didn't carry out repairs to the originals before we left, I would have to do so en route if I suffered another puncture. Images of trying to make a patch stick to a tube in a thunderstorm like last night's put paid to the instinctive desire to bury my head in the sand and ignore the problem. Yet I was in danger of causing considerable delay.

'Time for breakfast,' announced Per right on cue, and in the manner of a man for whom last night's vast meal was but a distant memory.

I told them I would have to join them later. They ambled off. Then, just as I had finally managed to locate my puncture repair kit, they all returned, looking rather downcast.

'What's up?' I asked.

'It's closed,' said Per.

'What's closed?' I asked.

'The shop and the café.'

'But the sign said shop and restaurant open for breakfast at 7 a.m.'

'Every day except Thursday,' Stephen corrected.

'What day is it?'

'It's Thursday.'

I began to get the feeling this was going to be a day to forget.

'What about the woman from last night who said it would be open?'

'Nowhere to be found.'

The café in fact would not open until midday. In the absence of last night's host, the shop would not be available to us for another hour at 8 a.m. A half-hearted debate about the possibility of continuing without re-stocking ensued, but common sense prevailed.

At least I was no longer the sole cause of our delay. After finishing my repairs, I went to the gas station to pump up my tyre. In keeping with the day so far, there was a sign reading 'no air'. The compressor was out of action. I walked back to our cabin through a disparate collection of trailers, some genuinely towable, others by now well-rooted in Sargents soil. It was a fate we seemed in danger of emulating. All were accompanied by enormous, shiny pick-ups and only slightly smaller but equally shiny quad bikes.

I inflated my tyre manually, an effort that made the café breakfast we now had to forego seem even more inviting. By the time I had finished it was 7.30 a.m. We twiddled our thumbs. We discovered a kettle in the cabin, but no tea or coffee. We found a toaster, but no bread.

'We could always go to the shop,' said Stephen with enforced irony.

Eventually, we did go to the shop. It was not really worth the wait. There was little to choose from, though there was hot coffee. Determined to make the best of it, we had an impromptu competition to find the highest calorific content of our preferred snacks. Trevor and I went for pastries: blueberry cheese Danish and bear claw (a generic term for an almond-flavoured confection purportedly shaped like a bear's claw). The cheese Danish won by a short head: 509 calories compared to 480 calories in a 4.5-ounce package. Stephen selected his personal favourite, Pearson's Salted Nut Roll, a sort of peanut butter, nougat and marshmallow bar, and pointed gleefully to that fact that they had an even better calorie-to-weight ratio: 760 calories in 5.5 ounces.

'You've not tried them?'

'No.'

'They're disgusting,' said Per, putting two into his shopping basket along with both pastries (cheese Danish and bear claw, just for the sake of comparison) and as many tortillas as the rest of us put together.

'Just a little something,' he smiled.

We went to pay.

'I thought you boys would have been gone by now,' said the woman at the till, who had also been behind the bar the previous night.

Clearly her alcohol-induced promise to be open for breakfast had been long forgotten.

It was 8.30 a.m. by the time we finally left.

'I'm beginning to get the feeling we're doomed never to make it to Antelope Wells,' I said as we rode along.

'Nonsense. We'll be finished in a week,' said Per.

'You're just saying that so you can catch your plane,' I objected. 'The rest of us could take two weeks more, if we wanted, and have a day off tomorrow.'

'Speak for yourself. I've got to get home so I can start my new job,' Stephen pointed out.

'And I just want to get to the finish as soon as possible so I can stop riding,' said Trevor.

This was the Catch-22 we were now in. With unfortunate timing, our enthusiasm for cycling was at something of a low ebb. We had made it past halfway, which had been a huge fillip. There was no escaping the fact, however, that this had meant we still had to do the same again. Recent experience demonstrated just how arduous that might be. Yet the longer we prevaricated, the longer we would have to keep riding.

So we kept riding. Until I had another puncture, that was. I had been dawdling behind the others so they were ignorant of my plight. I threw my bike disgustedly into the verge and watched forlornly as they rode over the brow of a hill and out of sight. Even repeated blasts on the bear whistle I was still carrying around my neck went unheeded. It was a good job I hadn't needed to use it in earnest.

With plenty of recent practice I was soon underway again. The enforced solitude was surprisingly agreeable. By lunch we were all reunited on the far side of Cochetopa Pass, the 'Buffalo Gate' of the native Ute Indians and another historically significant breach in the surrounding mountains, this time used as a stage route. With a gradient suited to coach and horses, it had not proved a major obstacle.

We were now in much more arid country, though the grey skies above suggested otherwise. We stopped to eat in a dry, rocky stream bed bereft of significant vegetation. As well as its aesthetic deficiencies, it was infested with mosquitoes.

'Yum. Salami tortillas with added insect,' said Per, through a buzzing cloud.

It was no place to linger. Yet there was good reason to ensure we ate our fill. It was in the nearby town of Saguache ('nearby' and 'town' being relative terms in Colorado as Saguache was more than an hour's ride away and had a population of a mere 500) that one of the Wild West's most heinous crimes first came to light. The crime in question was cannibalism, preceded by murder. The assumed perpetrator of both acts was Alfred G. Packer, a hapless prospector originally from Pennsylvania.

In spite of advice to the contrary, including from no less an authority than Ute Indian Chief Ouray, Packer and five companions set off into the surrounding mountains en route to Gunnison in February 1874. As was inevitable, they were caught in the winter weather, then became lost and snowbound. Only Packer survived. When the bodies of his companions were later discovered, all had died violently and all had had strips of flesh taken from legs and chest.

According to Packer, apprehended spending money from his companions' wallets in Saguache, another member of the party – Shannon Bell – had gone mad and killed the other three prior to eating parts of them. Packer said he had then been forced to kill Bell in self-defence, and to perpetuate the cannibalism in order to survive.

The courts thought otherwise. Packer also appeared to change his mind. He wrote a confession and was convicted of murder, but then escaped from jail. Nine years later he was caught again and convicted a second time, though this conviction was then reduced to manslaughter just prior to his intended execution. In spite of another written confession and his sentence being upheld by the Colorado Supreme Court, Packer died a free man, having earlier been paroled or pardoned, depending on which account you read.

With this in mind, it was with some trepidation that we embarked on the ascent of the dubiously named Carnero Pass. It sounded uncomfortably close to carnivorous to me. Fortunately, our overriding hunger was to reach our destination for the night, the Spanish-sounding town of Del Norte. Actually, it didn't sound Spanish at all. It looked Spanish but, like Salida, had a very Anglicised pronunciation. Del Norte, in fact, was Del Naught, not Del Nortay, while Salida now charmingly rhymed with saliva.

A long descent through dramatic, rocky scenery took us into another vast Colorado basin. Three separate storms could be seen on the horizon. The largest, darkest, most fearsome of these, of course, appeared to be directly on our route. Yet at the last moment our fortunes improved and we turned sharply to our right. Instead of a storm to contend with, we were now confronted with a landscape straight from a Western film as we skirted the basin's edge. Red soils and rocky bluffs made for perfect ambush territory. I began to hum the theme from *The Big Country*.

A narrowing track and stony ground also made for Stephen's idea of perfect cycling territory. He had been rather sluggish all day but he now cycled between the sagebrush as if the posse were on his trail. Trevor did a passable impression of hot pursuit, but Per and I were laggards once again.

It was of no consequence. We re-emerged between two prominent basalt towers onto the plain only a short time later with Del Norte in sight less than five miles away. At first glance it seemed about as appealing as Rawlins, without the glamour of its historical association with outlaws (even though it was, according to the town sign, the home of astronaut Kent Rominger – fame indeed).

On closer inspection, however, the town's broad, bland main street gave way to a grid of tree-lined residential roads with well tended houses and even better tended lawns. The sense of homeliness was reinforced by our accommodation for the night. The map had informed us that Gary Blakely and Patti Kelly offered basic services to passing cyclists. In a moment of inspiration, Stephen had called to see if that included sleeping space. To our collective surprise, it did.

'Hey, guys, come on in. How are you all feeling?' asked Gary.

A lot better for having arrived, was the consensus reaction. The house was a white, timber-framed, one-storey construction surrounded by manicured lawns dotted with trees and flowering bushes. At the back was a vegetable patch. Inside was equally immaculate. It didn't look designed to accommodate four such lumbering, noisome oafs. Yet Gary and Patti were undeterred. Perhaps their sense of the obnoxious had been diluted over years of similar hospitality to passing cyclists.

Whatever the reason, the warmth of their welcome was genuine. Along with all domestic facilities, including clean towels and hot water, Gary provided us with some more race updates. We had confirmation that Matthew Lee had won, and that Kurt, Chris and the Petervarys on their 'Love Shack' had also finished.

'Matthew stopped by last Wednesday,' said Gary, kindly not

mentioning the fact it was now Thursday over a week later. 'He wasn't going to stop long as he thought there were a couple of guys only a few hours behind him, but we told him they'd dropped back so he relaxed a bit and stopped for a shower and something to eat.'

Alan, Steve and John had also passed through a good while ago in a group of eight riders. They had all now almost certainly finished as well. Jill Homer and Jamie Thomson had been through more recently, though were too far ahead for us to consider catching them. Then there was Cricket.

'She's called the race,' said Gary.

'There are plenty of things I'd like to call the race at times,' I said, assuming I'd missed the crucial adjective.

'It means she's pulled out,' explained Stephen.

All the while, Patti inadvertently emphasised my sense of cumbersome gaucheness by performing effortless and elegant stretches. It made my inability to summon the coordination to take my shoes off even more pitiful, though Patti kindly refrained from pity. She also expressed a surprising degree of enthusiasm for the South West Coast Path back home. It seemed incongruous to be talking of something so mundane while in such impressive surroundings, but one man's backyard is another's exotic playground.

We asked about options for eating.

'There are two,' said Gary. 'There's a nice, organic place that's great but where the portions are a little on the light side, and there's Boogie's diner that's good too and might suit your needs better if you're wanting something more substantial.'

He looked at us and read our minds.

'I'd go for the diner.'

....

CHAPTER 25

IT'S ALL DOWNHILL FROM HERE

DAY 22

There were, it turned out, two downsides to staying with Gary and Patti.

The first was the quality of the night's sleep. This was not something that could be blamed on our hosts. Rather, it was a combination of too much roast beef dinner the night before and too many people having consumed too much roast beef dinner trying to sleep in too small a space. The attic bedroom was simultaneously hot and cold. Any covers were too many; no covers were too few. Space was at a premium. The room had a double bed in it, which I shared with Per; Stephen and Trevor had already bagged the comfort of the floor. Moving was not an option.

The second problem was also not the fault of Gary and Patti. We were once more slow to depart, though this time the obstacles were psychological rather than practical. Gary had been as good as his word and got up at 5 a.m. to provide fresh, hot coffee to speed us on our way, but the warmth of the hospitality and the natural desire not to leave a cosy kitchen on a cold morning combined to make us tarry. Six croissants for my breakfast alone didn't help.

Our sloth might also have been inspired by the prospect of what lay ahead. Indiana Pass, at a breath-shortening 11,910 feet, was the highest point of the whole Tour Divide and was only 23 almost exclusively uphill miles away. It was also probably the biggest climb on the route in terms of altitude gain in one go, towering more than 4,000 feet above Del Norte. What's more, while the first 800 feet came in the

11 miles of paved road straight out of town, the remaining 3,300 came in 12 miles of dirt and gravel. It was clearly going to be hard work.

At 6.20 a.m. we could delay no longer. We rode out of town past the Colorado hair emporium and 'shoppe', the Del Norte National Bank and a 'drive-thru' ATM. The morning was chill with high, grey clouds. Perfect cycling conditions.

The paved part of the climb went smoothly. Then the real ascent began. It took just under two hours, but it seemed to pass in a flash. In spite, or maybe because, of the six croissants, I settled immediately into a comfortable rhythm. It was the exact opposite of my travails on Boreas Pass. Within minutes I was absorbed by the existential simplicity of cycling uphill. Life was reduced to nothing more than turning the pedals. The power of conscious thought seemed to disappear, to be replaced instead by an abstract concentration on the task in hand. Yet my senses were heightened. I was consumed by an animalistic awareness of the surroundings that defied conventional powers of observation and description.

I arrived at the top a man refreshed. Five minutes later I was a man refrigerated. The energy expended combined with the thin air and the cold, damp conditions quickly reduced me to a shivering wreck. By the time Trevor arrived, still hot from his endeavours, I was clad in all available clothes and cowering out of the chilling wind.

'Good climb,' he beamed in typically laidback fashion.

'It's downhill all the way to Mexico now,' I replied.

Then bravado got the better of me.

'I'm tempted to ride up the hill a bit just to say I've exceeded 12,000 feet.'

'Go on, then,' said Trevor, calling my bluff.

I hesitated.

'Not that tempted,' Trevor observed.

We were joined first by Per and then Stephen. Per's knee troubles had now been transformed from acute pain to merely persistent soreness and aching. Yet he seemed to have become able to accept the throbbing base beat of discomfort as simply a backdrop for the rest of the wear and tear incurred on such a long ride. Stephen, on the other hand, was now suffering in Per's place, his knee causing him considerable concern. He had also, he revealed at Gary and Patti's, lost 12 pounds since the race started, which was not necessarily a good thing.

'I can see it now – the Tour Divide diet book,' said Trevor.

I gradually returned to my senses. We were sat on top of a broad, grassy pass. Around us, the San Juan mountains continued to rise above even our lofty position, their heads lost in the cloud. Patches of winter snow remained. It was a delightful setting, seemingly removed from all human influences other than the dirt road we were on.

Just how far this was from the truth was revealed less than 5 miles later as we descended into the erstwhile mining town of Summitville, the highest town in the whole of Colorado and still above 11,000 feet. Ahead of us, above the town, were the scars inflicted by 140 years of gold mining in the area. Worse still, however, were the invisible scars inflicted by the most recent mining operations, which only ground to a halt in 1991. The process of using sodium cyanide to leach gold from a pyritic ore had gone so badly awry that water in the whole of the surrounding river drainage had been declared unsafe for human consumption. The guidebook described it as 'too contaminated for human ingestion even after filtering'.

The nearby hamlet of Platoro, on the other hand, had a reputation as a pleasant pitstop. We rode on, enthused. The description of 'pleasant' turned out to be accurate, but that of 'nearby' proved well short of the mark. We had conveniently ignored the density of the squiggles on the map, which in turn disguised the fact it was more than 20 miles away. Somehow we had also overlooked the presence of two four-mile climbs. To miss one climb may be regarded as a misfortune; to miss both looked like carelessness.

Yet the riding between the two was through some of the most picturesque mountain scenery of the whole trip, with grassy meadows and clearings complemented by streams and wild flowers. When we finally arrived we were also rewarded by a warm welcome at the Skyline Lodge.

'Ah, you must be in the race,' said a wiry, long-bearded man leaning on the porch.

We confessed as much.

'Everyone else has been through,' he explained, pointing to a list of times and dates by the bar. 'We check them in and check them out again.'

A serving of peach cobbler with cream and ice cream, the best dessert since the pies in Lima, a cup of tea and the opportunity to phone home completed the picture of loveliness. The waitress then burst the bubble by explaining breezily how everyone else had eaten more and more speedily.

'You can tell you guys aren't in a rush.'

The slight on our consumption levels came as a much bigger blow than that on our credentials as racers.

From Plataro we rolled gently down the valley of the nascent Conejos River for 20 easy miles. Our plan was to call in the last short day of our ride and spend the night where the valley met the main road in the equally small hamlet of Horca. That would leave six more days to meet Per's deadline.

The plan seemed sound. According to the map, Horca had a motel, a restaurant and a grocery store. We let ourselves become excited by the prospect of an early night, laundry and cool beer. In spite of the heat, I began to salivate – about the beer, not the laundry.

The map was wrong. Horca, which was pronounced more like a killer whale than a peddler, was in fact a damp squib. The motel had closed and the cabins were for sale. The restaurant was not open and, to judge from its dingy exterior, would have held no appeal anyway. What passed for the shop was little more than a moribund collection of out-of-date tins and jars.

Things were looking bleak. Sleeping rough would be tricky enough near a main road. But the biggest concern was the lack of food. The cupboard was bare, which was difficult to swallow, and the next services of any kind were more than 100 miles ahead. Even then their existence was questionable.

The miserable man at the till when we arrived had been replaced by his equally miserable-looking wife, inspiring Stephen to exercise his Southern charm. The rest of us had no desire to cast aspersions on his talents, but we had already started calculating whether we could subsist on snacks for another 12-hour day plus dinner that night. Perhaps inspired by our lack of faith, Stephen came back triumphant.

'She says there's a caravan site with cabins two miles down the road, and she thinks it has a shop.'

There was, indeed, a caravan site with cabins, and it was two miles down the road, but the shop offered little more than chocolate bars. Still, two out of three wasn't bad. Unfortunately, it being the eve of

America's national holiday, no cabins were available. Even a space to pitch our tents was looking distinctly questionable until the owner asked where we'd come from and where we were headed.

'Canada to Mexico,' said Stephen.

That seemed to do the trick.

'Gee, that's some ride,' he said. 'There's a pitch over by the entrance that won't be filled until tomorrow morning. They said they'd be coming early so I kept it free tonight, but if you guys say you'll be out before lunchtime . . .'

We assured him we'd be gone before breakfast, though the prospect of missing the 'Fifth Annual Ponderosa Caravan Site Pancake Breakfast and Duck Race' caused a twinge of regret.

'John Bryant's famous sourdough pancakes,' murmured Per sadly as he read the notice.

The campsite was a gem. The owner, 'Uncle' Jack, said we could use the laundry and provided clean towels for the showers, all for the princely sum of $5 each. He also introduced us to just about every other camper, the regulars among whom had, like him, earned the honorary title 'uncle'.

The conversations followed a similar pattern.

'Hey, Uncle Herb (or Uncle Chuck, or Uncle JT), how ya doin'? Listen. D'ya hear what these boys are doin'? They're only cycling from Canada to Mexico,' said Uncle Jack.

'Is that so?' would reply Uncle Herb (or Uncle Chuck, or Uncle JT).

'It is so. Go on, young man, tell him what you're doing.'

We did, and a whole series of uncles demonstrated more enthusiasm for cycling than their pick-ups, trailers and quad bikes could ever have implied was possible.

The evening passed quickly in a series of chores, most related to trying to maintain what was a rapidly disintegrating relationship with the concept of cleanliness. It was reasonably successful. Our food situation had not improved markedly, but we would at least smell more presentable. Trevor revealed the extent of his hidden depths by unveiling a previously unworn cycling top.

Dinner was a picnic made up of random ingredients from the Horca shop. The determining factor was items that had not passed their sell-by date, or not by much, at least. Per had found jam and I had found Spam. With stale rolls we contrived main course and dessert.

'Mmm. This Spam's all right,' enthused Per, though his appetite was by now so vast as to betray a certain lack of discrimination.

'Ah, yes, canned in 2005. That was a good vintage and it has matured nicely into a full-bodied Spam with hints of forest fruits and a good finish,' I explained.

'Pardon?' said Per.

'Never mind.'

NEW MEXICO

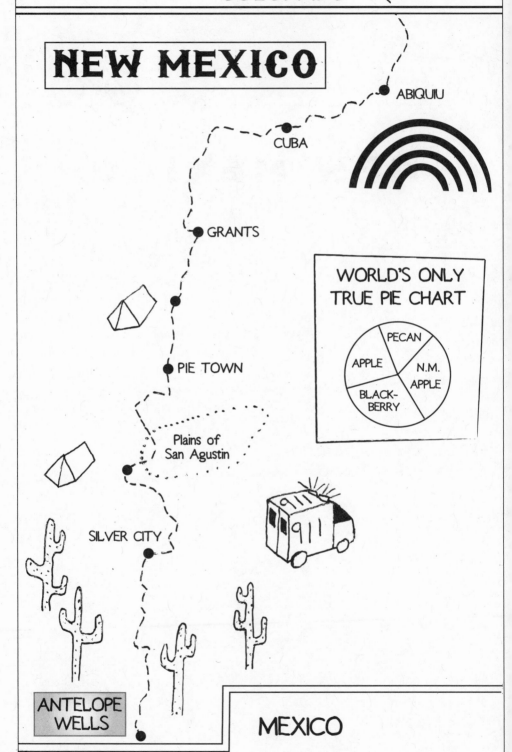

CHAPTER 26

....

INDEPENDENCE DAY

DAY 23

In spite of our impressive prevarication pedigree, we couldn't quite contrive a way to remain at the Ponderosa Caravan Site until the promised pancake breakfast. More Spam and jam was a less than satisfactory alternative, but it was better than nothing.

The day began cold and sunny with a long climb up State Highway 17 to La Manga Pass. I had another puncture. Stephen's knee was hurting, so we finally conquered the pass some time after Per and Trevor. A pick-up drove past with a screeching, burning rear wheel leaving a trail of sparks and smoke behind it.

'That looks how I feel,' I said.

'I wouldn't want to go down a pass like this in a car like that,' replied Stephen.

We passed the ghostly remnants of a gas station at which we had dreamed of having fresh coffee and pastries, then turned off the paved road. Three miles later we crossed into New Mexico.

The Land of Enchantment wasn't quite what I had been expecting. Of course, it was ridiculous to think that there would be an immediate change. The border between New Mexico and Colorado was typically American in its arbitrariness, following a straight line drawn on a map rather than geographical features on the ground. Yet it was the last state on our journey and its name confirmed its proximity to the finish. Accordingly, it had assumed such significance in our journey that I had been lulled into thinking we would immediately be surrounded by cacti and desert.

Instead, we continued to ride through some of the most beautiful semi-Alpine scenery of the whole trip. The brilliant sunshine and the azure sky provided a perfect backdrop for the bounty of wild flowers: dog roses, potentilla, dandelions, wild irises, Michaelmas daisies and geraniums, to name only those I could recognise. The forests that framed the meadows were made up of cottonwood trees, aspens, spruce and firs.

Even better than the immediate scenery was the fact that for almost the first time in the whole ride to date we were cycling along the top of the mountains rather than simply scaling passes between them. We rode for some 20 miles at more than 10,000 feet along Brazos Ridge. The panorama on all sides was spectacular.

The only problem was the exceptionally demanding terrain. It was punctuated by short, steep ups and downs. It was also incredibly rough going. When the trail wasn't among boulders it was stony and rutted. Progress uphill was juddering and tenuous. Progress downhill was juddering and dangerous. As usual, Stephen seemed unperturbed and recouped on the descents what he had lost on the uphills due to his sore knee. Per's rigid forks meant he was shaken, though not, he insisted, stirred.

The result was slow progress, with a knock-on effect on supplies. At midday it had taken five and a half hours to ride 40 miles. The only certain food was still 82 miles away. At the current rate of progress that would see us arriving at 11 p.m. Even Per's enthusiasm for Spam and jam was uncertain to last that long.

Shortly afterwards we were confronted with a reminder of the slenderness of our margin for error created by the decision to travel light. A large, profusely perspiring cycle tourist rode into view and hailed us heartily. It wasn't his size, however, that caused us to draw breath, though the effort he must have expended to haul his bulk to such an altitude was impressive enough. It was the size of his luggage. If he was large enough to make two of us, he had more stuff with him than the four of us combined. He had a full set of panniers to both front and rear, and a large rucksack. He also had a full bike trailer bouncing cumbersomely behind him. It was a heartening, if slightly disconcerting, sight.

'Hey, guys, how ya doin'?' he exclaimed, clearly pleased at a chance for a breather.

After exchanging pleasantries, we told him where we were heading; he said he was doing a similar thing in reverse.

'I'm just setting out to see how far I can get before winter,' he added.

At his self-proclaimed average of 30 miles a day, we calculated that he should arrive in Canada before the end of September. He seemed reassured. Then he broached the topic that had obviously been on all of our minds.

'How do you guys manage with such little stuff? Not tents and stuff, but food?'

It was, we admitted, a question we were beginning to ask ourselves. Then he asked about water. We carried about five litres each, which had so far been plenty.

'I carry more than two gallons,' he replied.

With all that extra weight to contend with, his presence at above 10,000 feet seemed nothing short of remarkable.

After a short spell so rocky that riding was impossible the terrain finally improved, first with five miles of paved roads, then with a dry, dusty forest trail. We rode through a succession of formal and informal campgrounds, full of locals celebrating their national holiday. The prerequisites for such a celebration were simple: beer, barbecues and quad bikes, though not, we hoped, in that order.

The first two ingredients were universal and understandable; the last a surprise and a growing annoyance. Far from being utilitarian tools for farmers, the quad bike had clearly become the latest must-have gadget for a patriotic, outdoorsy family. Around us, whole families indulged in quad bike safaris. Children not yet ten were let loose on machines that dwarfed them. Those younger still sat jauntily on mom or pop's knee.

You could see their appeal. When the enormous 4×4 pick-up that had been used to transport family and quad bike from the city to the mountains just couldn't go any further, they could now jump on their quads and desecrate (sorry, discover) vast new areas of erstwhile wilderness previously immune from the internal combustion engine. Why walk when you could quad bike?

'I see the 4th of July is actually national ride your quad bike day,' I said to Stephen.

He magnanimously agreed with this discourteous assessment.

The speed of our progress was increasing, but so was the temperature and the effort required. With only one round of Spam/jam sandwiches remaining, timing our last feed stop of the day would be crucial. At 3 p.m. we could wait no longer. A stray dog inadvertently herded us into a partial clearing in the forest, complete with shade to cool off in and logs to sit on. We were delighted. When he recognised the prospect of food and drink, so was the dog.

The poor mutt was clearly in a bad way: it was as desperate for Spam as we were. It was also covered in mange and was panting uncontrollably. It made a half-hearted effort to pester us before flopping exhausted to the ground.

'It doesn't look too good,' I said.

'There's not much we can do for it,' pointed out Per.

After a few minutes, a tell-tale buzzing noise alerted us to the impending arrival of yet another quad bike. It was do or die for the dog. I rushed to the road and flagged down the speeding machine. It was a young teenage couple. I explained about the dog.

'Aww, that's soo sad,' said the girl, looking in its direction.

The boy didn't look quite so moved.

'Do you know anyone who's lost a dog or can you take it with you?' I asked.

'Gee, we could ask when we get back to camp. Maybe someone could come back and pick it up,' she said, looking imploringly at her young beau.

'Maybe,' he replied, recognising the chance to at least temporarily avoid assuming responsibility for the situation.

It wasn't what the dog needed but it was the best we could think of.

After finishing our late lunch we embarked on a speedy descent that took us below the forests into dry scrubland that better conformed to my clichéd image of New Mexico. We were now below 8,000 feet and the temperature had continued to rise in proportion to the fall in altitude. We arrived in the picturesque Vallecitos River Valley at the hamlet of Cañon Plaza, the first of three settlements dating back to the late eighteenth century and the first Spanish colonisers in the area. It was far enough from anywhere to be rumoured to be entirely devoid of services, and I had tried in vain not to become too excited about the possibility of refreshments. Yet the map had offered one glimmer of hope to which I had clung disproportionately.

'Snack stand on left may be open.'

It wasn't. Nor was there anything on offer in the neighbouring hamlet of Vallecitos, which was little more than a collection of farm buildings and unintentional scrapyards full of disused farm machinery and pick-up trucks. This paucity of services did not augur well for El Rito, where it was suggested we would find food and shelter for the night. Yet we were temporarily distracted from self-pity by the rigours of the climb that we had to scale to get there. It was not the gradient that was the problem. Once again, it was the ground conditions. This time, in an unfortunate twist on the fate of the Ancient Mariner, we were compelled to ride through a rim-deep ribbon of quagmire while the rest of the surrounding forest was covered in tinder-dry leaves. The forest road was a sort of compacted goo that clearly turned to goulash after the heavy rain we had heard they had suffered in the area yesterday.

'Dryness, dryness everywhere, but not a yard to ride upon,' I murmured to myself as I fought a losing battle to maintain momentum.

The crest of the hill was a long time coming, and the following downhill offered little in the way of respite due to the slipperiness of the conditions. Yet we had now been riding for more than 13 hours, and it was late enough to cause concern about shops and restaurants shutting up for the night (we still naively clung to the belief that there would be shops and restaurants). The result was something of a kamikaze downhill, survived due to good fortune rather than skill.

That was where the good fortune ended, however. No sooner had the path led out of the forest into the great sweep of plains around El Rito than it became clear it would have little to offer the passing traveller. In fact, that turned out to be an overstatement. It had nothing. Even the grounds of the high school where the map suggested we would be able to camp were locked. In New Mexico at least, the information on the map was indicative rather than definitive.

Waiting for the others to arrive, I came across the tail-end of the town's 4th of July celebrations, which seemed to consist of open house at the volunteer fire station. A man with arms crossed looked on proprietorially. I asked if he knew of anywhere to eat in the village. He shook his head. Then he decided to expand on his answer.

'There used to be a nice place, but the health inspector paid a visit and decided it wasn't quite as nice after all. Things got worse when the owner disagreed with the health inspector's assessment and tried to shoot him. Now he's not at liberty to provide any food, whether good or bad.'

I had to admit that this was a turn of events for which the map could not be blamed.

'Are you from Britain?' asked the man, whose name turned out to be Malcolm Morrison.

'That's right.'

'My grandmother was from Stornoway on Lewis,' he said.

'A lovely spot.'

'She didn't think so. Full of midges and rain. She had nothing good to say about it.'

I was saved from further embarrassment by the arrival of the others, to whom I explained the situation. They didn't need to say anything for their disappointment to be obvious. Malcolm decided to propose a solution.

'I don't know if they'll be open, it being 4th of July and all, but there's a pizza place and a bar at the junction with the main road. You could try there.'

The junction was on our intended route, but it was 14 miles away. It was 7.50 p.m.

'We might make it by 8.30 p.m., they could still be open,' said Trevor.

'Let's go,' said Per.

We had little choice. Even our Spam supplies had now expired. The road to the junction was all downhill. Freewheeling through the red-soiled scrubland under the setting sun should have been a delight. Racing against an invisible clock for the outside possibility of something to eat took the edge off it a little.

At the junction, the pizzeria was closed. Trevor tried the bar. Three weeks of wearing Lycra in peculiar places had inured us to the occasional snide comment, but the latent hostility of the reaction as he walked in was palpable. Everybody stopped. Everybody stared.

'We done serving food,' said the barman.

Even in our hour of need, it was something of a relief.

'Let's go,' I said quickly.

Trevor didn't move. Taking what I hoped was the calculated risk of prolonging our stay, he then asked if there was anywhere else nearby. The silence seemed interminable.

'The Abiquiu Inn is a couple a miles up the road. They serve 'til quarter to nine.'

'Could you phone them to let them know we're coming?' asked Trevor.

'Nope. They'd just tell me to tell you not to bother,' said the barman.

It was the excuse I had been waiting for. Being nearest the door, I was first on the bike. It was now 8.33 p.m. We had 12 minutes. If it was only two miles we might be OK, I reasoned. I rode the bike like a man whose dinner depended on it, which was just as well. A precious minute was wasted exploring a derelict building with a B&B sign outside. It clearly wasn't an inn but, in desperation, anything seemed possible. Then the Inn appeared. At 8.40 p.m. precisely, I jumped off my bike and ran inside.

'Are . . . you . . . still . . . serving . . . food . . . ?' I panted.

The receptionist looked at the clock. Then she looked at me. I was not, I realised, a pretty sight. Dried mud and dead mosquitoes were fighting for space on my face and three-week beard. Perspiration ran in rivulets down my cheeks and dripped off my nose. The benefits of yesterday's laundry on the cleanliness of my cycling top had long since worn off. I tried a smile. To my surprise it seemed to work.

'Of course, sir, is it a table just for one?' she said, looking for all the world as if the arrival of a nearly hyperventilating cyclist was a daily occurrence.

'No . . . there . . . are . . . three . . . more . . . coming . . .'

This time there was not even a hint of hesitation.

'That's fine, sir. The waiter will be through to take you to your table shortly.'

'Thank . . . you . . .'

'You're welcome.'

After slowly regaining my composure and discovering that the inn also had one room remaining for the night, I stumbled back to the entrance to wait for the others. As I did so, it became clear this was far from your average roadside diner. In fact, it was a rather chic, almost boutique, hotel. The interior was elegantly whitewashed and adorned with Spanish and Native American artefacts. The tiled floor was artfully covered in a series of pristine rugs. Outside was a courtyard with a well-kept Hispanic garden.

The others arrived and we were shown through to the dining room. We tried hard not to disturb the two couples enjoying their 4th of July dinner in an atmosphere of studied romanticism. It was in vain.

The menu perplexed us with its temerity to deviate from the habitual fast food offerings.

'What, no Spam?' said Per.

Yet the food, once we had deciphered what was on offer, was delicious. I enjoyed tomato tortilla soup followed by a lamb kofta kebab with extra fries. The others were similarly extravagant. The coup de grâce, though, was the dessert: bread pudding with caramel sauce; and ice cream; and cream.

....

CHAPTER 27

THROUGH THE RAINBOW

DAY 24

Not surprisingly, I slept terribly.

'I scarcely slept at all,' I said loudly, just in case anybody had failed to notice my constant tossing and turning on the cold, tiled floor; the room had only one bed, and I had nobly volunteered to sacrifice comfort for some guarantee of uninvaded personal space.

'Not as badly as Stephen,' said Trevor.

'What do you mean?'

'You didn't hear him?'

'Didn't hear what? And where is he?'

'I thought you said you'd been awake all night?'

Just then, a disturbing retching noise emanated from the bathroom. Shortly after, an ashen-faced Stephen appeared. He had, it turned out, already been through a similar routine at 4 a.m. Yet he still professed some hope of being able to continue. He joined us for breakfast before we set off. It was a bad move.

Two miles down the road we stopped at Bode's store to restock for the day ahead. Cuba, the next town, was 80 miles away, and we didn't want to repeat yesterday's mistake. Trevor, Per and I went inside to acquaint ourselves with what was on offer. Stephen stayed outside and reacquainted himself with his breakfast. It looked considerably less appetising second time around.

We cleaned away the evidence as best we could. The process was disconcertingly reminiscent of sickness bugs at home, though Stephen had the great merit of being able to hold his own bucket and not cry incessantly for his mummy. But it was clear Stephen was not going any further, not today at least.

Fortunately, the owner of the store was sympathy personified, in spite of the fact this was not the first time a worn-out cyclist had vomited profusely on his forecourt.

'I had a girl here last year who had exactly the same thing happen to her. I had to take her to hospital in the end,' he said cheerily.

He offered Stephen the use of his sheltered veranda until he was feeling well enough to decide what he would do. He also offered to find a lift to take him to a doctor if that turned out to be necessary. There seemed nothing else the three of us could do. We had little option but to say goodbye.

'I'll stay here, maybe see if I'm better tomorrow,' said Stephen, manfully endeavouring to ease our departure.

'It might be for the best. Your knee might improve after a day's rest,' I suggested.

The sentiment was well intentioned, but the words rang hollow.

We left, and immediately embarked on a 30-mile climb. There were, in fact, a few minor descents between Abiquiu and the high-point of the Polvadera mesa, but we were in no mood to quibble. The ascent and the heat of a gloriously sunny day helped focus our minds on the task in hand rather than Stephen's misfortune.

The scenery was every bit as beautiful as yesterday's. The terrain every bit as rough. It came as something of a surprise, therefore, after two hours of riding into the middle of nowhere, to encounter a pick-up truck with an ancient caravan bobbing painfully along behind it. Even more surprising was the presence, on the open platform of the pick-up, of two young children sat happily in deck chairs. There was no obvious means of restraining either chairs or children.

We slowed to let the pick-up past, then stopped to check the directions. It read as we thought: 'swing right up steep and rocky climb, might be a pusher'.

'It can't be that bad, then,' said Trevor, motioning in the direction of the truck.

It was worse. We could not ride up it, yet somehow the caravan and pick-up with free-range children in the back had come down it.

'One of life's little mysteries,' said Trevor.

'Maybe we were hallucinating,' I suggested.

'All three of us?' asked Per.

At the top of the climb we stopped for another luxurious lunch of tortillas and salami. Our enjoyment was spoiled, however, by the arrival of a thunderstorm. Initially it seemed like it would merely be on a par with that experienced on Marshall Pass. Then it entered a league of its own as it started to hail. Lycra, we quickly discovered, proved an ineffectual defence against such an assault.

For 15 minutes the hail came and went, turning us into caricatures of plague victims with red weals on exposed flesh. Eventually we rode through the storm into clear skies.

'That was nice,' said Trevor.

'I hate New Mexico,' said Per enthusiastically, almost seeming to relish the disaffection.

Next came what we had anticipated would be one of the highlights of the trip. We were about to cycle through the location of this year's Rainbow Gathering, a peripatetic annual reunion of 'The Rainbow Family of Living Light' or the 'Rainbow Tribe' – otherwise known as hippies.

The first inkling of its proximity was the presence of an abandoned car with Connecticut licence plates lying at a jaunty angle across the road in the middle of the forest. On the back seat was a motley selection of beer and foodstuffs as well as that classic hippie giveaway: tie-dyed clothing.

'Gone for gas,' read a hand-scrawled sign in the windscreen.

Then came two guitar-toting teenagers who, in between a bewildering intensity of expressions like 'wow, man' and 'cool, man', asked if they were heading the right way to find the brothers. We assumed they meant the Gathering, rather than an unlikely offshoot of a religious order, and said that as we'd not yet passed them we assumed they were still ahead.

'Wow, man. Cool, man.'

Then they remembered their manners.

'Thanks, man.'

A couple of miles further on it became apparent the Gathering, a kind of Woodstock without the music, was near at hand. Instead of music, the focal point was a prayer for peace and a variety of activities designed to engender such hippy ideals as peace, love, freedom and harmony. It sounded great. Even better, a very encouraging report of an earlier Tour Divide encounter with the event had been posted on the race website.

'Expect to see somewhere around 15–20 THOUSAND naked hippies jammin' out in drum circles. Family members suggest that you should bring some "shiny rocks" for bartering items such as food, drinks, etc . . .'

Alas, reality did not match expectation. Such nourishment as was on offer held less appeal than yesterday's Spam, and nudity was noticeable only by its absence. This was probably a good thing. It was far from certain our sense of purpose could have resisted such siren charms. Indeed, there were few people at all, scantily clad or otherwise.

All we got instead was cars. And more cars. In fact, there were thousands of them, parked gaily on the verges. Those parked with gayest abandon were those you might most typically associate with hippies: ageing Volvos, bashed up VWs, converted school buses in psychedelic colours. Some gave the distinct impression they had found their final resting place in this particular patch of New Mexico forest.

Yet those parked with more circumspection betrayed the presence of a new breed of hippie. In fact, the roadside car park was dominated by an eye-watering fleet of expensive pick-ups and 4×4s that would not have looked out of place at a reunion of accountants. Or of 'hockey-moms'. Or both.

'Hippies just aren't the same as they used to be,' sighed Trevor.

The theme of vehicular excess continued once we were past the main concentration of the hippy camp. While all around me were celebrating freedom, the freedom I had experienced over the past three and a half weeks to cycle happily, day after day, without encountering a car, had been sorely curtailed. I began to feel a most unhippy-like rage coming to the boil. The pleasure of an undulating descent was being denied me by a trail of cars and pick-ups.

Eventually, I could stand the cloud of dust and exhaust fumes being belched in front of me no longer. Ahead was a queue of four vehicles behind a clapped-out saloon pulling a caravan far bigger than its engine capacity could manage. I resorted to the guerrilla tactics of an erstwhile London cycling commuter. Building my momentum nicely, I capitalised on one short descent to make it past the first two cars. Then I despatched the next two in similar fashion. The mask of determination I was now wearing did little to endear me to the chilled-out dudes in the back of each pick-up. But all that remained was the caravan. Suddenly I felt like Jeremy Clarkson, the only other person who could possibly suffer road rage in such an ostensibly tranquil setting.

'Get this heap of junk off the road,' I muttered.

Then I saw my chance. Throwing caution to the wind, I dived down the inside of a corner, narrowly avoided becoming the meat in a caravan-and-tree sandwich, and surged triumphant into the lead.

'Yeeha!' I hollered, to no one in particular. 'Take your stinking, cumbersome icons of consumerism and stick 'em up your peace pipe. I'm freeeeeee!'

Then I came to a hill. And another. And another. After three desperate attempts to retain my hard-won liberty I was compelled to accept the reality of a pyrrhic victory. Topography was against me. No amount of bravado and belligerence could compensate for a lack of horsepower. Even the spluttering, puttering, caravan-towing saloon soon overtook me, followed by a succession of pick-ups with noisome V8 engines. My freedom to obstruct and weave was as nothing compared to their freedom to accelerate uphill.

In the end I found inner peace by stopping for a chocolate bar. I sat and made unreciprocated peace signs at passing motorists.

The traffic thinned and Trevor and Per arrived. At the edge of the forest we enjoyed a rip-roaring, 10-mile, paved descent into the town of Cuba. In homage to Stephen's phenomenal downhill skills, I used Per's considerable frame as a windshield, then sling-shotted past him in an attempt to establish a new Tour Divide speed record. I passed a '40 mph' sign at 41.5 mph, still some way short of Stephen's best of 46 mph. I redoubled my efforts. Then I rounded a bend to find myself staring into the barrel of a policeman's gun. Fortunately it was a speed gun. Unfortunately, it was too late to slow down. I smiled instead. It had worked with the receptionist at the Abiquiu Inn. The police officer didn't move. I continued on my merry way. A couple of minutes passed. There were no sirens or flashing lights. I began to breathe more easily. The prospect of being hauled over by the local version of Sheriff J.D. Hogg from *The Dukes of Hazzard* was not something to be entertained lightly.

Like Rawlins, Cuba – pronounced 'Cooba' – was a town with a reputation. The guidebook said that as recently as the early 1900s, travellers were advised against being caught overnight there. The sign by the gas station door suggested it had not reformed quite as much as might have been hoped.

> FREE!
> Ride in a SHERIFF'S CAR if you shoplift from this store.
> Compliments of:
> Sheriff John Paul Trujillo and Undersheriff Tim Lucero
> Sandoval County Sheriff's Office.

I wondered if the local shoplifters knew the sheriffs were out catching speeding hippies.

It was only 6 p.m. but, in spite of Cuba's questionable charms, we decided to stop. We found the last room in a scruffy motel next to a scruffy diner. In order to make the most of our early finish we ordered food immediately. It was a good decision. Within minutes, the whole place was heaving with ravenous refugees from the Rainbow Gathering. Most seemed not to have eaten for a week; many seemed to have forgotten the purpose of tables and chairs. Unsurprisingly, chaos ensued, especially when the deleterious impact of the holiday weekend on the restaurant's supplies became evident.

The influx was not entirely a bad thing, however. Not only did our outlandish cycling attire now seem less incongruous. For the first time in three and a half weeks the dubious accolade of 'smelliest people in the room' could be awarded to someone else.

LOSING MY INNOCENCE IN WALMART

DAY 25

It was time to face up to the reality of our situation. There was still just over 500 miles to go until the finish, but we only had four days left to ensure we made it in time for Per's flight. The prospect of 125-mile days was no longer daunting in itself, but clearly some days were more suited to covering greater distances than others. The important thing was to know which.

According to the profile on the map, which we had pored over at length after last night's dinner and which we assumed couldn't be as erroneous as the information it provided about shops and diners, the next 200 miles would make for good going. The next 160 miles in particular looked promising, as we intended to exploit one of the few rules of the race that allowed us to follow a paved alternative to the main route. Thereafter we would be confronted with 180 miles through the Gila National Forest that had a profile bearing a depressing resemblance to a saw blade, and a reputation to match.

'Exceptionally steep and rugged mountains, where each steep descent is followed by an equally steep climb,' said the map, which for once we were quite happy to believe.

It sounded no place to be trying to make up time. Now, we concluded, was the moment to make a move. Accordingly, we boldly decided to ignore the off-site continuation of the Rainbow Gathering in the motel's neighbouring rooms and retired early in anticipation of a pre-dawn start. We surfaced at 4 a.m., even without the benefit of Stephen's errant mobile phone, and were underway within the hour.

It was a good decision, if only for the first, glorious hour spent riding on a deserted road through a deserted desert in the silvery twilight of a setting moon. Gradually, almost imperceptibly, silver turned to gold as the influence of the moon succumbed to the power of the rising sun. Mesas and buttes, great eruptions of rock from the surrounding plain, were first framed darkly against the horizon, then bathed in blazing light.

By 6 a.m. the sun was fully fledged. By 7 a.m. it had dispelled the morning chill and replaced it with burgeoning heat. We had already covered nearly 30 miles, and the route ahead was appealingly flat, but it was set to be a long day.

Entertainment was provided by the local wildlife. Or rather, we provided the local wildlife with some unintentional entertainment. The fact that the pack of feral dogs that decided to interpret our strange presence in their territory as a catalyst to regress to traditional hunting patterns were nominally domesticated was of little relevance. They certainly behaved like wild animals.

First to run the gauntlet was Per. He had the distinct disadvantage of having set the pace for the morning, the result of which was that he was caught unawares by the dastardly dog ambush. Trevor and I at least had the benefit of being forewarned.

Not that such preparation made it possible to avoid the confrontation. The best that could be hoped for was to encounter it on our own terms. Benefiting from the distraction provided by Trevor, I gathered momentum down a short hill and sprinted past the dogs' lair. Even though they had recently given up on Trevor, they were more than willing to try their luck on me. A dozen or so of the foulest, meanest, mangiest mutts ever to have disgraced a dog kennel came tearing down the verge in hot pursuit. Even the most vicious and ill-treated Yorkshire sheepdogs, with their seemingly inbred taste for cyclists' calves, had nothing on these apocalyptic fiends.

I now had the certain knowledge of what it felt like to be an elk pursued by wolves. Fortunately, I had also seen enough David

Attenborough natural history programmes to realise that they were likely to lose interest after a while, so I ploughed on. It was difficult to resist the temptation to unclip a foot and fend off the bravest of the hounds, but cycling uphill precluded such pre-emptive action. What's more, as they seemed to have forgotten the art of felling their prey before trying to devour it, I decided it would be wise not to remind them. Eventually my endurance told and I emerged unscathed.

Per and Trevor had wisely continued to make good their escape. We reconvened some miles later at a gas station with a grocery store. It was something of a relief, not only because of the opportunity it afforded to relive our canine capers.

'Nice dogs,' said Per.

'Lovely,' I agreed.

'They liked me so much they tried to eat me,' added Trevor.

We were also keen to replenish our drinking supplies. The sun was now high in the sky and shelter was a redundant concept in this barren, treeless land. The map had already promised one gas station (which turned out to be abandoned) and two stores, one that turned out to be a gas station without a shop and one store that had in fact been a Laundromat.

'A Laundromat? In the middle of the desert? Why?' I asked, though I knew there was no likelihood of an answer.

Even more inexplicable had been the presence at the side of the road of four churches, roughly double the number of houses we had seen. Apart from the distinct smell of sulphur that we had encountered an hour or so previously, there seemed nothing to justify the existence of one church, let alone four. Yet four there were, all with suitably inspiring names: The Rock Springs Holiness Mission; the Angel Food Ministries; the Tinion Baptist Church; and last, but far from least, God's Mighty Warriors Church. The free market in religion was obviously thriving. Or maybe the souls of local dog owners needed a lot of rescuing. There was even the North Fork Baptist Church Memorial Gardens, though evidence of a garden was somewhat thin on the ground. Either that or the gardeners were intent on cultivating the types of plants that grew in the surrounding desert. In which case it was a great success.

The sun continued to blaze in the sky. The temperatures continued to rise. We continued to pedal.

Four parched hours later, and 116 miles since Cuba, we arrived in Milan. Not the cultural and consumer capital of Italy but, judging by the presence of four well-drilling and welding company workshops and very little else, the small-scale engineering capital of this inhospitable corner of New Mexico. There was also a Cross Roads Motel, the appeal of which was lost on Trevor and Per.

Not in immediate need of having anything welded or any wells drilled, we continued to the neighbouring town of Grants, the charms of which we hoped would be more considerable. Things started brightly enough as we turned onto Route 66, America's most famous road and an essential element on any road trip such as ours. That was as good as it got, however.

The most flattering way to describe the rest of our experience of Grants would be 'unpleasant'. Downright miserable would be closer to the mark. Even the guidebook was less than effusive. After describing a past predicated on periodic mineral exploitation that had once earned it the slightly dubious title of 'Uranium capital of the world', it added: 'Today, as residents await the next boom, Grants plugs along as a service town, selling meals and motel rooms to travellers on Interstate 40.'

Even selling decent meals seemed to be beyond it, however. The sole virtue of the charmless concrete block dressed up as a Pizza Hut was that it had air conditioning. This more or less made up for the inability to serve pizzas that bore any resemblance to our order. Or even to food, unless pizzas were supposed to resemble the box in which they were dispatched to takeaway customers. The waitress, whose pained facial expression revealed that she had obviously had to suffer life in Grants far longer than we had, had no need to spell out that it was futile complaining.

After what passed for lunch, and with there being no evidence of any other grocery stores in town, our next port of call was Walmart.

'My first ever Walmart,' I announced.

'Me too,' said Per.

'Then we're all Walmart virgins,' said Trevor.

Unlike sex, however, it was not an experience you would wish to repeat. The expertly sycophantic 'greeter' on the door was the antithesis of the genuine hospitality experienced so far on the trip that had done so much to rid me of my European cynicism.

'Hello, hello, come in, come in, welcome, welcome.'

Clearly, everything had to be repeated twice for emphasis. Having been lulled over the past four weeks into dispensing with my native instinct to ignore such behaviour, I returned the greeting. It was a mistake. The pitiful wretch grasped both my hands and said she'd always wanted to shake hands with an Englishman; her eyes suggested sincerity, but it was sincerity bought at the minimum wage. It was nauseating.

Instead of being sick, however, I had a nosebleed. Maybe it was all the adulation. More likely it was the dry air. I managed to avoid despoiling the store, but only through the expedient of bleeding into my cycling top. It seemed to make little difference to my already unappealing appearance.

Inside, the choice was overwhelming, and any useful provisions that could be found invariably came in multipacks. Even in my thirsty state I realised I would struggle to consume six cans of Coke, though I bought them anyway. It was not a place to linger, but the soaring afternoon temperature deterred us from leaving. Eventually our role of novelty attraction for passing gang members circling the car park in their pimped-up rides lost its appeal. The New Mexico furnace seemed the lesser of two evils.

As we left town, we rode over the railway tracks, though which side was the wrong side was not evident.

'Did you see that guy scamming outside the store?' asked Trevor.

'You mean the guy doing the competition?'

'That's what he was saying.'

I'd noticed someone purporting to offer the chance to win an exotic holiday. I'd also noticed the practised ease of his patter, targeted exclusively at attractive young women ('You have two choices, you just have to tell me where you'd like to go, Acapulco or Paris? I bet you're a Paris woman. I'm right? You'd go to Paris? Oh, that's where I'd choose myself, it would be so romantic. I've never been lucky enough to have the chance to go like you, but I'm told it's beautiful. Would you take your husband? You're not married? I can't believe someone hasn't fallen for you yet . . .').

'They could only enter "the competition" by providing their bank details,' Trevor explained.

The good news was that we were leaving all this behind us. The bad news was that we were riding into El Malpais – the badlands. Not just any old badlands either. The area had been awarded its own special accolade. This was the El Malpais National Monument.

Fortunately, the lands were only bad if you wanted to farm or live there. As cycling terrain went, they were pretty much perfect. Once the heat of the day finally began to wane we were able to admire the stunning scenery caused by an ancient volcanic eruption. To our left was an abrupt escarpment turned a thousand hues of red by the lowering sun. At least 10 miles long, the otherwise impenetrable wall was temporarily breached by a vast, natural arch, the proportions of which dwarfed the greatest cathedrals. To our right, the lava flowed horizontally across a broad valley clad only in the sparsest, hardiest shrubs.

Eventually the structure of the valley was lost as the cliffs to either side diverged and we rode into another broad plain. We were now in ranch land, though the absence of any cattle confirmed the impression that this was still unforgiving terrain.

It was past 8 p.m. and our increasingly southern latitude meant the sun was setting fast. We had left Grants with no particular plan, which had been peculiarly liberating. There were no towns or campsites for another 70 miles, a distance that we knew was beyond us. Instead we simply intended to pitch our tents at a suitable spot at a suitable time. That time had now come.

We rode off the paved surface and began another long section of dirt road. After two miles, with no change in the topography likely, we decided to call it a day. We had ridden 165 miles.

'That's further than I've ever ridden in a day before.'

'Me too,' said Per.

'And me,' said Trevor.

Perhaps we were beginning to pass muster as cyclists.

The sagebrush and grasses were sufficiently sparse to make it easy to pitch our tent on the sandy soil at the side of the road. I looked for a piece of wood with which to sweep the ground, Ray Mears-style, and deter arachnids and insects.

'Don't worry. They'll get me first,' Per said pointedly, unfurling his bivvy bag.

Day turned swiftly to night. To the west was the setting sun. To the east, silhouetting the now distant escarpment, rose a full moon. For the first time, New Mexico was living up to its nickname. It was, for now at least, a land of enchantment.

CHAPTER 29

....

PIE TOWN

DAY 26

With not enough candlepower to be able to ride the desert trails in the dark, we let ourselves enjoy the natural pleasure of waking up to the dawn, Per having survived the night unmolested. The sun and moon had swapped roles and places, the sun now rising to the east as the moon set in the west. Under an achingly clear sky it was scarcely above freezing, yet it was already destined to be another hot day.

Breakfast was a perfunctory affair. It mattered not. Thirty miles away lay the glittering oasis of Pie Town, where such luxuries as a cooked breakfast and, we hoped, pie, lay waiting.

Actually, glittering oasis was something of an overstatement. The 'town' part of Pie Town was another misnomer. It boasted, according to its own website, little more than a few far-flung dwellings, and the essential services of a post office and a chiropractor; living in New Mexico was, we all agreed, back-breaking work. But there were also two 'world famous' cafés specialising in pies. 'Home Cooking on the Great Divide', as the town's resident marketing gurus put it.

In fact, it was the pie specialisation of Texan immigrant and World War One veteran Clyde Norman in the 1920s that earned the town its name. Capitalising on the designation of the town's US Highway 60 as a transcontinental route, his well-advertised wares came to symbolise the town itself. The association was then formalised by the US Postal Service, arbiter of all habitation nomenclature in the US, and a town was born.

When we arrived, the choice of cafés was reduced by 50 per cent. It was Tuesday, so the Pie-O-Neer Café was closed. That left the Daily Pie, which was welcoming and warm and suffused by the smell of freshly baked pies. It was, in fact, a wonderful place.

On a white board behind the counter was drawn 'the world's only true pie chart'. There were actually three pie charts, each detailing some of the delicacies to hand.

The largest was 'Standard Flavors': Apple; New Mexico Apple (with added chilli pepper and piñon); Peanut Butter; and Key Lime Cheesecake, all for $3.99 per slice.

Then came 'Primo Flavours': Cherry; Peach; Blueberry; Coconut Crème; Blackberry; and Vanilla Crème, slightly dearer at $4.75 per slice.

Finally there were 'Pielets': Piñon and Pecan for the princely sum of $3.00 each.

There was also a slightly alarming injunction to 'please order pies with a 48-hour notice', though the array under the counter suggested this wouldn't be necessary for hungry passing cyclists.

Perversely, in spite of all these pie riches, we ordered cooked breakfasts. I chose sausages, bacon, scrambled eggs, toast and pancakes. All together – I had succumbed at last.

'When in Rome,' I said quietly to myself as I watched Trevor pour maple syrup on his pancakes and his bacon.

We also had coffee, which came in mugs outlining the café's unique pricing plan: 'One cup $1.50; one hour $2.00; half day $2.50; full day $5.00 and keep the cup ($4.50 if you go home for lunch). Finger snappers and spoon knockers all pay double.'

Clearly, neither Pie Town nor the Daily Pie Café were places for the impatient.

It was catching. Although we were keen to finish, we had by now become sufficiently confident about what lay ahead to enjoy the relaxation. Indeed, yesterday's record mileage meant for the first time since Banff we had dared to let ourselves think of how close we now were to our goal. By the end of the next day we should be in Silver City. Although that was not the finish, there remained just 120 more or less flat miles until Antelope Wells, 80 of which were on paved roads. In any other circumstances it would have seemed a considerable challenge. Now it seemed a walk in the park.

It also seemed we were not the only people thinking about our imminent arrival at the finish. Midway through breakfast I returned from the bathroom to find Per wearing a gnomic smile.

'What's up?' I asked.

'I've just had a nice conversation with your wife.'

Thanks to the wonders of modern technology through our SPOT tracker, and in spite of the fact that I hadn't spoken to her since Sargents, Catherine had not only been able to ascertain our precise location but then to find the phone number of the Daily Pie Café as well. And I had chosen that precise moment to answer a call of nature.

'Would you like to use the phone to ring her back?' offered the woman behind the bar, sensing my disappointment.

'Well, if you don't mind. I have a phone card so it shouldn't cost anything.'

'Oh, don't worry about that.'

The reason behind Catherine's call was an offer from her cousin Steve, he of the 'rather remarkable reach', to help extricate us from Antelope Wells, or 'that shit hole in the desert' as he picturesquely described it. Per and Trevor looked suitably impressed when I told them he might be able to re-route a truck off Interstate 40 to collect us and deliver us straight to Phoenix for our return flights. I said I would ring him when we arrived in Silver City. I also told them that Stephen was officially out of the race. He had called from Albuquerque saying neither his stomach nor his knee was sufficiently remedied for him to consider riding any further, though his intestines had subsequently been restored to full working order.

It was with high spirits, therefore, that we eventually summoned the motivation to leave the Daily Pie. It was also with a slice of pie 'to go'. It seemed impossible to leave without any. It had also seemed impossible to choose from the myriad varieties, so I didn't. I defied my three and a half decades spent learning that, in terms of culinary experience, less is more, and selected 'mixed berry' pie. It contained the unlikely combination of apple, blackberry, blueberry and strawberry. It was delicious.

For the next couple of hours our journey was as nice as the pie. It was mainly spent riding on undulating, hard-packed dirt and gravel roads through stands of piñon and juniper trees. We passed the occasional ranch, as well as signs offering land for sale: 'Big Parcels: contact Pie Town realty'. The American homesteading dream was still alive and well; there could hardly have been a better location than Pie Town for getting away from it all and demonstrating your self-reliance.

We were also passing through another slice – excuse the pun – of the history of the exploitation of the West. This was the land once covered by cowboys and their herds on the Beefsteak Trail that brought animals from grazing lands in New Mexico and Arizona to the railhead at the town of Magdalena, a few dozen miles to the north-east. The Beefsteak Trail was the last regularly used major cattle drive in the country, surviving right up until the 1950s. At its height, in 1919, more than 20,000 cattle and 150,000 sheep passed along it in one season.

After three hours of increasing heat and decreasing shade we began to know how the cowboys felt. Or perhaps the cows. A long descent from Continental Divide crossing number twenty-three (only six more remained) brought us to a particularly desolate spot.

We were at the crossroads with State Highway 12. The by-now anticipated absence of the promised gas station, the last chance to restock for nearly 120 miles, was but a minor frustration. Of far greater concern was what lay ahead: the Plains of San Agustin.

A former lake bed, now long since desiccated, the pan-flat plains extended more than 50 miles from north-east to south-west and were up to 15 miles wide. Vegetation was conspicuous only by its absence. There were no trees. There was no shade. Even the sage scrub of the Great Divide Basin had been beaten into submission by the sun's brutality. All that replaced it were reluctant clumps of grass that clearly demanded a lot of personal space, such was their distance from their neighbours.

It was featureless and terrifying. What San Agustin, or Saint Augustine for that matter, had done to deserve the association could only be guessed at. Nothing could have been better designed to deter a roaming Yorkshireman. For the first time since the lonely forests of Montana, my presence here seemed questionable. And, frankly, ludicrous. Riding out into such inhospitable terrain at 2 p.m. seemed utter folly.

Still, there was little point in getting cold feet now. Not that cold feet was likely to be a problem. Under a white-blue sky and an armada of clouds like those seen in documentaries of African droughts – full of unfulfilled promises – we rode forth. This was *The Good, The Bad and The Ugly* territory, though which roles we might each assume remained to be seen. At least there was no pot of gold for us to fight over.

The heat bore down on us like a drill. Brows sweated, eyes stung, mouths parched. Yet the sense of desolation was so great as to be seductive. I stopped to try and capture it in a photograph. Then I noticed a peculiar, blowsy, white flower that had a prickly stem. It was, it seemed, half thistle and half poppy.

'Pistle, or thoppy?' I wondered to myself, Per and Trevor having wisely continued.

Thoppy, I concluded, sounded better. 'Howard's Thoppy' sounded better still. I bent over to record my discovery (or conceit, if you prefer) for posterity, and immediately regretted it. Somehow, even though I was no longer actually riding my bike, I managed to fall off it. Or fall over it might have been more accurate. Either way, I sprawled miserably onto the dusty ground, looking round for somebody to blame like a five year old who has just tripped over his own feet. There was no one. Vultures circled, if not above my head then certainly in it.

The blow to my pride and the damage to my left shin, in which was imprinted a mirror image of my front chain ring, coloured with oil and oozing blood, was nothing, however, compared with the blow to my supplies. I had left my snack pack open and had now lost most of my supply of Skittles. With an appetite that was finally beginning to wane due to the past few days of heat, the loss of such sweet, easily digestible calories was verging on a disaster.

In a fit of pique, I grabbed the bike and made to ride off as quickly as possible. That, too, was a mistake. Impatience caused me to miss the pedal, as a result of which I only narrowly missed castrating myself on the cross bar. I then overcompensated and, for the second time in as many minutes, fell off, or rather over, the bike while not actually riding it. The remainder of my Skittles disappeared into the dust at my feet. I nearly cried.

I rejoined Per and Trevor just as the route turned away from the plains at last and into La Jolla Canyon. A few miles later and we were once again riding through the shade of trees. Under one particularly fine example of a Ponderosa Pine we called a halt. It was siesta time. Before attempting to doze, I unpacked my bags in search of food as appetising as Skittles. I found none. I did, however, find the still pristine shirt I had purchased in Steamboat Springs. It would have proved ideal for the past two hours. Now it served equally well as a pillow. It was 4 p.m.

The rest was fantastic, but it was, by normal siesta standards, shortlived. Less than two hours later we resumed our trek. Per, clearly benefiting from his rest and the slight waning of the sun's power, set a fearsome pace. We sped through delightful open forest below rugged, rocky peaks. We saw one, then two, then thirty head of elk, both cows and calves. Then the forest gave way to the broad, grassy valley of the imaginatively named O-Bar-O Canyon. The isolation was splendid. White butterflies flocked around us like an incongruous snow flurry. As dusk descended, last night's beguiling courting between moon and sun resumed. We pitched camp for what we hoped would be the last time on the entire ride.

....

GERONIMO!

DAY 27

It was something of a incident-packed night.

The first disturbance was a rather alarming dream about Johnny Cash. Before we pitched camp I had pointed out to Trevor and Per that the Man in Black had first been arrested for possession of amphetamines in El Paso, which wasn't a million miles away. Cycling, after all, has something of a long and rather chequered association with such artificial stimulants.

Now, in the middle of the night, I was riding a bike that magically grew into a tandem to accommodate Cash himself, who had appeared, somewhat flustered, carrying a concealed package. As sweaty as if he were in the middle of a live performance, he urged me to pedal faster and faster.

Obligingly I turned forward to redouble my efforts, only to find we were not alone. Sandra Bullock was miraculously seated alongside me, the bike having become a sort of tandem rickshaw, though the exact design remained unclear. At first I was delighted to find I had such a charming travelling companion. It soon became clear, however, that Sandra was here on business rather than pleasure. She kept motioning to my bicycle computer and saying 'Speed! Speed!'

I responded by saying 'Yes! Yes! And it also tells me how many calories I've consumed', which was in fact a lie but I was keen to make an impression. But Sandra was unmoved.

'It's Johnny.'

Beguiled, I'd forgotten he was even with us.

'If we don't keep above 15 mph all the way to the Mexico border he'll explode.'

I woke up in a cold sweat. There was a lot I would be prepared to do for Miss Bullock, but this seemed too much. Even Per hadn't been quite so demanding, though as far as I knew he wasn't carrying a small explosive device.

I had scarcely recovered from this disconcerting interruption when I found myself aware of another peculiar intruder into my subconscious. This time it was not Johnny Cash. Instead, it was a loud, haunting howl that came, if not from inside my tent, then from very near to it. I dismissed it as another dream, only to realise that I was already awake.

Apprehension began to mount. Then, belatedly, it crossed my mind that it wasn't me the coyote-wolf-monster-whatever-it-was would be interested in but Per. I pricked up my ears and listened for anything that suggested he was being mauled but there was only silence. I would like to be able to say that I then got out of my tent to reassure myself of Per's continued safety and that we weren't surrounded by a pack of the hungry Mexican wolves that had just been reintroduced to New Mexico from over the border and which had already established themselves in the Gila. But I didn't. I simply fell straight back to sleep.

The next disturbance was equally unwelcome, yet more expected. It was the alarm clock, which meant it was 4.30 a.m. and time to rise. There was no evidence of our howling companion, and Per was, again, still intact.

'Did you see what it was?' I asked.

'No,' he said.

In fact he seemed more pleased that he'd managed to go back to sleep afterwards than that he'd not been the victim of a midnight feast in the first place.

'I heard it, then nothing happened, and the next thing I knew was being woken again by your alarm.'

Our first port of call was Beaverhead Work Centre, 10 miles away. We didn't know what a Work Centre was but, as even the regularly over-optimistic map didn't predict any services, our expectations weren't high. First impressions suggested we were right to have been cautious. There was a collection of utilitarian buildings that seemed designed to provide facilities for forest service employees, as well as what appeared to be a visitor information point.

There was also an interpretive sign detailing the links between the surrounding area and one of its most famous inhabitants, the great Apache war chief Geronimo. He had been born nearby and, along with other leaders such as Cochise and Mangas Colorado, had regularly sought refuge in these hills during his long-running guerrilla campaign against encroaching settlers and the US and Mexican armies. Nothing could have given a better indication of the inhospitable, chaotic nature of the terrain, and his ability to survive and even thrive here enhanced my own feelings of inadequacy. Until we found a fully-functioning, refrigerated drinks machine, that was.

'Aha. I bet Geronimo wouldn't have been able to figure out how to get hold of a nice cold can of Dr Pepper!' I exclaimed.

It turned out to be something of a struggle for us too. The machine said 'exact change only' and it required prolonged rummaging through bags and pockets for us each to find the requisite 80 cents. That none of us was particularly thirsty at such an early hour of the morning seemed beside the point.

After Beaverhead the terrain became even more challenging. Whereas the route had previously seemed to follow the path of least resistance, now it had decided, or been compelled, to traverse an incessant series of ridges between steep-sided drainage basins. The result was an arduous and seemingly endless series of ups and downs, neither of which offered any respite from the other due to the roughness and the gradients encountered. Every now and then the trail topped a rise and provided dramatic views of the tortured landscape. Even more dramatic were distant plumes of smoke.

'A forest fire?' I asked.

'Maybe,' said Trevor, once again demonstrating the sanguinity with which he had faced every obstacle on our journey thus far. It seemed unfair. He still had a much better beard than I did as well.

Then, 50 miles and more than six hours after we had started, we finally came to the long descent to the Mimbres River Valley and something approaching civilisation. Initially that civilisation seemed quite sinister, in spite of the delightful greenery of the valley itself, with large, handsome cottonwood and willow trees standing on the riverbanks. First came what appeared to be an arms race in the naming of the steep gorges feeding in to the main valley. 'Soldier Canyon' was followed by 'Big Gun Canyon' and then by 'Six-Shooter Canyon'. Reassuringly in the face of such bravado, a sign at the entrance to Big Gun Canyon said 'No Shooting'.

Less reassuring was the advert for the Gila Rangers, whoever they were: 'Live Cowboy Action Shooting. Every Second Saturday.'

To my mind, this could be read two ways, at least one of which was somewhat alarming. Was it the 'action shooting of live cowboys'? Or was it the more innocuous 'live, cowboy-action shooting'? It wasn't Saturday so we didn't have the opportunity to find out.

It was a relief, nevertheless, to find the store in Mimbres village considerably more hospitable. Indeed, Per and I were once again confronted with being minor celebrities due to the unmistakable 'foreignness' of our accents. Surprisingly, Per's origins were quickly determined. Mine took a little more time.

'Are you Australian?' asked the friendly woman behind the counter.

I explained that I wasn't.

'That's a shame. I don't like our new president too much and I was hoping to move to Australia but they said I was too old and too dumb,' she added before immediately descending with her two colleagues into gales of laughter.

I was in the middle of searching for the right combination of words to assure her that this surely wasn't the case when I was confronted by new evidence to the contrary.

'Do you know if Australia has a socialist economy?' she asked. 'It's just I know it has a queen and a parliament.'

I was, I sensed, treading on thin ice. I said I was pretty sure that having a queen and a parliament didn't mean it was necessarily socialist, and that as far as I was aware it had a fairly robust enthusiasm for the free market. I waited anxiously for the reaction. There was none, which was fine by me. Instead, conversation now turned to soft fruit.

'Would you like some peaches?' she said, pointing to the plump, ripe fruit that were filling a basket by the door and for which she had just been attempting to determine a price. We appeared to be about to eat her profit margin, but she was resolutely unconcerned. Whatever the merits of the assessment made by Australian immigration officials, lack of generosity was certainly not one of her failings.

With Silver City now only just over 20 miles away, we allowed ourselves the luxury of eating our peaches on the veranda. If there had been any activity to entertain us we could have said we were watching the world go by. As it was, the pace of life in Mimbres seemed to be on a par with that in Pie Town.

After one last, unpaved climb past the abandoned settlement of Georgetown, and another disturbingly vast copper mine, we reached US Highway 180. This was the main road into Silver City, a town that had become so closely associated in our minds with the end of the ride that it could not have been more keenly anticipated had it been called El Dorado. As if to heighten our expectancy still further, the city itself arrived as in a series of very slow jump cuts from a French 'New Wave' movie. The road was as straight as an arrow, but it was also cruelly undulating. Every dip caused our goal to be rendered once again invisible; each summit seemed to bring it only fractionally closer.

The monotony was broken most unexpectedly. A slightly battered pick-up truck drove slowly by and then pulled onto the hard shoulder. The driver wound down his window and beckoned me to stop. At first it seemed a rather dubious invitation, but as there was no evidence of road rage or ill intent, and because I was thankful for an excuse for a rest, I decided to stop.

'Hi, are you Paul?'

It was not a difficult question but the surprise made me struggle to answer.

'Er, yes.'

'I'm Jeff. I'm part of the unofficial welcome committee for Tour Divide riders in Silver.'

I was once again speechless. Jeff explained that he and a whole host of others in the town had been following the race on the Internet. Every time a racer made it to Silver they would try and meet them to offer encouragement for the final push. Silver City, it seemed, was not just El Dorado. It was also a cycling Mecca.

'I'm going to the bike shop. I'll let them know you're coming,' he said before driving off.

Refreshed, I caught Per and Trevor on the edge of town. Initially we were disheartened. The outskirts were little different from so many towns en route: a selection of prefabricated motels, chain restaurants and out-of-town salesrooms. Downtown, however, was another matter entirely. It had managed to retain the majority of the original buildings from its early days as a mining and frontier town (it had been a lively place – Billy the Kid called it home when he was just a, ahem, kid). These had now assumed an air of faded grandeur that nicely offset the bohemian stores and organic cafés they housed along with more functional emporia.

We found the bike shop – Gila Hike and Bike – where the owner, Jack Brennan, and his colleagues were, not surprisingly, not surprised to see us. As we made arrangements for boxing our bikes prior to flying home and enquired about how we could be collected from the finish tomorrow – we had no intention of riding back – we were also greeted by other members of the welcoming committee. After four weeks of isolation from such social interaction it was an almost overwhelming whirl of new faces and new names. After Jeff in the pick-up, another Jeff rode up with his son on a tandem and single-handedly took charge of arranging tomorrow's transport arrangements. Then a mysterious character known variously as Mimbres Man and Barin Beard (which I misheard as Baron Beard), arrived to take our pictures. It was heady stuff and we kept reminding ourselves we hadn't even finished yet.

We sought refuge from our own over-inflating egos in a nearby Mexican restaurant. In between mouthfuls of bean and cheese burritos – three of them – I raised the previously unspoken prospect of us continuing to ride that night in order to record as fast a finish time as possible.

'We could finish in less than 27 days,' I pointed out.

It was a dangerous move. I had no particular desire to carry on, yet I was aware that the perceived constraints of politeness often involve respondents replying more enthusiastically than they would otherwise wish to such suggestions in order not to appear rude. In extreme circumstances this can even lead to outcomes that are the polar opposite of the desires of everybody involved, simply because a subject is innocently mooted and nobody dares to say what they actually think. I once nearly had to cook Christmas dinner for 11 people on such a sketchy basis.

Fortunately, three weeks in each other's company had removed any sense of obligation to follow peculiar social niceties. The discussion was frank. The decision was unanimous.

'I'm quite happy with 27 days,' said Trevor.

'As long as I catch my plane I'm satisifed,' Per added.

Just as we were about to leave the restaurant to find a motel, we received yet another surprise visitor. This was no Tour Divide fan, though. This was Jamie Thomson, Silver City's very own Tour Divide racer.

'Hey, guys, how ya doing?'

Having finished just the previous day, Jamie was clearly now doing very well indeed. Even through the sloth generated by too much Mexican cuisine and our decision to postpone further movement until tomorrow, his energy and enthusiasm was infectious. He had also, according to Catherine, become something of a legend of the race, or at least to listeners to his entertaining call-ins made to the website.

'I hope you meet him. He sounds like a real character. He's been in love with a mosquito and described chipmunks as being like Tour de France groupies,' she had said when we spoke in Pie Town.

It rapidly became apparent that the description of him as a character was a considerable understatement. He had, it transpired, only participated in the race because he was offered a lift to Canada in time to make it to the start. The offer had been made at lunchtime with departure set for early evening. That had given him about three hours to make his preparations. Even Per's minimalist planning seemed meticulous in comparison.

'I just went home and grabbed my stuff then went to the bike shop and said what else I needed and they lent me some gear. Then I got in the back of the van and that was it.'

Not surprisingly, he had suffered a bewildering array of mechanical problems, all of which had been overcome, including using dental floss to stitch a tyre sidewall that had been slashed by a rock.

'That's an old Jack Brennan trick,' he said modestly.

We also learnt something about Jamie's earlier adventures, including getting caught in a nighttime thunderstorm near the Plains of San Agustin.

'I didn't have any lights and it was so dark that the only time I could see where the road went was when lightning flashed. I had to get into the middle of the road, then run as far as I could until I eventually fell off the verge again.'

He managed several miles in this unlikely fashion until he eventually sought refuge in a disused bus at the HQ of the Very Large Array, a vast collection of satellite dishes in the middle of the desert.

'I woke up just as everyone was coming in for work, so I had to sneak back out again.'

Then he asked if we'd like to stay at his house for the night to save some money on a motel. Not only that, he pointed out that he lived less than half a mile away, whereas all the motels were back on the outskirts of town. It was a simple decision.

The house was instantly recognisable. The exterior was decorated with dozens of bikes, some leant artfully against the chain-link fence, others abandoned in the front garden as if waiting to be repaired. Inside, the cycling associations continued: a poster of two grizzled Belgian professionals from the 1930s sharing a cigarette while racing; thousands, it seemed, of bicycle-related magazines and articles; the odd bike. In the circumstances, the addition of three distinctly odd cyclists seemed quite normal.

....

CHAPTER 31

THE FALL

DAY 28

It was Thursday, 9 July. It was the twenty-eighth day of our race, and hopefully the last. All that remained was 120 seemingly straightforward miles between Silver City and Antelope Wells. Our only anxiety was the fact that we were now about to enter a real desert. The Great Divide Basin and the Plains of San Agustin had been challenging enough. Now we were faced with a desert that could be located in atlases and on globes. The Chihuahuan Desert was the third largest in the entire Western hemisphere. It even had a dog named after it.

Accordingly, we set a new record for early starts and rose swiftly as the alarm sounded at the ungodly hour of 3.00 a.m. The plan was to avoid as much of the anticipated heat as possible – July daytime temperatures of between 35° and 40°C were the norm – by tackling the first 18 miles of pavement in the hour before dawn. Without any major mishaps, we reckoned we would then be able to make it to Antelope Wells between midday and 2 p.m. Jamie had told us it would be a piece of cake, but for a man of Jamie's enthusiasm and energy, everything was a piece of cake. Even so, we dared to let ourselves feel optimistic.

To start with, the plan went well. Pet cockroaches in the sink and the arrival through an open window of a luna moth caused minor frights, but we succeeded in leaving as planned within the hour. We cycled out of a silent Silver City on State Highway 90 and made good progress along the rolling road in the dark. A distinctive rattling at the side of the road reminded us of the wisdom of having refrained from the temptation to ride through the unpaved section of the desert at night.

Nevertheless, our plan worked almost too well. Within another hour we had arrived at the junction with the day's first dirt road. It was still not light. In fact, dawn had scarcely begun to break, and it was with some trepidation that we began to feel our way gingerly through the desert. It was difficult to distinguish the sand of the road from the sand that purported to be soil.

The situation deteriorated further when we rode across what the map described as a 'canyon wash'. It was, it seemed, a seasonal river bed. The amount of soft sand through which we were now blindly wading suggested it was out of season. It would have been funny had I not kept slithering to an ignominious halt. To Per and Trevor it seemed quite amusing anyway.

I was saved from further embarrassment by our southern latitudes and the speedy arrival of the sun. As we climbed out of the wash, we stopped to take in the magnificence of the scenery and the sunrise. To the east, over a huge plain culminating in suitably serrated mountains, the sky had turned an infinite variety of oranges and mauves. Indigo clouds, like giant ink spots, scurried away from the imminent heat.

More importantly, we could now see where we were going. We rode easily along the winding road. Spirits were high. We began to discuss our celebratory dinner.

Then, disaster struck. On what was possibly the most innocuous part of the Tour Divide, just as we were freewheeling down a long, gentle hill under a now fully fledged sun, Per somehow contrived to ride straight into the only treacherous part of the whole, hard-packed, well-surfaced road.

Everything happened so quickly that it was difficult to recall the precise order of events. Nevertheless, the starting point seemed to be when Per's front wheel ploughed into an unexpected patch of soft sand. As we were by now travelling at considerable speed – 20 mph, maybe more – this resulted in a rapid loss of momentum and his bike being tugged violently to one side. This I knew for sure as I suddenly found Per careering across the road towards me.

'Watch where you're . . .'

I didn't get the chance to finish the sentence before Per corrected himself. My sense of relief was shortlived. Per had in fact over-corrected himself. From suddenly travelling at 45 degrees to the left of our initial direction of travel he had now turned back through 90 degrees and seemed set for an unintended excursion into the undergrowth. That was to forget the effect of the momentum acquired by the rest of his considerable frame, however. The front wheel might have been intent on some off-roading; the rest of his bike and every-thing associated with it was still charging forwards.

At some indefinable point in this instantaneous yet seemingly interminable battle, the back of the bike won. Out of the corner of my eye, my own forward progress not having suffered such a rude interruption, I saw Per flip over his handlebars. I did not see his landing, but I heard it.

I stopped. Laughing nervously, I looked back. Trevor, who had been riding a short distance behind us, had slithered to a halt a few feet from Per.

'All right, Per? That was exciting.'

No response. I looked at Trevor. His expression was not encouraging.

'Per, are you all right?' he asked.

Still no response. I put down my bike and ran back to where he lay. It was not a happy sight. He was face down in the dusty road, with legs and arms splayed at awkward angles beneath him. In fact, being 6 foot 6 inches tall, his arms and legs seemed to be everywhere except where they should have been.

'Per! Per!' said Trevor, more urgently this time.

Still no response. Things were looking bleak. My first aid knowledge was rudimentary – cuts, stings, maybe a broken bone or two. Uncon-sciousness was something different. Trevor was of a similar opinion.

'Per!' I shouted, trying to suppress a sense of panic and iniquity. It was all right for him. He was fast asleep. Trevor and I were the ones who had to tidy up the mess. At least he was still breathing.

'Should we move him?' I asked.

Fortunately, Per saved us from the responsibility of deciding between the merits of the recovery position and the possibility of aggravating the potentially serious back or neck injuries that were suggested by his current posture by moving himself. Unfortunately, it was not voluntary movement. Instead, he began to convulse violently. We could do little but try and stop further injury by moving the bike away.

After a minute at most – though it seemed like an hour – Per stopped twitching. His eyes opened. He tried to sit up. It was an abortive attempt. He relapsed into unconsciousness. Eventually, after several more tries, and with both our help, Per made it into a sitting position. Awareness of his surroundings, of who we were, of who he was, took slightly longer.

Five minutes later, with Per now able to answer simple questions with a little prompting, we took stock. Miraculously, nothing seemed broken, though one collarbone and several ribs were very sore. Per also had a large bump on his head, just underneath the crack that had gone clean through his helmet.

'You've very cleverly saved yourself by landing on your head,' said Trevor.

There was a ghost of a smile. This was reassuring. Less so was the realisation that Per's bike was going nowhere. Both wheels were far too buckled to be either turned or mended.

'I guess we need to get some help,' I suggested.

With Per still struggling to remember exactly why he was sitting in the middle of the desert with a sore head, Trevor and I decided that he needed to be taken to hospital. Silver City was 30 miles behind us and there had been little evidence of any habitation thereafter. Ahead, however, about eight miles away, was a ranch. We decided that I should try there while Trevor kept Per company.

'Are you sure you don't mind staying with him?' I asked.

It sounded mean, but any relapse would be an awful responsibility.

'I'll be fine,' said Trevor.

In half an hour, after my fastest period of sustained riding during the whole race, I arrived at Thorn Ranch. A collection of single-storey farm buildings surrounded a central, bare-earth yard. At the far end was access to a much more substantial adobe building, itself surrounded by tall trees. There were a couple of pick-up trucks but there was no sign of life.

Then a dog started barking enthusiastically in one of the farm buildings. At least I decided to interpret its barking as enthusiastic, rather than ferocious. 'Sorry, Per, I was about to get help but there was a scary dog, so you'll have to walk to hospital instead' just didn't seem to wash.

I knocked on the door. To my surprise a man's voice shouted and the dog stopped barking. The door was open, so I went in. A friendly face motioned me to wait while he finished his phone conversation. Then he came and introduced himself. His name, he said in broken English with a strong Mexican accent, was Oscar Peña.

'Sorry. I just speak my boss. How can I help you?'

I explained the situation.

'I wondered if we could use your phone to call for an ambulance and then maybe use a pick-up to take Per to meet the ambulance.'

'No problem,' he smiled, ushering me out of his office and away from the phone.

He helped me put my bike in the back of his pick-up. Then we drove off. After five minutes I felt compelled to remind Oscar about calling an ambulance.

'No problem,' he smiled again.

I was just about to suggest that there did, in fact, appear to be a problem, as we were now ten minutes away from the phone I had very distinctly seen him use, when he fished a mobile phone from his pocket. He waved to the surrounding hills and kept driving. Finally, as we crested a ridge, he gave me the phone.

'Reception,' he beamed.

I called 911 and again explained the situation. It was quite a struggle to persuade the operator that it wasn't me who had been injured but, eventually, I was told an ambulance would be dispatched to meet us. I handed the phone back to Oscar.

'No problem,' he smiled.

Just then the phone rang, almost causing Oscar to drive into a ditch. It was the 911 operator. He asked how badly I was injured.

'I'm not injured at all.'

'Then why do you need an ambulance?'

This was becoming tiresome.

'I'm not injured. A friend of mine has fallen off a bike and has knocked himself unconscious.'

'Where are you?'

'I'm in a pick-up truck.'

'So you don't need an ambulance?'

'I don't need an ambulance for me,' I bellowed, much to Oscar's surprise. 'I need it for my friend who's fallen off his bike and who's unconscious.'

'OK, sir, no need to get cross, it's important to get things clear.'

My sentiments entirely. Five minutes later we found Trevor and Per, who was now clearly conscious.

'How are you?'

'I've got a sore head,' he said rather sheepishly.

'What news?' said Trevor.

'There's an ambulance coming down from Silver City, and Oscar has kindly agreed to take Per up to meet it.'

The only thing to resolve was whether Trevor and I should accompany Per to hospital.

'Don't do that,' said Per in a way that implied he felt as though it were really not necessary for him to go, let alone the rest of us. 'You've got to get to the finish. You can't come all this way and then stop.'

Coming from Per it did not seem a particularly persuasive argument, but he was adamant. We compromised. I went with Per and Oscar to meet the ambulance.

A few miles down the track we were flagged down by a small fire truck with three people in it. They seemed surprised to see us.

'Have you guys seen a cyclist who has fallen off his bike?'

We stopped to let Per out so he could be assessed. I wondered quite how they were going to take him back to hospital in a vehicle with only three seats, all of which seemed to be taken. Then an ambulance arrived, all flashing lights and wailing sirens. The crew seemed surprised to see us. They were even more surprised to see the fire truck.

'Have you guys seen a cyclist who has fallen off his bike?'

Keystone Cops sprang to mind. Even Per was smiling. Finally, we were joined by a local sheriff's department pick-up, which by this point was no surprise at all. At least there would be no problem in getting Per to hospital.

Convinced at last that he was in safe hands, though exactly whose it was difficult to tell, and with Per still adamant that I needn't go with him, Oscar and I returned to Trevor.

'Thank you very much,' I said as we arrived.
'No problem,' he smiled.

We started to ride south again.
'And then there were two,' said Trevor with a forced smile.
'He had me worried there for a minute,' I said.
'Me too.'
We covered the next 20 miles in glum silence. At Separ, which was not so much a town as a cheesy souvenir shop at the intersection with the Interstate, we stopped for refreshments. It was nearly 10 a.m., two hours later than planned, and already baking hot. Spirits could hardly have been lower.

From Separ we rode silently alongside the Interstate for 45 minutes. Cars and trucks flashed past with consummate ease while we toiled on the soft, dusty road. It seemed the very definition of pointlessness. Dangerous questions floated in and out of my head. If it was so pointless, why was I still riding? We had, after all, already achieved what we set out to do. Or at least I had. I'd had an adventure. I'd ridden the length of the Rockies. I'd not been eaten by a bear. What possible reason could there be to tempt fate still further by riding into a desert in the heat of the day? Who cared if I stopped now or in 60 miles? Why should Per get the day off?

'We might as well keep going now we've come so far,' said Trevor the mind-reader.

He was right, of course. But the logic of continuing didn't assuage all of my anxieties. Even if I wanted to keep riding, I wasn't entirely sure that I could. It was already so hot that I could hardly see through eyes stinging with perspiration and steamed-up sunglasses. The exposed skin that I had assumed was now inured to the sun's rays gave me a unique insight into how a cow felt when branded. I was also consuming liquid at an alarming rate. I didn't really want to add to the day's casualty list by collapsing from dehydration only a stone's throw from the finish.

We turned right onto the paved road that now led all the way to Antelope Wells. Trevor miraculously pulled an iPod and earphones from somewhere deep in his luggage.

'Do you mind if I put them on?' he asked.
'Not at all,' I said, aware that my company was not great.

It was that sort of road. Long, straight and relentless. I decided to make my own music. I cycled past a sign saying 'Antelope Wells 59 miles'. That was the cue I had been looking for.

'Fifty-nine green bottles, hanging on a wall, fifty-nine green bottles, hanging on a wall, and if one green bottle should accidentally fall, there'll be fifty-eight green bottles, hanging on a wall . . .'

Seven miles later I had successfully disposed of all the green bottles. I had also demonstrated to myself that the arbitrary accomplishment of a seemingly futile task could be a satisfactory end in itself. Maybe there was some point in making it to Antelope Wells after all.

After seven more miles my spirits received another boost. As did my parched throat. I arrived in the ghost town of Hachita to find not only Trevor but also an open, welcoming grocery store. It had air conditioning. It had chilled drinks. It had Danish pastries. It was heaven. The map, of course, denied its existence entirely.

All of a sudden finishing seemed like a real possibility. A probability, even.

'Trevor. You keep riding to the finish. Don't worry about waiting for me. You ride at your pace, I'll ride at mine and I'll see you at the border.'

'I'll see you before that,' he replied kindly.

We cycled out of town past the conspicuously beautiful and incongruous Saint Catherine of Sienna Catholic Church. In spite of its dilapidated, almost derelict, state – both windows and doors were smashed – its impressive stone tower with ornately traced pointing suggested an air of permanence at odds with the rest of Hachita's fragile existence.

Trevor again rode off into the distance. My relative lethargy was no longer anything to do with uncertainty about continuing. It was now all about ensuring that I would be able to continue all the way to the finish. At least we each had the 'Lonely Highway' to ourselves.

I passed another road sign.

'Antelope Wells Port of Entry. 45 miles. Open 8 a.m. to 4 p.m. Travel Time 1 Hour.'

That seemed wishful thinking. It was gone midday. Just arriving before the border post closed for the night would be enough for me.

I contemplated the desert landscape. To the right were the Little Hatchet Mountains, to the left and slightly ahead their Big Hatchet cousins. Their arid slopes seemed vaguely reassuring, confining the featureless plain through which we rode. The plain itself was populated by creosote and mesquite plants as well as miserable-looking cattle. Even here, it seemed, ranching was big business.

More notable still were the yucca plants. Their spiky headdresses gave the distinct impression I was cycling through a punk reunion. After the Rainbow Gathering, anything seemed possible. Brightly coloured but inedible gourds lay temptingly at the roadside.

To pass the time I resorted once more to musical distraction. With my internal jukebox stuck, I could do no better than embark on another repetitive children's song.

'One man went to mow, went to mow a meadow, one man and his dog and a packet of crisps, went to mow a meadow.'

Sung at an appropriate rhythm, I reached the conventional end of the song – ten men going to mow – after a mile. I persisted for 4 more miles and 40 more men before I could mow no more.

The route passed through the gap between the two branches of the Hatchet Mountains. Less than 30 miles remained. Further excitement was provided by a vast monsoon storm breaking over the imposing Animas Mountains that had replaced the Little Hatchets to my right. Towering cumulonimbus clouds cast rain and lightning against the ridges and peaks as if trying to obliterate them from the face of the earth. I was still bathed in merciless sunlight.

Then the real countdown began. Twenty-five miles. Twenty miles. I was now holding Trevor steady a mile or so ahead of me. 'I could get used to this desert-cycling lark,' I thought to myself. Fifteen miles. I started to shout out each milepost as I cycled by.

'Fourteen. Thirteen. Twelve. Eleven.'

To make such gratuitous noise in the overwhelming silence was strangely therapeutic. At 10 miles to go, I could see Trevor waiting at the roadside. Just as I arrived within hailing distance I heard a tell-tale 'pssss' noise. He started to ride off; I skidded to a halt. Trevor realised I wasn't with him.

'What's up?'

'Puncture.'

In spite of scarcely being able to wield the tyre levers because of the sweat on my hands, I managed to change the inner tube and began to pump up the tyre. Nothing happened. The tyre remained stubbornly deflated. I looked at Trevor. He looked at me. I looked in my saddle bag. I had used an un-repaired inner tube.

I didn't know whether to laugh or cry. The only reason Trevor didn't have to physically restrain me from throwing the bike into the desert was the fact that I was by now almost completely bereft of energy. I started again. Eventually, the tyre began to fill out.

'You could get a job doing that,' said Trevor.

'I've had plenty of practice.'

'I've still not had a puncture,' Trevor added.

'Thanks for the reminder.'

We cycled the last 10 miles together, silently reminiscing about all that had gone before. It didn't seem possible that we were about to finish. With five miles to go we spotted the border post. Never has a scratchy collection of concrete buildings with air conditioning and stony-faced border guards seemed more welcoming.

At 3.41 p.m. precisely we rode into the compound. There, before us, was the sign we had been waiting for.

'Boundary of the United States of America. Limite de los Estados Unidos Mexicanos.'

CHAPTER 32

....

SATISFACTION

We celebrated our arrival with utter disbelief. If Trevor had not been with me I might well have assumed I was dreaming. The million things that could have gone wrong, that had already gone wrong for some, had not gone wrong for us. We had made it.

We celebrated with cheap champagne bought the day before and that Mike, the chauffeur for our return journey, had brought with him; cousin Steve's offer of our own lorry had been great in theory but too complicated in practice. The champagne had a screw top. It was hardly the podium moment of imagination, but I shook the bottle and sprayed it anyway. It had only been out of the fridge a couple of hours yet it was disgustingly warm. No matter, it was not for drinking.

We celebrated again when the border guards were shocked into revealing their latent humanity and let us ring home. We celebrated more still when I spoke to Catherine and she said Per had phoned in to say he'd been discharged from hospital with nothing worse than concussion and a headache.

We celebrated silently all the way back to Silver City as Mike's jeep whisked us at incredible speeds along roads down which we had just laboured. Even his rant against the injustices meted out by the industrial-military complex seemed celebratory, at least for a while.

Back in Silver City, Per celebrated with us at Jamie's house. His face spoke of headaches and the fatigue to which Trevor and I would not succumb until tomorrow. Yet he bore his fate with enviable and typical stoicism.

'It seems like it was quite a bad crash so I'm just glad I didn't do myself any more damage,' he said happily.

Viewed in such a light, it was another cause for celebration. We treated ourselves to a slap-up dinner at Jalisto's restaurant. We didn't quite go the whole hog, but I did manage half a chicken. At the brew pub next door to the bike shop we were offered free beer. I was almost too worn out to accept it. Almost.

The next day passed quickly in a blur of preparations for our journey home. We took leave of Jamie's fabulous cycling cornucopia. Bikes had to be boxed, travel to Phoenix had to be arranged. In a country in which the concept of public transport was perceived as an affront to individual freedom, this was no mean feat. In the end we hired a car. The close-knit cycling community of Silver City provided a driver to return it after we'd been delivered to the airport. It was none other than Barin Beard, Mimbres Man himself; Mimbres Man, it turned out, related to a previous life as an originator of a brand of cool cycling clothing.

'I'm on holiday so I can drive for a day and talk about cycling, it'll be fun.'

It was, though the complexity of finding somewhere to sleep at Phoenix airport was mind-boggling.

'It must be the only airport in the whole world not to be surrounded by hotels,' I fumed as we drove around it for the third time.

We eventually found one. After dinner, and bidding farewell to Mimbres Man, we checked the Tour Divide website and discovered that Trevor and I had, in fact, failed in our bid to finish last, though only by one place. Clearly poisoning Stephen and causing Per to crash had not been enough. The man set to save us from such indignity – and take home the coveted prize of *Lanterne Rouge* – was Michael Komp. He had, it turned out, been handicapped from the start by the fact his bike had been delayed in Canadian customs. As a result, he had not even managed to depart with all the other riders, eventually leaving Banff nearly seven hours after the race had officially begun. He finally reached Antelope Wells in thirty-one days, twenty-two hours and thirty-five minutes, four days after Trevor and I had passed through. Our official finishing time was twenty-seven days, five hours and forty-two minutes.

More than a week and a half earlier, Matthew Lee had won the race in just under eighteen days. Kurt Refsnider took second in eighteen days and eleven hours, only two hours ahead of the Petervarys on their 'Love Shack'. Steve, Alan and John from the UK all safely finished within a couple of hours of each other, in less than twenty-two days. Jill Homer, although only the second woman to finish after Tracy Petervary, set a new female course record of twenty-four days, seven hours and twenty-four minutes.

Of the other riders I encountered on the way, Cadet abandoned the race in Eureka, unable to ride any further on his sprained knee. He gallantly let Rick and Deanna depart in high spirits in the belief that he was going to set off shortly after them before pulling the plug. Arizona Jeff called it a day in Butte to go home to his pregnant wife. Martin from Austria turned his race into a touring ride before eventually flying home from Colorado. Rick continued in spite of his sore knee and rode the best part of 1,000 miles into Wyoming before deciding to call it a day. Ray's self-inflicted cut turned out to be even worse than it had seemed. He had severed an artery in his hand which required surgery to fix. The surgery was a success. Bruce persisted for 36 days and made it all the way to the finish in spite of missing a small section of the route and disqualifying himself from the race. Deanna also made it to the finish but was relegated from the final leaderboard for similarly going off-route for some 50 miles north of Helena.

Some of those who didn't make it expressed an immediate desire to return to the race, including Stephen Huddle and Cadet. Steve McGuire said he would complete the route one way or another, maybe taking a bit more time to appreciate the scenery and surroundings in the process. Even Trevor and Per – both successful in my book – said they would consider returning to ride it. Quicker.

Racing faster – or maybe just racing – was certainly a seductive notion. I told myself I could probably go faster. Matthew Lee took 30 days to ride from border to border in 2004 before returning the following year to win in 19 days. Greater speed would, in itself, certainly increase the level of adventurousness, if that was the motive. To ride as fast as Matthew Lee or the other front-runners did exposed them so much more to the risks inherent in the ride: bad weather; untimely mechanicals; running out of food and water; running out of energy. It was the cycling equivalent of scaling a higher mountain. I was in the Rockies. They were in the Himalayas.

Yet one of the most appealing aspects of the whole event was the element of the unknown. I now knew the route, which removed much of the novelty factor. I could also no longer claim to be a mountain bike novice, even though I had still only ridden one race.

The result was to conclude that once was probably enough. I toyed with the idea of passing this off as the result of the Tour Divide being a form of immersion therapy; or possibly aversion therapy. Making it to Antelope Wells, I conjectured, meant that I was now so at ease with my phobia of actually completing tasks (just ask my wife) that I could henceforth avoid undertaking anything more challenging than getting up in the morning. Or perhaps I could explain my future abstinence as the consequence of day after day of endless pedalling having cured me of the desire to ride long distances off-road for a month.

Neither really carried much weight. Laziness and the desire to protect my 100 per cent success rate were probably more significant factors. As was the view of the four children and wife I had left behind for over a month for the sake of a bike race, for whom once was also enough. Unless they could come too, though the bike hasn't yet been built that could allow us to do it together (if any enterprising designer wants to organise a road test – make that an off-road test – drop me a line).

Nevertheless, even one day of 'normality' was sufficient to have me yearning once again for the existential simplicity of life on the Tour Divide. Eat. Sleep. Ride. Great Divide. That was the motto devised by the route's creators at the Adventure Cycling Association. It would make a fine philosophy.

But for now, at least, that was it. The adventure was over. Trevor flew home to Montreal on Saturday morning. Per caught his flight that evening. I had to wait until Sunday, but I was home in time for school sports day. I entered the fathers' race. I couldn't find a way of coming last in that either.